CRE▲TIVE
HOMEOWNER®

# COZY
# COTTAGE
# HOME DESIGNS

CREATIVE HOMEOWNER®, Upper Saddle River, New Jersey

VP/Business Development: Brian H. Toolan
VP/Editorial Director: Timothy O. Bakke
Production Manager: Kimberly H. Vivas

Home Plans Publishing Consultant: James D. McNair III
Editorial Assistant: Jennifer Doolittle

Design and Layout: Arrowhead Direct (David Kroha, Cindy DiPierdomenico, Judith Kroha)

Cover Design: David Geer

Current Printing (last digit)
10 9 8 7 6 5 4 3 2 1

Cozy Cottage Home Designs
Library of Congress Control Number: 2004103760
ISBN: 1-58011-222-6

CREATIVE HOMEOWNER®
A Division of Federal Marketing Corp.
24 Park Way
Upper Saddle River, NJ 07458
**www.creativehomeowner.com**

Printed in China

*Note: The homes as shown in the photographs and renderings in this book may differ from the actual blueprints. When studying the house of your choice, please check the floor plans carefully.*

# Contents

# Getting Started

**M**aybe you can't wait to bang the first nail. Or you may be just as happy leaving town until the windows are cleaned. The extent of your involvement with the construction phase is up to you. Your time, interests, and abilities can help you decide how to get the project from lines on paper to reality. But building a house requires more than putting pieces together. Whoever is in charge of the process must competently manage people as well as supplies, materials, and construction. He or she will have to

- Make a project schedule to plan the orderly progress of the work. This can be a bar chart that shows the time period of activity by each trade.
- Establish a budget for each category of work, such as foundation, framing, and finish carpentry.
- Arrange for a source of construction financing.
- Get a building permit and post it conspicuously at the construction site.
- Line up supply sources and order materials.
- Find subcontractors and negotiate their contracts.
- Coordinate the work so that it progresses smoothly with the fewest conflicts.
- Notify inspectors at the appropriate milestones.
- Make payments to suppliers and subcontractors.

## You as the Builder

You'll have to take care of every logistical detail yourself if you decide to act as your own builder or general contractor. But along with the responsibilities of managing the project, you gain the flexibility to do as much of your own work as you want and subcontract out the rest. Before taking this path, however, be sure you have the time and capabilities. Do you also have the

time and ability to schedule the work, hire and coordinate subs, order materials, and keep ahead of the accounting required to manage the project successfully? If you do, you stand to save the amount that a general contractor would charge to take on these responsibilities, normally 15 to 30 percent of the construction cost. If you take this responsibility on but mismanage the project, the potential savings will erode and may even cost you more than if you had hired a builder in the first place. A subcontractor might charge extra for hav-

**The first step** to a new home, above, requires choosing a plan that suits your needs.

**Building a home,** opposite, includes the need to schedule building inspections at the appropriate milestones.

ing to return to the site to complete work that was originally scheduled for an earlier date. Or perhaps because you didn't order the windows at the beginning, you now have to pay for a recent cost increase. (If you had hired a builder in the first place he or she would absorb the increase.)

## Hiring a Builder to Handle Construction

A builder or general contractor will manage every aspect of the construction process. Your role after signing the construction contract will be to make regular progress payments and ensure that the work for which you are paying has been completed. You will also consult with the builder and agree to any changes that may have to be made along the way.

Leads for finding builders might come from friends or neighbors who have had contractors build, remodel, or add to their homes. Real-estate agents and bankers may have some names handy but are more likely familiar with the builder's ability to complete projects on time and budget than the quality of the work itself.

The next step is to narrow your list of candidates to three or four who you think can do a quality job and work harmoniously with you. Phone each builder to see whether he or she is interested in being considered for your project. If so, invite the builder to an interview at your home. The meeting will serve two purposes. You'll be able to ask the candidate about his or her experience, and you'll be able to see whether or not your personalities are compatible. Go over the plans with the builder to make certain that he or she understands the scope of the project. Ask if they have constructed similar houses. Get references, and check the builder's standing with the Better Business Bureau. Develop a short list of builders, say three, and ask them to submit bids for the project.

## Contracts

### Lump-Sum Contracts

A lump-sum, or fixed-fee, contract lets you know from the beginning just what the project will cost, barring any changes made because of your requests or unforeseen conditions. This form works well for projects that promise few surprises and are well defined from the outset by a complete set of contract documents. You can enter into a fixed-price contract by negotiating with a single builder on your short list or by obtaining bids from three or four builders. If you go the latter route, give each bidder a set of documents and allow at least two weeks for them to submit their bids. When you get the bids, decide who you want and call the others to thank them for their efforts. You don't have to accept the lowest bid, but it probably makes sense to do so since you have already honed the list to builders you trust. Inform this builder of your intentions to finalize a contract.

### Cost-Plus-Fee Contracts

Under a cost-plus-fee contract, you agree to pay the builder for the costs of labor and materials, as verified by receipts, plus a fee that represents the builder's overhead and profit. This arrangement is sometimes referred to as "time and materials." The fee can range between 15 and 30 percent of the incurred costs. Because you ultimately pick up the tab—whatever the costs—the contractor is never at risk, as he is with a lump-sum contract. You won't know the final total cost of a cost-plus-fee contract until the project is built and paid for. If you can live with that uncertainty, there are offsetting advantages. First, this form allows you to accommodate unknown conditions much more easily than does a lump-sum contract. And rather than being tied down by the project documents, you will be free to make changes at any point along the way. This can be a trap, though. Watching the project take shape will spark the desire to add something or do something differently. Each change costs more, and the accumulation can easily exceed your budget. Because of the uncertainty of the final tab and the built-in advantage to the contractor, you should think twice before entering into this form of contract.

### Contract Content

The conditions of your agreement should be spelled out thoroughly in writing and signed by both parties, whatever contractual arrangement you make with your builder. Your contract should include provisions for the following:

- The names and addresses of the owner and builder.
- A description of the work to be included ("As described in the plans and specifications dated . . .").
- The date that the work will be completed if time is of the essence.
- The contract price for lump-sum contracts and the builder's allowed profit and overhead costs for changes.
- The builder's fee for cost-plus-fee contracts and the method of accounting and requesting payment.
- The criteria for progress payments (monthly, by project milestones) and the conditions of final payment.
- A list of each drawing and specification section that is to be included as part of the contract.
- Requirements for guarantees. (One year is the standard period for which contractors guarantee the entire project, but you may require specific guarantees on

**When submitting bids,** all of the builders should base their estimates on the same specifications. Once the work begins, communicate with your builder to keep the work proceeding smoothly.

**Inspect your newly built home,** if possible, before the builder closes it up and finishes it.

certain parts of the project, such as a 20-year guarantee on the roofing.)
- Provisions for insurance.
- A description of how changes in the work orders will be handled.

The builder may have a standard contract that you can tailor to the specifics of your project. These contain complete specific conditions with blanks that you can fill in to fit your project and a set of "general conditions" that cover a host of issues from insurance to termination provisions. It's always a good idea to have an attorney review the draft of your completed contract before signing it.

## Working with Your Builder

The construction phase officially begins when you have a signed copy of the contract and copies of any insurance required from the builder. It's not unheard of for a builder to request an initial payment of 10 to 20 percent of the total cost to cover mobilization costs, those costs associated with obtaining permits and getting set up to begin the actual construction. If you agree to this, keep a careful eye on the progress of the work to ensure that the total paid out at any one time doesn't get too far out of sync with the actual work completed.

What about changes? From here on, it's up to you and your builder to proceed in good faith and to keep the channels of communication open. Even so, changes of one sort or another beset every project, and they usually add to its cost.

### Light at the End of the Tunnel.

The builder's request for a final inspection marks the end of the construction phase—almost. At the final inspection meeting, you and the builder will inspect the work, noting any defects or incomplete items on a "punch list." When the builder tidies up the punch list items, you should reinspect. Sometimes, builders go on to another job and take forever to clean up the last few details, so only after all items on the list have been completed satisfactorily should you release the final payment, which often accounts for the builder's profit.

## Some Final Words

Having a positive attitude is important when undertaking a project as large as building a home. A positive attitude can help you ride out the rigors and stress of the construction process.

**Stay Flexible.** Expect problems, because they certainly will occur. Weather can upset the schedule you have established for subcontractors. A supplier may get behind on deliveries, which also affects the schedule. An unexpected pipe may surprise you during excavation. Just as certain, every problem that comes along has a solution if you are open to it.

**Be Patient.** The extra days it may take to resolve a construction problem will be forgotten once the project is completed.

**Express Yourself.** If what you see isn't exactly what you thought you were getting, don't be afraid to look into changing it. Or you may spot an unforeseen opportunity for an improvement. Changes usually cost more money, though, so don't make frivolous decisions.

Finally, watching your home go up is exciting, so stay upbeat. Get away from your project from time to time. Dine out. Take time to relax. A positive attitude will make for smoother relations with your builder. An optimistic outlook will yield better-quality work if you are doing your own construction. And though the project might seem endless while it is under way, keep in mind that all the planning and construction will fade to a faint memory at some time in the future, and you will be getting a lifetime of pleasure from a home that is just right for you.

## Plan #211013

**Dimensions:** 48' W x 29' D
**Levels:** 1
**Square Footage:** 998
**Bedrooms:** 3
**Bathrooms:** 1
**Foundation:** Slab, optional crawl space, or basement
**Materials List Available:** Yes
**Price Category:** A

If you're looking for a well-designed, space-efficient small home, you'll love this traditional beauty.

**Features:**

- Ceiling Height: 8 ft.

- Living Room: Large enough to make entertaining easy, this room is positioned so that friends and family will naturally gather here.

- Kitchen: This galley kitchen streamlines your work patterns and provides good storage areas as well as counter space.

- Patio: Walk from the kitchen straight onto this patio in the morning to enjoy your breakfast in the sunshine or in the afternoon and evening when you're entertaining guests or grilling for the family.

- Master Bedroom: A large walk-in closet gives good storage space here, and direct access to the bathroom adds convenience.

*Images provided by designer/architect.*

*Copyright by designer/architect.*

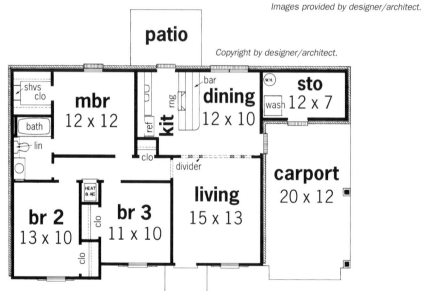

## SMARTtip

### Mixing Patterns

A trick for mixing patterns is to provide links of scale, motif, and color. The regularity of checks, stripes, textural looks, and geometrics, particularly if small-scale and low-contrast, tends to make them easy-to-mix "neutral" patterns. A small floral can play off a thin ticking stripe, while a cabbage-rose chintz may require a bolder stripe as a same-scale foil. Use the same or similar patterns in varying sizes, or develop them by focusing on florals, geometric, or ethnic prints.

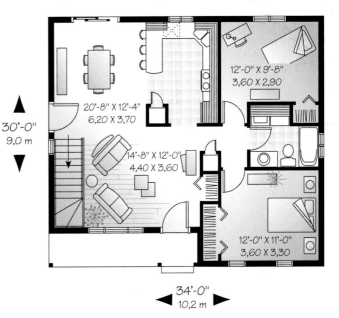

## Plan #181010

**Dimensions:** 48' W x 30' D

**Levels:** 1

**Square Footage:** 947

**Bedrooms:** 2

**Bathrooms:** 1

**Foundation:** Full basement

**Materials List Available:** Yes

**Price Category:** A

*Images provided by designer/architect.*

30'-0"
9,0 m

20'-8" X 12'-4"
6,20 X 3,70

12'-0" X 9'-8"
3,60 X 2,90

14'-8" X 12'-0"
4,40 X 3,60

12'-0" X 11'-0"
3,60 X 3,30

34'-0"
10,2 m

*Copyright by designer/architect.*

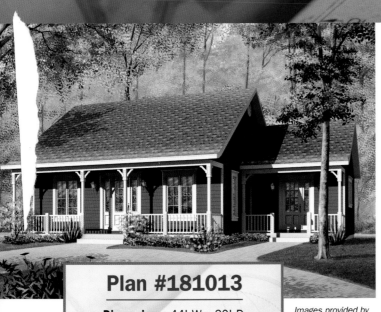

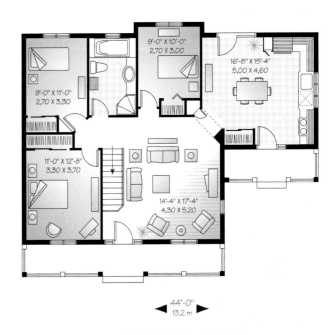

## Plan #181013

**Dimensions:** 44' W x 30' D

**Levels:** 1

**Square Footage:** 1,147

**Bedrooms:** 3

**Bathrooms:** 1

**Foundation:** Full basement

**Materials List Available:** Yes

**Price Category:** B

*Images provided by designer/architect.*

9'-0" X 10'-0"
2,70 X 3,00

16'-8" X 15'-4"
5,00 X 4,60

9'-0" X 11'-0"
2,70 X 3,30

11'-0" X 12'-8"
3,30 X 3,70

14'-4" X 17'-4"
4,30 X 5,20

44'-0"
13,2 m

*Copyright by designer/architect.*

## Plan #281010

**Dimensions:** 34' W x 31' D

**Levels:** 1

**Square Footage:** 884

**Bedrooms:** 2

**Bathrooms:** 1

**Foundation:** Crawl space

**Materials List Available:** Yes

**Price Category:** A

This cute vacation or retirement home is modest in size yet contains all the necessary amenities.

**Features:**

- Ceiling Height: 8 ft.

- Open Plan: The living room, dining room, and kitchen are all contained in one open space. This makes the space versatile and allows plenty of room for entertaining despite the home's small size.

- Covered Deck: Step outdoors and enjoy warm breezes on this covered deck, which is accessible from the open main living area.

- Master Bedroom: This master bedroom is separated from the other bedroom to allow maximum privacy.

- Second Bedroom: This bedroom is perfect for when friends and family come to spend the night.

- Cedar Siding: This vertical cedar siding weathers to a beautiful silver gray when left unstained.

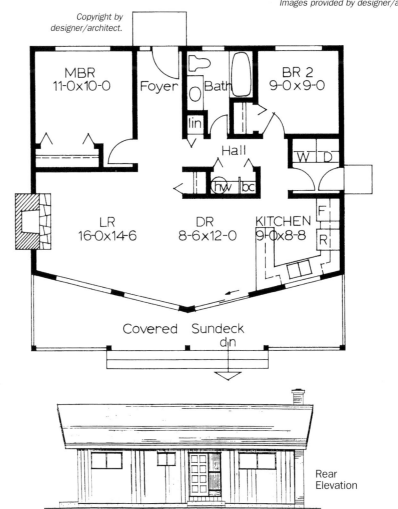

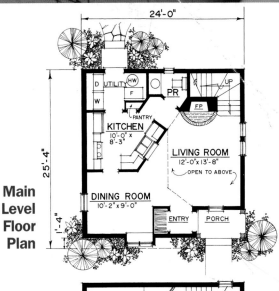

## Plan #291006

**Dimensions:** 24' W x 25'4" D

**Levels:** 2

**Square Footage:** 965

**Main Level Sq. Ft.:** 547

**Upper Level Sq. Ft.:** 418

**Bedrooms:** 1

**Bathrooms:** 1½

**Foundation:** Crawl space

**Materials List Available:** No

**Price Category:** A

*Images provided by designer/architect.*

**Main Level Floor Plan**

KITCHEN 10'-0" x 8'-3"

LIVING ROOM 12'-0"x13'-8"
OPEN TO ABOVE

DINING ROOM 10'-2" x 9'-0"

ENTRY   PORCH

24'-0"

25'-4"

**Upper Level Floor Plan**

LOFT 12'-0"x 8'-0" (8'-0" CLG)
OPEN TO ABOVE

RIDGE BEAM

OPEN TO BELOW

TUB/SHWR   BATH

MASTER BEDROOM 12'-0"x11'-0" (12'-0" CEILING)

W.I.C.

PLANT SHELF

*Copyright by designer/architect.*

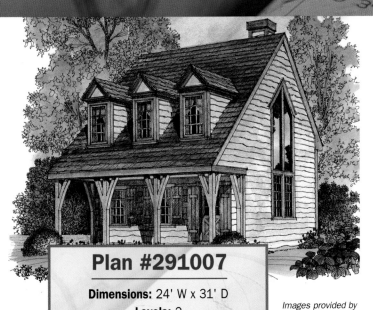

## Plan #291007

**Dimensions:** 24' W x 31' D

**Levels:** 2

**Square Footage:** 1,065

**Main Level Sq. Ft.:** 576

**Upper Level Sq. Ft.:** 489

**Bedrooms:** 1

**Bathrooms:** 1½

**Foundation:** Crawl space

**Materials List Available:** No

**Price Category:** B

*Images provided by designer/architect.*

**Upper Level Floor Plan**

5'-0" KNEEWALL
CEILING CLIP
LOFT 12'-4"x8'-0"

BATH

WOOD RAIL

EXPOSED BEAM

MASTER BED 13'-2"x11'-0"
CEILING CLIP

W.I.C.

5'-0" KNEEWALL

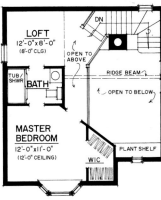

24'-0"

31'-0"

UTIL.   PR

KITCHEN 11'-0"x 8'-4"

FP

LIVING ROOM 13'-0"x13'-8"
OPEN TO ABOVE

DINING 15'-0"x 9'-0"

ENTRY

PORCH 24'-0"x7'-0"

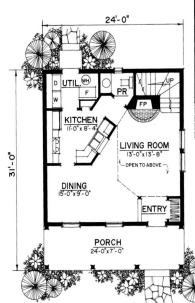

**Main Level Floor Plan**

*Copyright by designer/architect.*

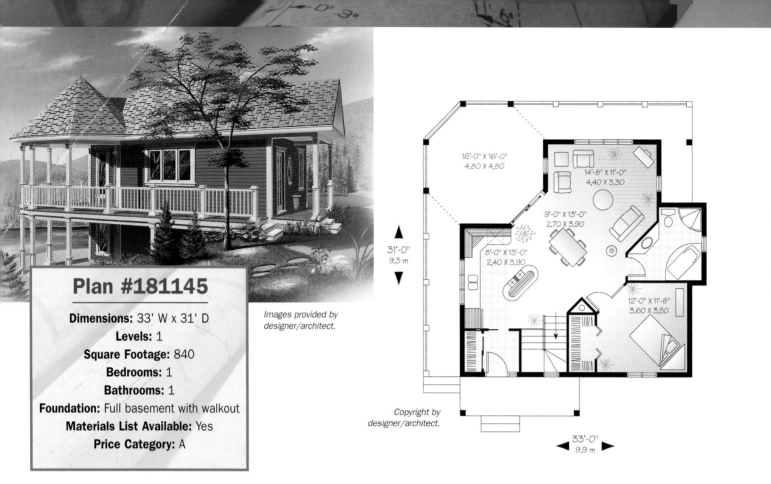

# Plan #181145

**Dimensions:** 33' W x 31' D
**Levels:** 1
**Square Footage:** 840
**Bedrooms:** 1
**Bathrooms:** 1
**Foundation:** Full basement with walkout
**Materials List Available:** Yes
**Price Category:** A

*Images provided by designer/architect.*

16'-0" X 16'-0"
4,80 X 4,80

14'-8" X 11'-0"
4,40 X 3,30

9'-0" X 13'-0"
2,70 X 3,90

8'-0" X 13'-0"
2,40 X 3,90

12'-0" X 11'-8"
3,60 X 3,50

31'-0"
9,3 m

33'-0"
9,9 m

*Copyright by designer/architect.*

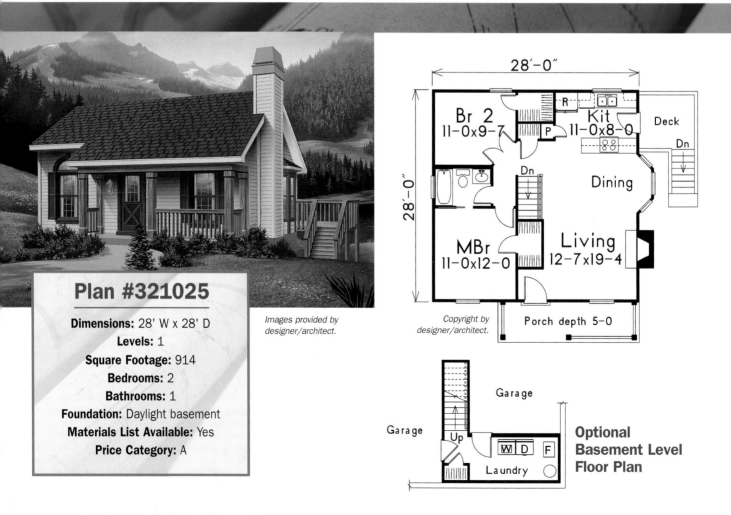

# Plan #321025

**Dimensions:** 28' W x 28' D
**Levels:** 1
**Square Footage:** 914
**Bedrooms:** 2
**Bathrooms:** 1
**Foundation:** Daylight basement
**Materials List Available:** Yes
**Price Category:** A

*Images provided by designer/architect.*

28'-0"

28'-0"

Br 2
11-0x9-7

Kit
11-0x8-0

Deck

Dn

Dn

Dining

MBr
11-0x12-0

Living
12-7x19-4

*Copyright by designer/architect.*

Porch depth 5-0

Garage

Garage

Up

W D F

Laundry

**Optional Basement Level Floor Plan**

## Plan #211004

**Dimensions:** 64' W x 62' D

**Levels:** 1

**Square Footage:** 1,828

**Bedrooms:** 4

**Bathrooms:** 2

**Foundation:** Slab, crawl space, basement

**Materials List Available:** Yes

**Price Category:** D

This super-energy-efficient home has the curb appeal of a much larger house.

**Features:**

• Ceiling Height: 9 ft.

• Kitchen: You will love cooking in this bright, airy, and efficient kitchen. It features an angled layout that allows a great view to the outside through a window wall in the breakfast area.

• Breakfast Area: With morning sunlight streaming through the wall of windows in

this area, you won't be able to resist lingering over a cup of coffee.

• Rear Porch: This breezy rear porch is designed to accommodate the pleasure of old-fashioned rockers or swings.

• Master Bedroom: Retreat at the end of a long day to this bedroom, which is isolated for privacy yet conveniently located a few steps from the kitchen and utility area.

• Attic Storage: No need to fuss with creaky pull-down stairs. This attic has a permanent stairwell to provide easy access to its abundant storage.

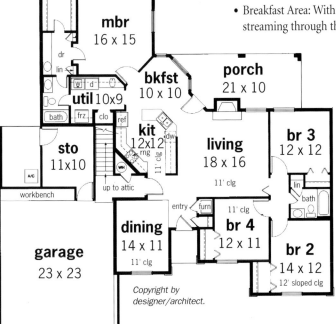

Copyright by designer/architect.

## SMARTtip

### Resin Furniture

Resin furniture is made of molded plastic. Most resin pieces are quite affordable, but lacquered resin with brass fittings is a high-end item. Resin doesn't corrode and cleans easily, but a scratched finish cannot be repaired. However, lacquered resin can be touched up.

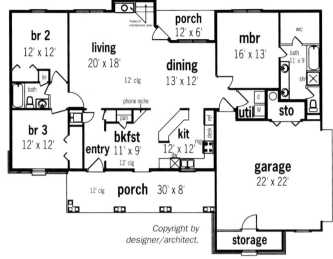

*Images provided by designer/architect.*

*Copyright by designer/architect.*

## Plan #211035

**Dimensions:** 64' W x 48' D

**Levels:** 1

**Square Footage:** 1,770

**Bedrooms:** 3

**Bathrooms:** 2

**Foundation:** Slab

**Materials List Available:** Yes

**Price Category:** C

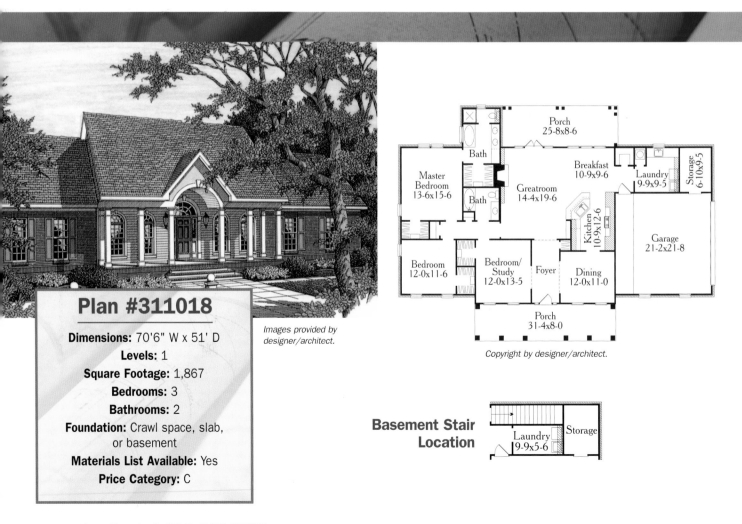

*Images provided by designer/architect.*

*Copyright by designer/architect.*

**Basement Stair Location**

## Plan #311018

**Dimensions:** 70'6" W x 51' D

**Levels:** 1

**Square Footage:** 1,867

**Bedrooms:** 3

**Bathrooms:** 2

**Foundation:** Crawl space, slab, or basement

**Materials List Available:** Yes

**Price Category:** C

## Main Level Floor Plan

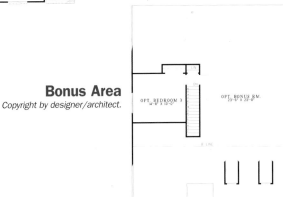

### Plan #151104

**Dimensions:** 43' W x 55' D

**Levels:** 1

**Square Footage:** 1,860

**Bedrooms:** 3

**Bathrooms:** 2

**Foundation:** Crawl space, slab with basement option for fee

**Materials List Available:** Yes

**Price Category:** D

*Images provided by designer/architect.*

## Bonus Area
*Copyright by designer/architect.*

### Plan #181153

**Dimensions:** 46' W x 34' D

**Levels:** 1

**Square Footage:** 1,478

**Bedrooms:** 3

**Bathrooms:** 1

**Foundation:** Full basement

**Materials List Available:** Yes

**Price Category:** B

*Images provided by designer/architect.*

*Copyright by designer/architect.*

## Plan #121004

**Dimensions:** 55'4" W x 48' D
**Levels:** 1
**Square Footage:** 1,666
**Bedrooms:** 3
**Bathrooms:** 2
**Foundation:** Basement
**Materials List Available:** Yes
**Price Category:** C

*Images provided by designer/architect.*

An efficient floor plan and plenty of amenities create a luxurious lifestyle.

**Features:**

• Ceiling Height: 8 ft. except as noted.

• Entry: Enjoy summer breezes on the porch; then step inside the entry where sidelights and an arched transom create a bright, cheery welcome.

• Great Room: The 10-ft. ceiling and the transom-topped windows flooding the room with light provide a sense of spaciousness. The fireplace adds warmth and style.

• Dining Room: You'll usher your guests into this room located just off the great room.

• Breakfast Area: Also located off the great room, the breakfast area offers another dining option.

• Master Suite: The master bedroom is highlighted by a tray ceiling and a large walk-in closet. Luxuriate in the private bath with its sunlit whirlpool, separate shower, and double vanity.

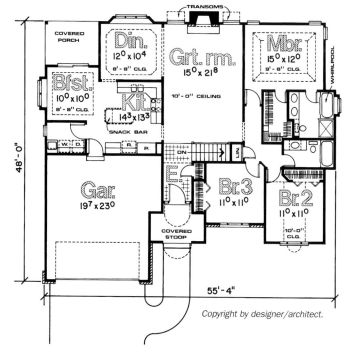

*Copyright by designer/architect.*

SMARTtip
### Carpeting

Install the best underlayment padding available, as well as the highest grade of carpeting you can afford. This will guarantee a feeling of softness beneath your feet and protect your investment for years to come by reducing wear and tear on the carpet.

## Plan #121005

**Dimensions:** 48' W x 52' D

**Levels:** 1

**Square Footage:** 1,496

**Bedrooms:** 3

**Bathrooms:** 2

**Foundation:** Basement

**Materials List Available:** Yes

**Price Category:** B

A beautiful starter or retirement home with all the amenities you'd expect in a much bigger house.

**Features:**

- Ceiling Height: 8 ft.

- Great Room: A cathedral ceiling visually expands the great room making it the perfect place for family gatherings or formal entertaining.

- Formal Dining Room: This elegant room is ideal for entertaining dinner guests. It conveniently shares a wet bar and service counter with a bayed breakfast area next door.

- Breakfast Area: In addition to the service area shared with the dining room, this cozy area features a snack bar, pantry, and desk that's perfect for household paperwork.

- Master Suite: The master bedroom features special ceiling details. It's joined by a private bath with a whirlpool, shower, and spacious walk-in closet.

- Garage: The two-bay garage offers plenty of storage space.

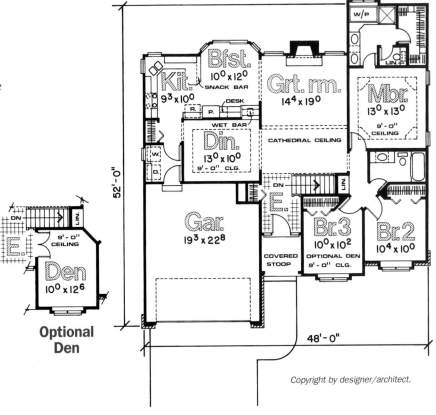

**Optional Den**

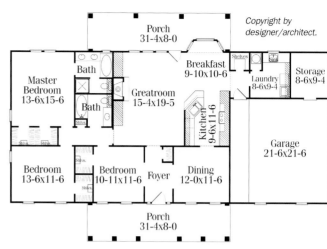

Porch
31-4x8-0

*Copyright by designer/architect.*

Master Bedroom
13-6x15-6

Bath

Bath

Greatroom
15-4x19-5

Breakfast
9-10x10-6

Kitchen
9-6x11-6

Laundry
8-6x9-4

Shelves

Storage
8-6x9-4

Garage
21-6x21-6

Bedroom
13-6x11-6

Bedroom
10-11x11-6

Foyer

Dining
12-0x11-6

Porch
31-4x8-0

## Plan #311008

**Dimensions:** 70'1" W x 48' D

**Levels:** 1

**Square Footage:** 1,688

**Bedrooms:** 3

**Bathrooms:** 2

**Foundation:** Basement, crawl space, or slab

**Materials List Available:** Yes

**Price Category:** C

*Images provided by designer/architect.*

Laun.
8-6x5-6

Storage

**Basement Stair Option**

---

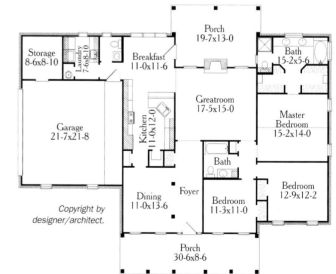

Storage
8-6x8-10

Laundry
7-6x8-10

Porch
19-7x13-0

Bath
15-2x5-6

Breakfast
11-0x11-6

Garage
21-7x21-8

Kitchen
11-0x12-0

Greatroom
17-5x15-0

Master Bedroom
15-2x14-0

Bath

Dining
11-0x13-6

Foyer

Bedroom
11-3x11-0

Bedroom
12-9x12-2

*Copyright by designer/architect.*

Porch
30-6x8-6

## Plan #311009

**Dimensions:** 68' W x 56'6" D

**Levels:** 1

**Square Footage:** 1,894

**Bedrooms:** 3

**Bathrooms:** 2½

**Foundation:** Basement, crawl space, or slab

**Materials List Available:** Yes

**Price Category:** D

*Images provided by designer/architect.*

Laun.
7-6x5-5

**Basement Stair Option**

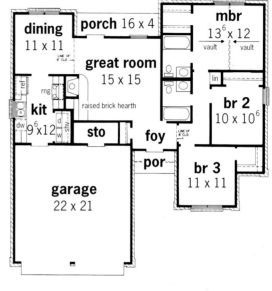

*Images provided by designer/architect.*

## Plan #201011

**Dimensions:** 46'10" W x 46'10" D

**Levels:** 1

**Square Footage:** 1,205

**Bedrooms:** 3

**Bathrooms:** 2

**Foundation:** Crawl space, slab, or basement

**Materials List Available:** Yes

**Price Category:** B

*Copyright by designer/architect.*

---

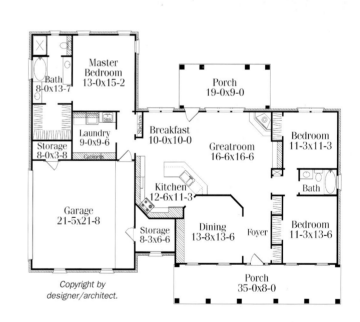

*Images provided by designer/architect.*

*Copyright by designer/architect.*

## Plan #311012

**Dimensions:** 65'8" W x 55' D

**Levels:** 1

**Square Footage:** 1,836

**Bedrooms:** 3

**Bathrooms:** 2

**Foundation:** Basement, crawl space, or slab

**Materials List Available:** Yes

**Price Category:** D

**Basement Stair Location**

## Plan #121006

**Dimensions:** 46' W x 58' D

**Levels:** 1

**Square Footage:** 1,762

**Bedrooms:** 3

**Bathrooms:** 2

**Foundation:** Slab

**Materials List Available:** Yes

**Price Category:** C

The entry has a trio of arched openings that leads you to other areas of this amenity-packed home.

### Features:

- Ceiling Height: 8 ft. except as noted.

- Eating Bar: Conveniently located between the kitchen and family room, this is sure to be a favorite spot for informal entertaining and family gatherings.

- Family room: A wall of windows, a fireplace, and a vaulted ceiling stretching to 11 ft. work together to make this a bright and warm room.

- Kitchen: There's no shortage of counter space in this well-planned kitchen that features a center island in addition to the eating bar.

- Master Suite: Luxuriate at the end of the day in this large bedroom with its decorative tray ceiling and walk-in closet. Enjoy the pampering bath with its sunlit corner whirlpool flanked by vanities.

- Garage: Two bays provide room for cars and plenty of storage as well.

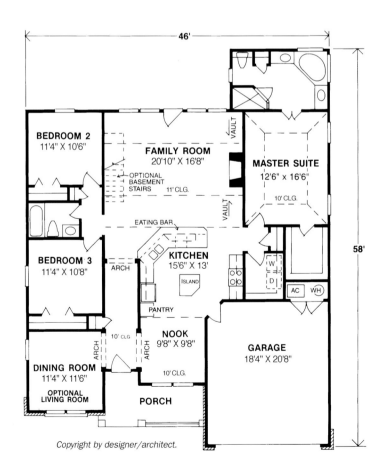

## Plan #121008

**Dimensions:** 62' W x 56' D
**Levels:** 1
**Square Footage:** 1,651
**Bedrooms:** 2
**Bathrooms:** 2
**Foundation:** Basement
**Materials List Available:** Yes
**Price Category:** C

*Images provided by designer/architect.*

This elegant home is packed with amenities that belie its compact size.

**Features:**

- Ceiling Height: 8 ft.

- Dining Room: The foyer opens into a view of the dining room, with its distinctive boxed ceiling.

- Great Room: The whole family will want to gather around the fireplace and enjoy the views and sunlight streaming through the transom-topped window.

- Breakfast Area: Next to the great room and sharing the transom-topped windows, this cozy area invites you to linger over morning coffee.

- Covered Porch: When the weather is nice, take your coffee through the door in the breakfast area and enjoy this large covered porch.

- Master Suite: French doors lead to this comfortable suite featuring a walk-in. Enjoy long, luxurious soaks in the corner whirlpool accented with boxed windows.

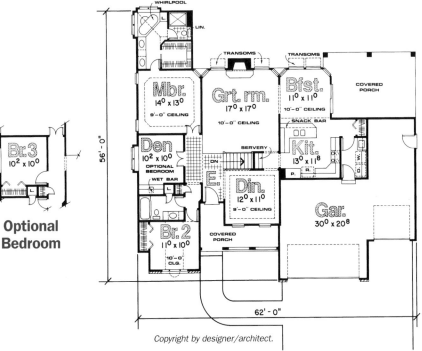

**Optional Bedroom**

*Copyright by designer/architect.*

## SMARTtip
## Finishing Your Fireplace with Tile

An excellent finishing material for a fireplace is tile. Luckily, there are reproductions of art tiles today. Most showrooms carry examples of Arts and Crafts, Art Nouveau, California, Delft, and other European tiles. Granite, limestone, and marble tiles are affordable alternatives to custom stone slabs.

# Plan #201034

**Dimensions:** 66'10" W x 46'10" D

**Levels:** 1

**Square Footage:** 1,660

**Bedrooms:** 3

**Bathrooms:** 2

**Foundation:** Crawl space, slab, or basement

**Materials List Available:** Yes

**Price Category:** C

This warm and inviting traditional country-style home, which features a delightful front porch that's perfect for relaxing on warm evenings, is a great choice for a growing family.

**Features:**

• Ceiling Height: 9 ft.

• Den: From the covered front porch, guests proceed through an entry foyer to this spacious den, which features a vaulted ceiling, built-in bookshelves and cabinets, and a handsome fireplace.

• Kitchen: This kitchen which is designed for convenience and easy work patterns, features abundant counter space, a breakfast bar, a large eating area, and access to the covered rear patio.

• Master Bedroom: Separated for privacy, this master bedroom features a whirlpool tub, separate shower, and large closet.

• Garage: The two-bay attached garage features a large storage room and has immediate access to the utility room.

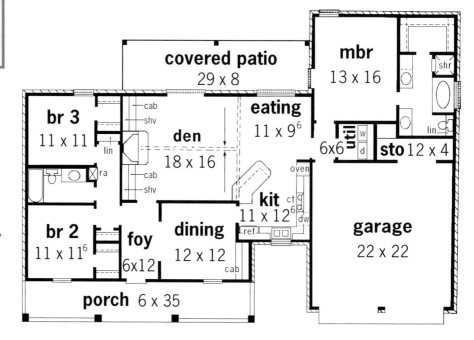

*Copyright by designer/architect.*

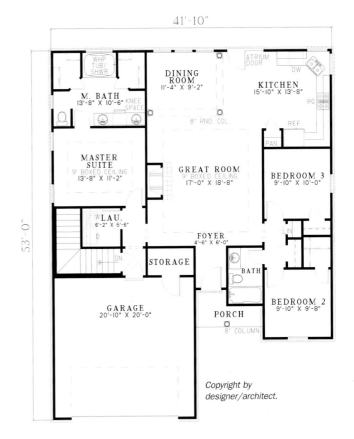

Images provided by
designer/architect.

## Plan #151059

**Dimensions:** 41'10" W x 53' D

**Levels:** 1

**Square Footage:** 1,382

**Bedrooms:** 3

**Bathrooms:** 2

**Foundation:** Crawl space, slab, with basement option for fee

**Materials List Available:** Yes

**Price Category:** B

Copyright by
designer/architect.

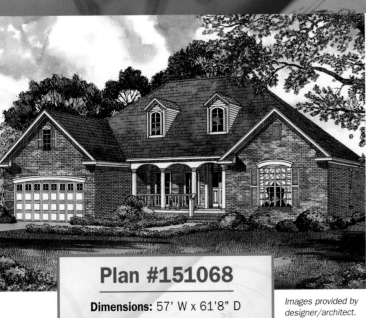

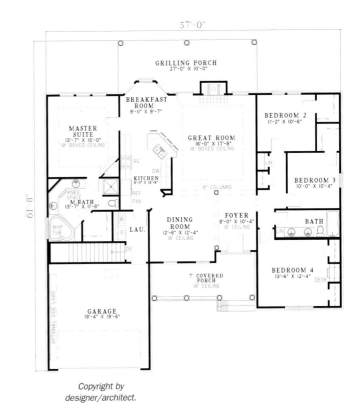

Images provided by
designer/architect.

## Plan #151068

**Dimensions:** 57' W x 61'8" D

**Levels:** 1

**Square Footage:** 1,880

**Bedrooms:** 4

**Bathrooms:** 2

**Foundation:** Crawl space, slab, or basement

**Materials List Available:** Yes

**Price Category:** D

Copyright by
designer/architect.

## Plan #131005

**Dimensions:** 70' W x 37'4" D
**Levels:** 1
**Square Footage:** 1,595
**Bedrooms:** 3
**Bathrooms:** 2
**Foundation:** Basement, crawl space, or slab
**Materials List Available:** Yes
**Price Category:** D

### SMARTtip

### Create a Courtyard

Create a private walled-garden retreat with fences covered by climbing vines. Add height with trellises, and divide spaces with clipped boxwood hedges. Include an (almost) instant patio by digging away an area of sod and then covering it with a layer of sand and landscaping mesh to discourage weeds. Then cover it with pea gravel, and add a garden bench, statuary, and perhaps an antique or two. The result? European ambiance for even the most nondescript suburban yard.

*Images provided by designer/architect.*

With the finest features of an open design in the main living areas, this home gives privacy where you need it. Best of all, it's wheelchair accessible.

**Features:**

• Foyer: A high ceiling gives this area real presence and serves to blend it seamlessly with the great room and the dining room.

• Great Room: The open design allows you to use this room as an extension of the dining room or, if you wish, furnish it to create a private reading nook or visually separate media center.

• Breakfast Room: Both this room and the adjacent well-appointed kitchen flow into the rest of the living area. However, access to the rear porch, where you can sit out and enjoy the weather while you eat, distinguishes this room.

• Master Suite: Located in the same wing as the other bedrooms, this suite has a separate entrance and features a vaulted ceiling, three closets, and a compartmented bath.

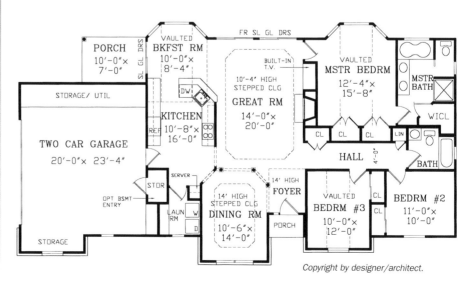

*Copyright by designer/architect.*

Foyer

Dining Room

Great Room

Living Room

## SMARTtip

### Natural Trellis

Create a natural rustic trellis that might even, if growing conditions are right, produce its own pretty blooms. Cut and place saplings in the ground as uprights. Then weave old grapevines with smaller saplings for the lattice.

## Plan #271078

**Dimensions:** 83' W x 52' D

**Levels:** 1

**Square Footage:** 1,855

**Bedrooms:** 1-2

**Bathrooms:** 1½-2½

**Foundation:** Daylight basement

**Materials List Available:** No

**Price Category:** D

*Images provided by designer/architect.*

**Optional
Basement Level
Floor Plan**

*Copyright by designer/architect.*

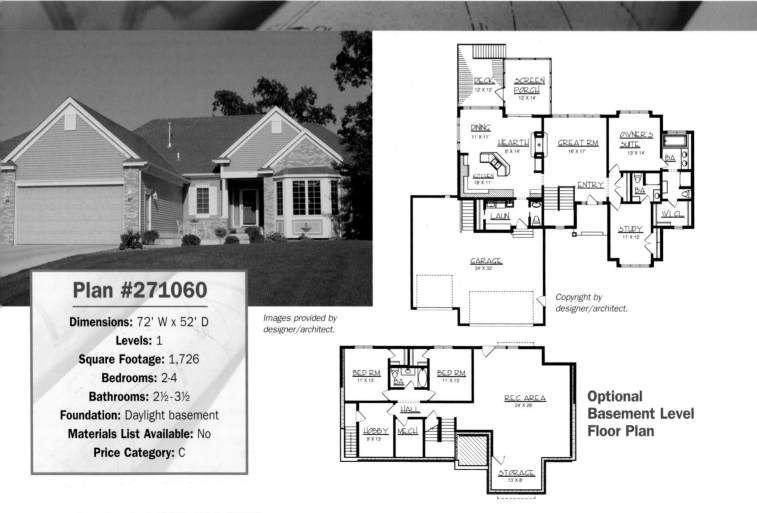

## Plan #271060

**Dimensions:** 72' W x 52' D

**Levels:** 1

**Square Footage:** 1,726

**Bedrooms:** 2-4

**Bathrooms:** 2½-3½

**Foundation:** Daylight basement

**Materials List Available:** No

**Price Category:** C

*Images provided by designer/architect.*

*Copyright by designer/architect.*

**Optional
Basement Level
Floor Plan**

## Plan #271077

**Dimensions:** 70' W x 53' D

**Levels:** 1

**Square Footage:** 1,786

**Bedrooms:** 1-4

**Bathrooms:** 1½-2½

**Foundation:** Daylight basement

**Materials List Available:** No

**Price Category:** C

*Images provided by designer/architect.*

**Optional Basement Level Floor Plan**

*Copyright by designer/architect.*

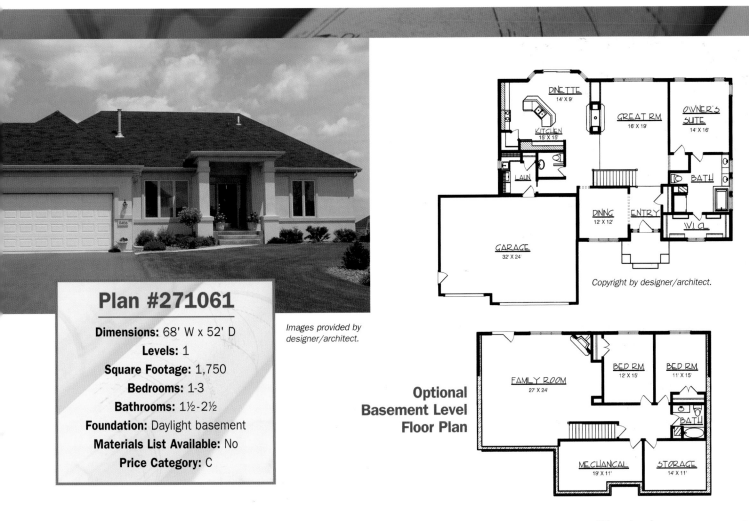

## Plan #271061

**Dimensions:** 68' W x 52' D

**Levels:** 1

**Square Footage:** 1,750

**Bedrooms:** 1-3

**Bathrooms:** 1½-2½

**Foundation:** Daylight basement

**Materials List Available:** No

**Price Category:** C

*Images provided by designer/architect.*

*Copyright by designer/architect.*

**Optional Basement Level Floor Plan**

## Plan #121009

**Dimensions:** 50' W x 58' D
**Levels:** 1
**Square Footage:** 1,422
**Bedrooms:** 3
**Bathrooms:** 2
**Foundation:** Basement
**Materials List Available:** Yes
**Price Category:** B

*Images provided by designer/architect.*

This amenity-filled home is perfect for the growing family or as a retirement retreat.

**Features:**

- Ceiling Height: 8 ft. unless otherwise noted.
- Great Room: This inviting space is the perfect place for gatherings of all sizes. It shares 12-ft. ceilings with the dining room and kitchen.

- Dining Room: In addition to the 12-ft. ceiling, arched openings, and built-in book cases make this an elegant place to dine.
- Private Porch: After dinner, step through a door in the dining room to enjoy a summer breeze in this inviting porch.
- Master Suite: The boxed ceiling lends drama to this suite and a walk-in closet adds convenience. Luxury comes from the whirlpool bath.
- Garage: You won't be short of parking and storage space in this two-bay garage. As a bonus there is space for a workbench.

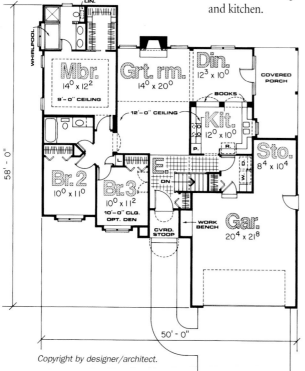

*Copyright by designer/architect.*

## SMARTtip
### Window Cornices

You can transform plain rooms by making jogs in cornice molding that will hold shades, blinds, and other window treatments. You can create individual pockets over each window or continue the molding past narrow wall sections between windows to form a more expansive detail. Housings below the cornice can be painted or papered.

## Plan #121092

**Dimensions:** 65'4" W x 52'8" D
**Levels:** 1
**Square Footage:** 1,887
**Bedrooms:** 3
**Bathrooms:** 2½
**Foundation:** Basement
**Materials List Available:** Yes
**Price Category:** D

*Images provided by designer/architect.*

This is the design if you want a home that will be easy to expand as your family grows.

**Features:**

• Entry: Both the dining room and great room are immediately accessible from this lovely entry.

• Great Room: The transom-topped bowed windows highlight the spacious feeling here.

• Gathering Room: Also with an angled ceiling, this room has a fireplace as well as built-in entertainment center and bookcases.

• Dining Room: This elegant room features a 13-ft. boxed ceiling and majestic window around which you'll love to decorate.

• Kitchen: Designed for convenience, this kitchen includes a lovely angled ceiling and gazebo-shaped breakfast area.

• Basement: Use the plans for finishing a family room and two bedrooms when the time is right.

## Main Level Floor Plan

## Lower Level Floor Plan

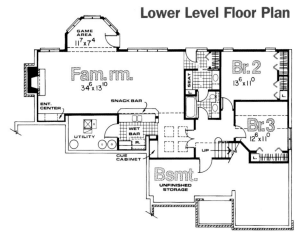

*Copyright by designer/architect.*

## Plan #321033

**Dimensions:** 38' W x 46' D
**Levels:** 1
**Square Footage:** 1,268
**Bedrooms:** 3
**Bathrooms:** 2
**Foundation:** Basement
**Materials List Available:** Yes
**Price Category:** B

*Images provided by designer/architect.*

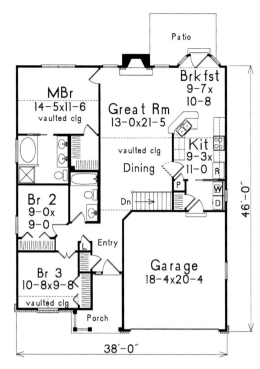

*Copyright by designer/architect.*

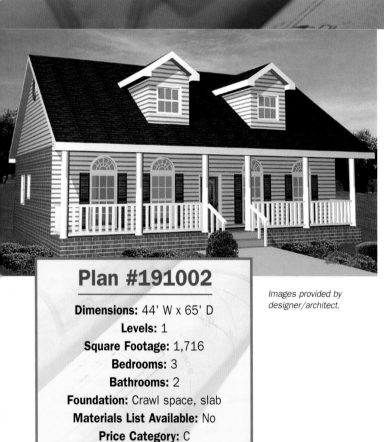

## Plan #191002

**Dimensions:** 44' W x 65' D
**Levels:** 1
**Square Footage:** 1,716
**Bedrooms:** 3
**Bathrooms:** 2
**Foundation:** Crawl space, slab
**Materials List Available:** No
**Price Category:** C

*Images provided by designer/architect.*

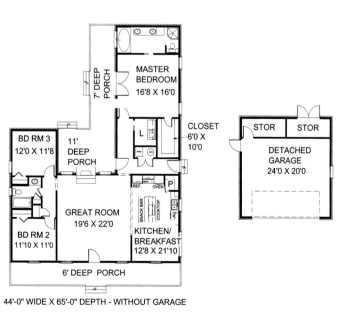

44'-0" WIDE X 65'-0" DEPTH - WITHOUT GARAGE

*Copyright by designer/architect.*

## Plan #341009

**Dimensions:** 44'5" W x 39'4" D

**Levels:** 1

**Square Footage:** 1,280

**Bedrooms:** 3

**Bathrooms:** 2

**Foundation:** Crawl space, slab, or basement

**Materials List Available:** Yes

**Price Category:** B

If you admire the exterior features of this home — the L-shaped front porch, nested gables, and transom lights — you'll love its interior.

**Features:**

- Ceiling Height: Ceilings are 9-ft. high to enhance this home's spacious feeling.

- Living Room: A fireplace creates a cozy feeling in this open, spacious room.

- Dining Room: Decorative columns grace the transition between this room and the living room.

- Kitchen: This open kitchen features a serving bar, a large pantry, and access to the back deck.

- Laundry: The washer and dryer are housed in a large utility closet to minimize noise.

- Master Suite: A designer window, vaulted ceiling, and walk-in closet make the bedroom luxurious, and the garden tub and shower make the private bath a true retreat.

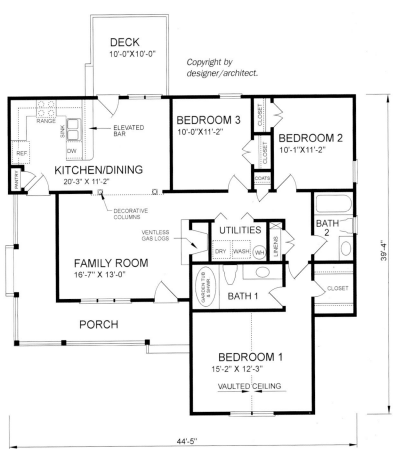

*Copyright by designer/architect.*

# Plans and Ideas for Your Landscape

L andscapes change over the years. As plants grow, the overall look evolves from sparse to lush. Trees cast cool shade where the sun used to shine. Shrubs and hedges grow tall and dense enough to provide privacy. Perennials and ground covers spread to form colorful patches of foliage and flowers. Meanwhile, paths, arbors, fences, and other structures gain the patina of age.

Constant change over the years—sometimes rapid and dramatic, sometimes slow and subtle—is one of the joys of landscaping. It is also one of the challenges. Anticipating how fast plants will grow and how big they will eventually get is difficult, even for professional designers, and was a major concern in formulating the designs for this book.

To illustrate the kinds of changes to expect in a planting, these pages show a landscape design at three different "ages." Even though a new planting may look sparse at first, it will soon fill in. And because of careful spacing, the planting will look as good in 10 to 15 years as it does after 3 to 5. It will, of course, look different, but that's part of the fun.

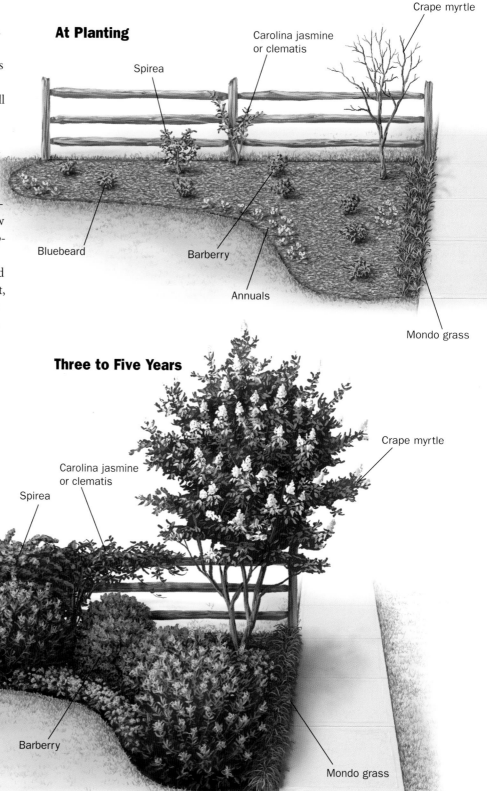

**At Planting**

Crape myrtle

Carolina jasmine or clematis

Spirea

Bluebeard

Barberry

Annuals

Mondo grass

**Three to Five Years**

Carolina jasmine or clematis

Crape myrtle

Spirea

Barberry

Mondo grass

**At Planting**—Here's how a corner planting might appear in spring immediately after planting. The fence and mulch look conspicuously fresh, new, and unweathered. The crape myrtle is only 4 to 5 ft. tall, with trunks no thicker than broomsticks. It hasn't leafed out yet. The spirea and barberries are 12 to 18 in. tall and wide, and the Carolina jasmine (or clematis) just reaches the bottom rail of the fence. Evenly spaced tufts of mondo grass edge the sidewalk. The bluebeards are stubby now but will grow 2 to 3 ft. tall by late summer, when they bloom. Annuals such as vinca and ageratum start flowering right away and soon form solid patches of color. The first year after planting, be sure to water during dry spells and to pull or spray any weeds that pop through the mulch.

**Three to Five Years**—Shown in summer now, the planting has begun to mature. The mondo grass has spread to make a continuous, weed-proof patch. The Carolina jasmine (or clematis) reaches partway along the fence. The spirea and barberries have grown into bushy, rounded specimens. From now on, they'll get wider but not much taller. The crape myrtle will keep growing about 1 ft. taller every year, and its crown will broaden. As you continue replacing the annuals twice a year, keep adding compost or organic matter to the soil and spreading fresh mulch on top.

**Ten to Fifteen Years**—As shown here in late summer, the crape myrtle is now a fine specimen, about 15 ft. tall, with a handsome silhouette, beautiful flowers, and colorful bark on its trunks. The bluebeards recover from an annual spring pruning to form bushy mounds covered with blooms. The Carolina jasmine, (or clematis) spirea, and barberry have reached their mature size. Keep them neat and healthy by pruning out old, weak, or dead stems every spring. If you get tired of replanting annuals, substitute low-growing perennials or shrubs in those positions.

## Ten to Fifteen Years

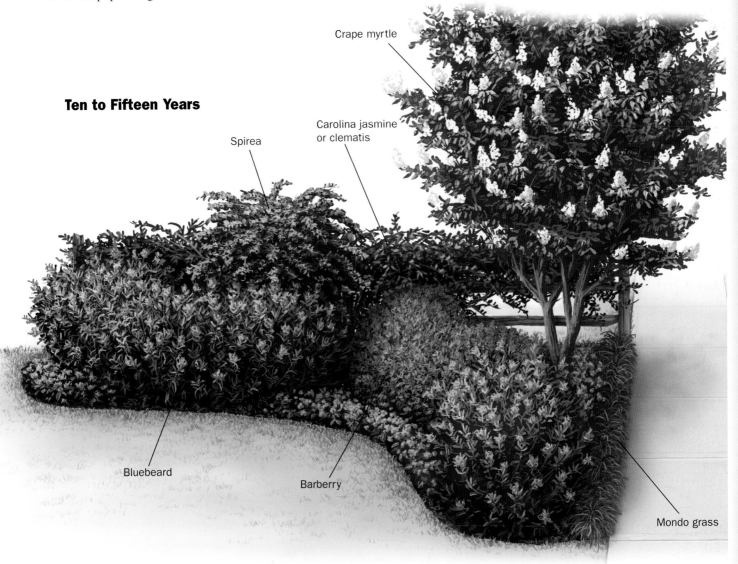

Crape myrtle

Carolina jasmine or clematis

Spirea

Bluebeard

Barberry

Mondo grass

# "Around Back"

## Dress Up the Area between Cottage and Detached Garage

When people think of landscaping the entrance to their home, the public entry at the front of the house comes immediately to mind. It's easy to forget that the back door often gets more use. If you make the journey between back door and driveway or garage many times each day, why not make it as pleasant a trip as possible? For many properties, a simple planting can transform the space bounded by the house, garage, and driveway, making it at once more inviting and more functional.

In a high-traffic area frequented by ball-bouncing, bicycle-riding children as well as busy adults, delicate, fussy plants have no place. The design shown here employs a few types of tough low-care plants, all of which look good year-round. The low yew hedge links the house and the garage and separates the more private backyard from the busy driveway. The star magnolia is just the right size for its spot. Its early-spring flowers will be a delight whether viewed coming up the driveway or from a window overlooking the backyard. The wide walk makes passage to and from the car easy—even with your arms full of groceries.

*Note: All plants are appropriate for USDA Hardiness Zones 5, 6, and 7*

**A** Star magnolia

See site plan for **F**

**Site:** Sunny
**Season:** Summer
**Concept:** A planting to raise spirits weighed down by shopping bags and to separate activities in the backyard from the driveway.

'Steeds' **C**
Japanese holly

**B** 'Hicksii'
hybrid yew

**D** 'Hidcote'
hypericum

**E** 'Big Blue' lilyturf

Walkway **G**

'Big Blue' lilyturf **E**

# Plants & Projects

The watchword in this planting is evergreen. Except for the magolia, all the plants here are fully evergreen or are nearly so. Spring and summer see lovely flowers from the magnolia and hypericum, and the carpet of lilyturf turns a handsome blue in August. For a bigger splash in spring, underplant the lily-turf with daffodils. Choose a single variety for uniform color, or select several varieties for a mix of colors and bloom times. Other than shearing the hedge, the only maintenance required is cutting back the lilyturf and hypericum in late winter.

**A** **Star magnolia** *Magnolia stellata* (use 1 plant)
Lovely white flowers cover this small deciduous tree before the leaves appear. Starlike blooms, slightly fragrant and sometimes tinged with pink, appear in early spring and last up to two weeks. In summer, the dense leafy crown of dark green leaves helps provide privacy in the backyard. A multi-trunked specimen will fill the space better and display more of the interesting winter bark.

**B** **'Hicksii' hybrid yew** *Taxus x media* (use 9)
A fast-growing evergreen shrub that is ideal for this 3-ft.-tall, neatly sheared hedge. Needles are glossy dark green and soft, not prickly. Eight plants form the L-shaped portion, while a single sheared plant extends the hedge on the other side of the walk connecting it to the house. (If the hedge needs to play a part in confining a family pet, you could easily set posts either side of the walk and add a gate.)

**C** **'Steeds' Japanese holly** *Ilex crenata* (use 3 or more)
Several of these dense, upright evergreen shrubs can be grouped at the corner as specimen plants or to tie into an existing foundation planting. You could also extend them along the house to create a foundation planting, as shown here. The small dark green leaves are thick and leathery and have tiny spines. Plants attain a pleasing form when left to their own devices. Resist the urge to shear them; just prune to control size if necessary.

**D** **'Hidcote' hypericum** *Hypericum* (use 1)
All summer long, clusters of large golden flowers cover the arching stems of this tidy semievergreen shrub, brightening the entrance to the backyard.

**E** **'Big Blue' lilyturf** *Liriope muscari* (use 40 or more)
Grasslike evergreen clumps of this perennial ground cover grow together to carpet the ground flanking the driveway and walk. (Extend the planting as far down the drive as you like.) Slim spires of tiny blue flowers rise above the dark green leaves in June. Lilyturf doesn't stand up to repeated tromping. If the drive is also a basketball court, substitute periwinkle (Vinca minor, p. 197), a tough ground cover with late-spring lilac flowers.

**F** **Stinking hellebore** *Helleborus foetidus* (use 5 or more)
This clump-forming perennial is ideal for filling the space between the walk and house on the backyard side of the hedge. (You might also consider extending the planting along the L-shaped side of the hedge.) Its pale green flowers are among the first to bloom in the spring and continue for many weeks; dark green leaves are attractive year-round.

**G** **Walkway**
Precast concrete pavers, 2 ft. by 2 ft., replace an existing walk or form a new one.

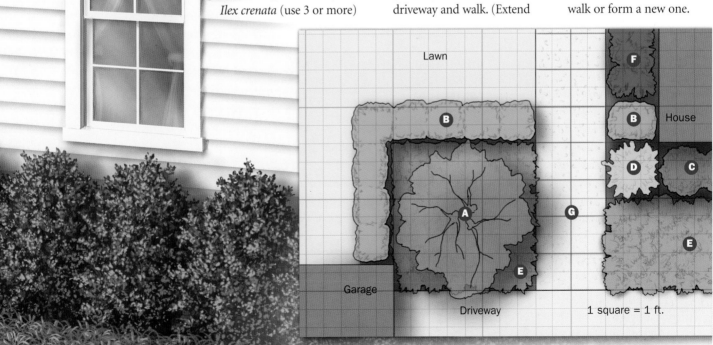

Lawn · House · Garage · Driveway · 1 square = 1 ft.

# Beautify Your Cottage's Garden Shed

Just as you enhance your living room by hanging paintings on the walls, you can decorate blank walls in your outdoor "living rooms." The design shown here transforms a nondescript shed wall into a living fresco, showcasing lovely plants in a framework of roses and flowering vines. Instead of a view of peeling paint, imagine gazing at this scene from a nearby patio, deck, or kitchen window.

This symmetrical composition frames two crape myrtles between arched latticework trellises. Handsome multitrunked shrubs, the crape myrtles perform year-round, providing sumptuous pink flowers in summer, orange-red foliage in fall, and attractive bark in winter. On either side of the crape myrtles, roses and clematis scramble over the trellis in a profusion of yellow and purple flowers.

A tidy low boxwood hedge sets off a shallow border of shrubs and perennials at the bottom of the "frame." Cheerful long-blooming daylilies and asters, airy Russian sage, and elegant daphne make sure that the ground-level attractions hold their own with the aerial performers covering the wall above. The flowers hew to a color scheme of yellows, pinks, blues, and purples.

Wider or narrower walls can be accommodated by expanding the design to include additional "panels," or by reducing it to one central panel. To set off the plants, consider painting or staining the wall and trellises in an off-white, an earth tone, or a light gray color.

Jackman clematis

'Golden Showers' rose

'Carol Mackie' daphne

'Happy Returns' daylily

'Green Beauty' littleleaf boxwood

## Plants and Projects

These plants will all do well in the hot, dry conditions often found near a wall with a sunny exposure. Other than training and pruning the vines, roses, and hedge, maintenance involves little more than fall and spring cleanup. The trellises, supported by 4x4 posts and attached to the garage, are well within the reach of average do-it-yourselfers.

**A** **'Hopi' crape myrtle** *Lagerstroemia indica* (use 2 plants) Large multitrunked deciduous shrubs produce papery pink flowers for weeks in summer. They also contribute colorful fall foliage and attractive flaky bark for winter interest.

**B** **'Golden Showers' rose** *Rosa* (use 3) Tied to each trellis, the long canes of these climbers dis-

play large, fragrant, double yellow flowers in abundance all summer long.

**C** **Golden clematis** *Clematis tangutica* (use 1) Twining up through the rose canes, this deciduous vine adds masses of small yellow flowers to the larger, more elaborate roses all summer. Feathery silver seed heads in fall.

**D** **Jackman clematis** *Clematis x jackmanii* (use 2) These deciduous vines clamber among the rose canes at the corners of the wall. The combination of their large but simple purple flowers and the double yellow roses is spectacular.

**E** **'Green Beauty' littleleaf boxwood** *Buxus microphylla* (use 15) Small evergreen leaves make this an ideal shrub for this

neat hedge. The leaves stay bright green all winter. Trim it about 12 to 18 in. high so it won't obscure the plants behind.

**F** **Carol Mackie' daphne** *Daphne x burkwoodii* (use 2) This small rounded shrub marks the far end of the bed with year-round green-and-cream variegated foliage. In spring, pale pink flowers fill the yard with their perfume.

**G** **Russian sage** *Perovskia atriplicifolia* (use 7) Silver-green foliage and tiers of tiny blue flowers create a light airy effect in the center of the design from midsummer until fall. Cut stems back partway in early summer to control the size and spread of this tall perennial.

**H** **'Happy Returns' daylily** *Hemerocallis* (use 6) These compact grassy-

leaved perennials provide yellow trumpet-shaped flowers from early June to frost. A striking combination of color and texture with the Russian sage behind.

**I** **'Monch' aster** *Aster x frikartii* (use 4) Pale purple daisylike flowers bloom gaily from June until frost on these knee-high perennials. Cut stems partway back in midsummer if they start to flop over the hedge.

**J** **Trellis** Simple panels of wooden lattice frame the crape myrtles while supporting the roses and clematis.

**K** **Steppingstones** Rectangular flagstone slabs provide a place to stand while pruning and tying nearby shrubs and vines.

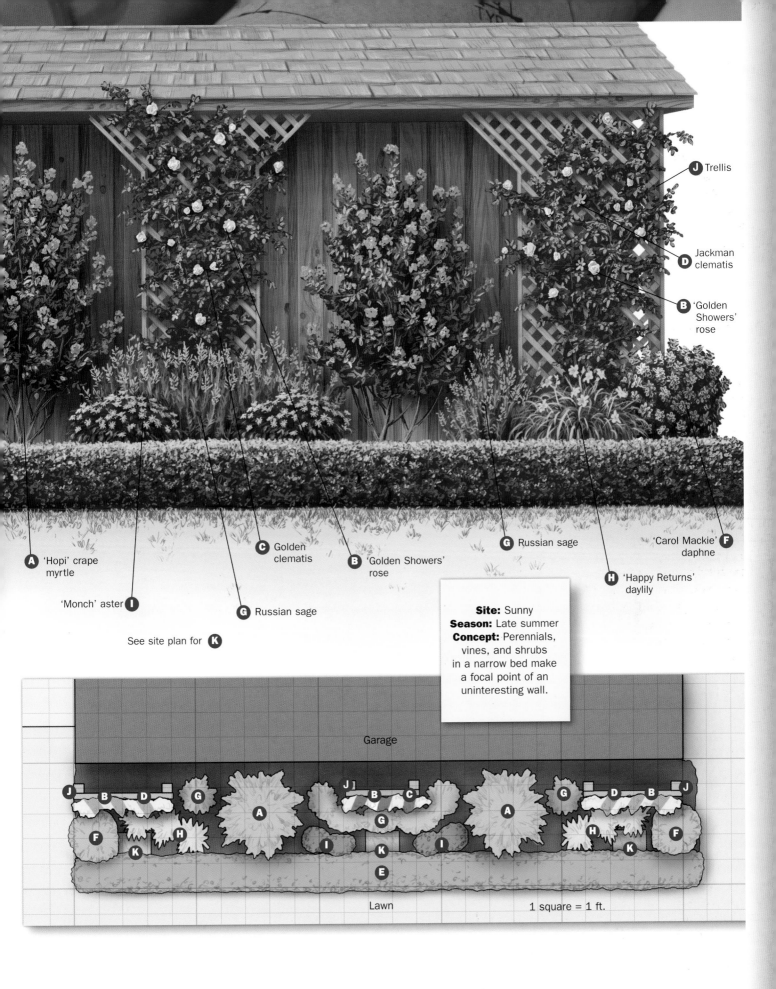

**J** Trellis

**D** Jackman clematis

**B** 'Golden Showers' rose

**A** 'Hopi' crape myrtle

**C** Golden clematis

**B** 'Golden Showers' rose

**G** Russian sage

**'Carol Mackie' F** daphne

**'Monch' aster I**

**G** Russian sage

**H** 'Happy Returns' daylily

See site plan for **K**

**Site:** Sunny
**Season:** Late summer
**Concept:** Perennials, vines, and shrubs in a narrow bed make a focal point of an uninteresting wall.

Garage

**J** **B** **D** **G** **J** **B** **C** **G** **D** **B** **J**
**F** **A** **A** **F**
**H** **G** **H**
**K** **I** **K** **I** **K**
**E**

Lawn          1 square = 1 ft.

# Pleasing Passage to a Cottage Landscape

Entrances are an important part of any landscape. They can welcome visitors onto your property; highlight a special feature, such as a rose garden; or mark passage between two areas with different character or function. The design shown here can serve in any of these situations. A picket fence and perennial plantings create a friendly, attractive barrier, just enough to signal the confines of the front

yard or contain the family dog. The vine-covered arbor provides welcoming access.

The design combines uncomplicated elements imaginatively, creating interesting details to catch the eye and a slightly formal but comfortable overall effect. Picketed enclosures and compact evergreen shrubs

broaden the arbor, giving it greater presence. The wide flagstone apron, flanked by neat deciduous shrubs, reinforces this effect and frames the entrance. Massed perennial plantings lend substance to the fence, which serves as a backdrop to their handsome foliage and colorful flowers.

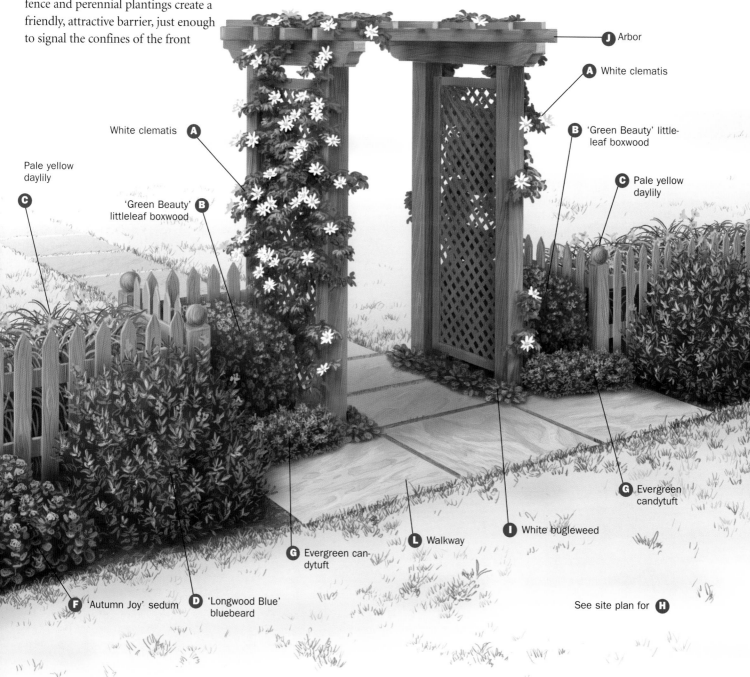

White clematis **A**

Pale yellow daylily **C**

'Green Beauty' littleleaf boxwood **B**

**J** Arbor

**A** White clematis

**B** 'Green Beauty' little-leaf boxwood

**C** Pale yellow daylily

**G** Evergreen candytuft

**I** White bugleweed

**L** Walkway

**G** Evergreen candytuft

**F** 'Autumn Joy' sedum

**D** 'Longwood Blue' bluebeard

See site plan for **H**

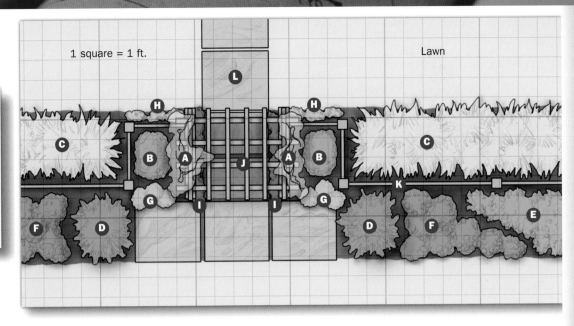

1 square = 1 ft.

Lawn

K Picket fence

E 'Wargrave Pink' geranium

F 'Autumn Joy' sedum

D 'Longwood Blue' bluebeard

## Plants and Projects

For many people, a picket fence and vine-covered arbor represent old-fashioned "Cottage" style. The plantings here further encourage this feeling.

Pretty white flowers cover the arbor for much of the summer. Massed plantings of daylilies, geraniums, and sedums along the fence produce wide swaths of flowers and attractive foliage from early summer to fall. Plant drifts of snowdrops in these beds; their late-winter flowers are a welcome sign that spring will soon come.

The structures and plantings are easy to build, install, and care for. You can extend the fence and plantings as needed. To use an existing concrete walk, just pour pads either side to create the wide apron in front of the arbor.

**A** **White clematis** *Clematis* (use 4 plants)
Four of these deciduous climbing vines, one at each post, will cover the arbor in a few years. For large white flowers, try the cultivar 'Henryi', which blooms in early and late summer.

**B** **'Green Beauty' littleleaf boxwood** *Buxus microphylla* (use 2)
This evergreen shrub forms a neat ball of small bright green leaves without shearing. It is colorful in winter when the rest of the plants are dormant.

**C** **Pale yellow daylily** *Hemerocallis* (use 24)
A durable perennial whose cheerful trumpet-shaped flowers nod above clumps of arching foliage. Choose from the many yellow-flowered cultivars (some fragrant); mix several to extend the season of bloom.

**D** **'Longwood Blue' bluebeard** *Caryopteris x clandonensis* (use 2)
A pair of these small deciduous shrubs with soft gray foliage frame the entry. Sky blue late-summer flowers cover the plants for weeks.

**E** **'Wargrave Pink' geranium** *Geranium endressii* (use 9)
This perennial produces a mass of bright green leaves and a profusion of pink flowers in early summer. Cut it back in July and it will bloom intermittently until frost.

**F** **'Autumn Joy' sedum** *Sedum* (use 13)
This perennial forms a clump of upright stems with distinctive fleshy foliage. Pale flower buds that appear during summer are followed by pink flowers during fall and rusty seed heads that stand up in winter.

**G** **Evergreen candytuft** *Iberis sempervirens* (use 12)
A perennial ground cover that spreads to form a small welcome mat at the foot of the boxwoods. White flowers stand out against glossy evergreen leaves in spring.

**H** **Lamb's ears** *Stachys byzantina* (use 6)
Favorites of children, the long woolly gray leaves of this perennial form a soft carpet. In early summer, thick stalks carry scattered purple flowers.

**I** **White bugleweed** *Ajuga reptans* 'Alba' (use 20)
Edging the walk under the arbor, this perennial ground cover has pretty green leaves and, in late spring, short spikes of white flowers.

**J** **Arbor** Thick posts give this simple structure a sturdy visual presence. Paint or stain it, or make it of cedar and let it weather as shown here.

**K** **Picket fence** Low picket fence adds character to the planting; materials and finish should match the arbor.

**L** **Walkway** Flagstone walk can be large pavers, as shown here, or made up of smaller rectangular flags.

Images provided by designer/architect.

**porch** 33 x 5

**dining** 13 x 12

**mbr** 13 x 18

**living** 20 x 18

**kit** 13 x 12

shv
cab
ov
ct
pan
cab
shv
wet bar

lin
shr

**foy** 9x11

**sto** 5x8

**eating** 13 x 9

**br 2** 12 x 11⁶

lin

**br 3** 12 x 12

**por** 9x3⁶

**garage** 22 x 21

Copyright by designer/architect.

## Plan #201043

**Dimensions:** 57'10" W x 54'5" D

**Levels:** 1

**Square Footage:** 1,887

**Bedrooms:** 3

**Bathrooms:** 2

**Foundation:** Crawl space, slab, or basement

**Materials List Available:** Yes

**Price Category:** D

---

## SMARTtip

### Resin Outdoor Furniture

Resin furniture is made of molded plastic. Most resin pieces are quite affordable, but lacquered resin with brass fittings is a high-end item. Resin doesn't corrode and cleans easily, but a scratched finish cannot be repaired. Lacquered resin can be touched up, however.

Images provided by designer/architect.

**mbr** 13 x 16⁸

shvs
cab

**den** 19 x 20

**eating** 13 x 10

**util** 7 x 7

**sto** 11 x 7

shr
lin

**kit** 13 x 12

ct
dbl
ov
pan
ref
dw

**garage** 22 x 22

**br 2** 13 x 11⁶

**br 3** 13 x 11⁶

**foy** 6 x 8

**por**

**dining** 13 x 12

Copyright by designer/architect.

## Plan #201044

**Dimensions:** 74'10" W x 44'4" D

**Levels:** 1

**Square Footage:** 1,869

**Bedrooms:** 3

**Bathrooms:** 2

**Foundation:** Crawl space, slab, or basement

**Materials List Available:** Yes

**Price Category:** D

## Plan #211016

**Dimensions:** 44'6" W x 59' D

**Levels:** 1

**Square Footage:** 1,191

**Bedrooms:** 3

**Bathrooms:** 2

**Foundation:** Slab

**Materials List Available:** Yes

**Price Category:** B

*Images provided by designer/architect.*

*Copyright by designer/architect.*

garage 22 x 21

patio

sto 11x5

w 11x5 d

util

br 3 12 x 10

dining 12 x 12

kit 12x10

rng

ref pan dw

lin

a/c

lin

mbr 16 x 12

beam

living 18 x 16

slope clg

slope clg

br 2 12 x 10

**porch** 42 x 5

---

## Plan #211019

**Dimensions:** 73' W x 37' D

**Levels:** 1

**Square Footage:** 1,395

**Bedrooms:** 3

**Bathrooms:** 2

**Foundation:** Slab

**Materials List Available:** Yes

**Price Category:** B

*Images provided by designer/architect.*

*Copyright by designer/architect.*

SMARTtip

### Hose for Dishwasher

Most dishwashers come with a discharge hose. If the unit you buy does not have one, you'll need to supply the hose. Appliance supply stores may have what you need, but if they don't, automotive heater hose is a reasonable substitute. It can handle prolonged exposure to heat and detergent.

mbr 14 x 13

knee space

shv

w d

living 18 x 17

beam

stone

patio

wood box

shvs

sto

shvs

lin

br 2 12 x 11

br 3 12 x 11

a/c

foy

post w/rail

dining 12 x 11

drop clg

bar

kit 12x10

ref rng dw

garage 21 x 21

**porch** 42 x 7

# Plan #121055

**Dimensions:** 51' W x 52' D
**Levels:** 1
**Square Footage:** 1,622
**Bedrooms:** 3
**Bathrooms:** 2
**Foundation:** Basement
**Materials List Available:** Yes
**Price Category:** C

*Images provided by designer/architect.*

You'll be delighted by the attractive design features that are built into this compact home.

**Features:**

- **Entry:** A gracious U-shaped staircase greets you as you walk into this home.

- **Great Room:** Located just beyond the staircase, this great room is sure to be the family favorite, with 11-ft. ceilings and a large brick fireplace framed by built-in entertainment centers on both sides.

- **Den:** French doors in the front of the house open to this cozy den, which you can convert to an extra bedroom if you wish.

- **Kitchen:** An 11-ft. ceiling is unusual in a kitchen, but the good design and ample work and storage space you'll find here are becoming common.

- **Master Suite:** A decorative ceiling detail, walk-in closet, and whirlpool tub with glass blocks on the shower highlight this private area.

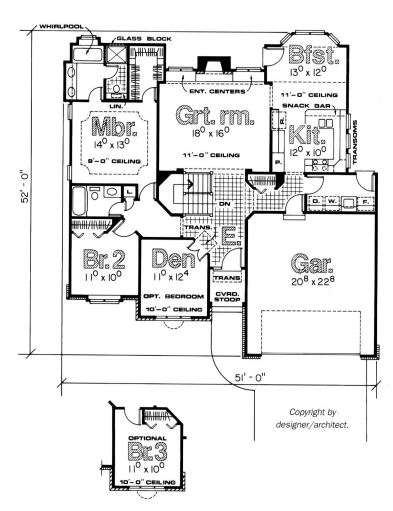

## Plan #121056

**Dimensions:** 48' W x 50' D
**Levels:** 1
**Square Footage:** 1,479
**Bedrooms:** 2
**Bathrooms:** 2
**Foundation:** Basement
**Materials List Available:** Yes
**Price Category:** B

*Images provided by designer/architect.*

This home is ideal if the size of your live-in family is increasing with the addition of a baby, or if it's decreasing as children leave the nest.

**Features:**

- **Entry:** This entry gives you a long view into the great room that it opens into.

- **Great Room:** An 11-ft. ceiling and a fireplace framed by transom-topped windows make this room comfortable in every season and any time of day or night.

- **Den:** French doors open to this den, with its picturesque window. This room would also make a lovely third bedroom.

- **Kitchen:** This kitchen has an island that can double as a snack bar, a pantry, and a door into the backyard.

- **Master Suite:** A large walk-in closet gives a practical touch; you'll find a sunlit whirlpool tub, dual lavatories, and a separate shower in the bath.

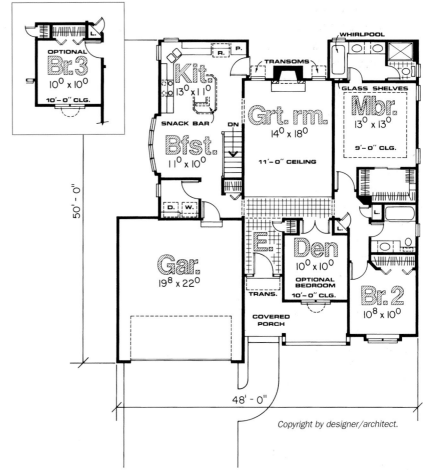

*Copyright by designer/architect.*

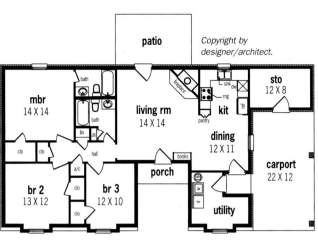

Copyright by designer/architect.

# Plan #211017

**Dimensions:** 60' W x 31' D
**Levels:** 1
**Square Footage:** 1,212
**Bedrooms:** 3
**Bathrooms:** 2
**Foundation:** Slab
**Materials List Available:** No
**Price Category:** B

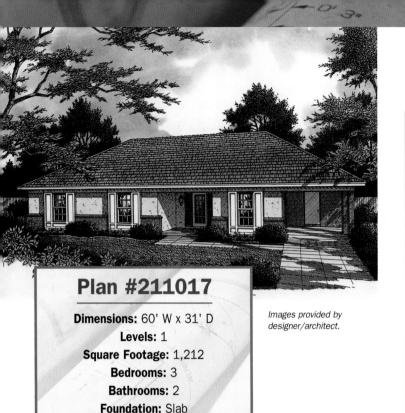

*Images provided by designer/architect.*

SMARTtip

## Adding Trim Accessories

Consider adding plinth and corner blocks to door and window casings. These relatively inexpensive elements add a decorative flourish to wall openings, bringing depth and richness to an interior space.

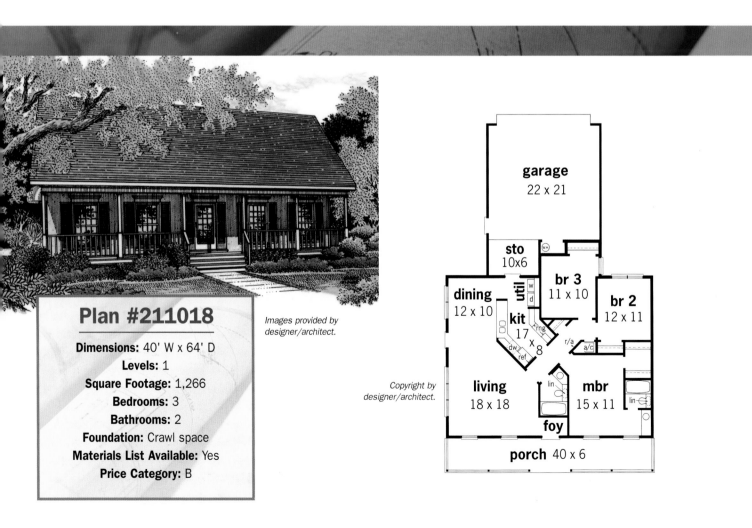

# Plan #211018

*Images provided by designer/architect.*

**Dimensions:** 40' W x 64' D
**Levels:** 1
**Square Footage:** 1,266
**Bedrooms:** 3
**Bathrooms:** 2
**Foundation:** Crawl space
**Materials List Available:** Yes
**Price Category:** B

Copyright by designer/architect.

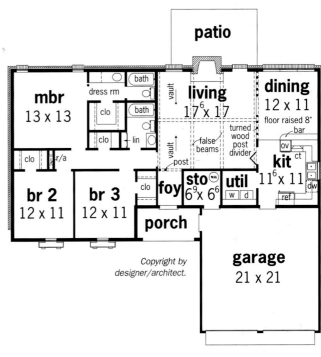

## Plan #211020

**Dimensions:** 54' W x 44'6" D

**Levels:** 1

**Square Footage:** 1,346

**Bedrooms:** 3

**Bathrooms:** 2

**Foundation:** Slab

**Materials List Available:** Yes

**Price Category:** B

*Images provided by designer/architect.*

*Copyright by designer/architect.*

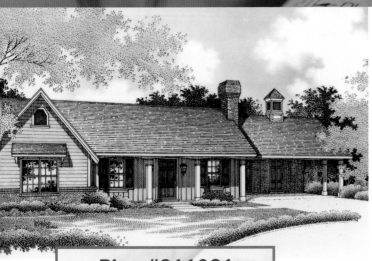

## Plan #211021

**Dimensions:** 61' W x 35' D

**Levels:** 1

**Square Footage:** 1,375

**Bedrooms:** 3

**Bathrooms:** 2

**Foundation:** Slab

**Materials List Available:** Yes

**Price Category:** B

*Images provided by designer/architect.*

*Copyright by designer/architect.*

## SMARTtip

### Creating Built-up Cornices

Combine various base, crown, and cove moldings to create an elaborate cornice that is both imaginative and tasteful. Use the pattern throughout your home to establish a unique architectural element having the appearance of being professionally designed.

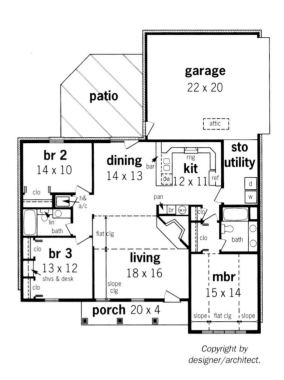

**garage**
22 x 20

**patio**

attic

**sto**
**utility**

**br 2**
14 x 10

**dining**
14 x 13

bar

rng

**kit**
12 x 11

dw

ref

d

w

clo

h&
a/c

lin

bath

pan

br

w

clo

clo

**bath**

**br 3**
13 x 12

shvs & desk

clo

clo

flat clg

**living**
18 x 16

slope
clg

**mbr**
15 x 14

slope

flat clg

slope

**porch** 20 x 4

*Copyright by
designer/architect.*

# Plan #211022

**Dimensions:** 46' W x 56' D

**Levels:** 1

**Square Footage:** 1,380

**Bedrooms:** 3

**Bathrooms:** 2

**Foundation:** Slab

**Materials List Available:** Yes

**Price Category:** B

*Images provided by
designer/architect.*

---

# Plan #211025

**Dimensions:** 70' W x 44' D

**Levels:** 1

**Square Footage:** 1,434

**Bedrooms:** 3

**Bathrooms:** 2

**Foundations:** Crawl space

**Materials List Available:** Yes

**Price Category:** B

*Images provided by
designer/architect.*

## SMARTtip

### Kitchen Peninsulas & Islands

If a peninsula or island separates the kitchen work area from the eating or living area in a great room, consider installing a 48-inch-high snack bar along the dividing line and standard height counters everywhere else. The high counter will help keep dirty dishes, pots, and pans out of sight while you are dining.

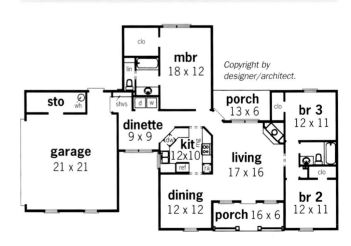

clo

**mbr**
18 x 12

lin

*Copyright by
designer/architect.*

shvs

d

w

**sto**
wh

**porch**
13 x 6

clo

**br 3**
12 x 11

**garage**
21 x 21

**dinette**
9 x 9

dw

**kit**
12x10

rng

ref

**living**
17 x 16

clo

**dining**
12 x 12

**porch** 16 x 6

**br 2**
12 x 11

Images provided by designer/architect.

## Plan #211024

**Dimensions:** 61' W x 44' D

**Levels:** 1

**Square Footage:** 1,418

**Bedrooms:** 3

**Bathrooms:** 2

**Foundation:** Slab

**Materials List Available:** Yes

**Price Category:** B

Copyright by designer/architect.

## Plan #211030

**Dimensions:** 75' W x 37' D

**Levels:** 1

**Square Footage:** 1,600

**Bedrooms:** 3

**Bathrooms:** 2

**Foundation:** Slab

**Materials List Available:** Yes

**Price Category:** C

Images provided by designer/architect.

SMARTtip

## Brackets in Window Treatments

Although it is rarely noticed, a bracket plays an important role in supporting rods and poles. If a treatment rubs against a window frame, an extension bracket solves the problem. It projects from the wall at an adjustable length, providing enough clearance. A hold-down bracket anchors a cellular shade or a blind to the bottom of a door, preventing the treatment from moving when the door is opened or closed.

Copyright by designer/architect.

# Plan #121051

**Dimensions:** 64' W x 44' D
**Levels:** 1
**Square Footage:** 1,808
**Bedrooms:** 3
**Bathrooms:** 2½
**Foundation:** Basement
**Materials List Available:** Yes
**Price Category:** D

*Images provided by designer/architect.*

You'll love the way that natural light pours into this home from the gorgeous windows you'll find in room after room.

**Features:**

- **Great Room:** You'll notice the bayed, transom-topped window in the great room as soon as you step into this lovely home. A wet-bar makes this great room a natural place for entertaining, and the see-through fireplace makes it cozy on chilly days and winter evenings.

- **Kitchen:** This well-designed kitchen will be a delight for everyone who cooks here, not only because of the ample counter and cabinet space but also because of its location in the home.

- **Master Suite:** Angled ceilings in both the bedroom and the bathroom of this suite make it feel luxurious, and the picturesque window in the bedroom gives it character. The bath includes a corner whirlpool tub where you'll love to relax at the end of the day.

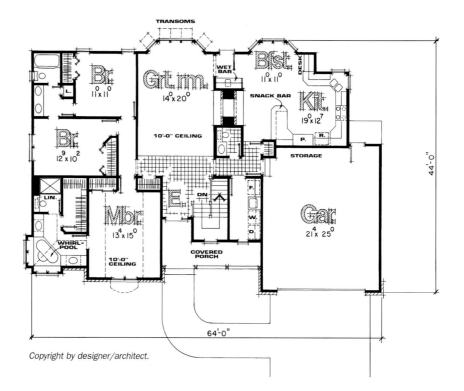

*Copyright by designer/architect.*

## Plan #121002

**Dimensions:** 42' W x 54' D
**Levels:** 1
**Square Footage:** 1,347
**Bedrooms:** 3
**Bathrooms:** 2
**Foundation:** Basement
**Materials List Available:** Yes
**Price Category:** B

*Images provided by designer/architect.*

This home's convenient single level and luxury amenities are a recipe for gracious living.

**Features:**

- Ceiling Height: 8 ft. except as noted.

- Great Room: The entry enjoys a long view into this great room where a pair of transom-topped windows flanks the fireplace and a 10-ft. ceiling visually expands the space.

- Snack Bar: This special feature adjoins the great room, making it a real plus for informal entertaining, as well as the perfect spot for family get-togethers.

- Kitchen: An island is the centerpiece of this well-designed convenient kitchen that features an island, a door to the backyard, a pantry, and convenient access to the laundry room.

- Master Suite: Located at the back of the home for extra privacy, the master suite feels like its own world. It features a tiered ceiling and sunlit corner whirlpool.

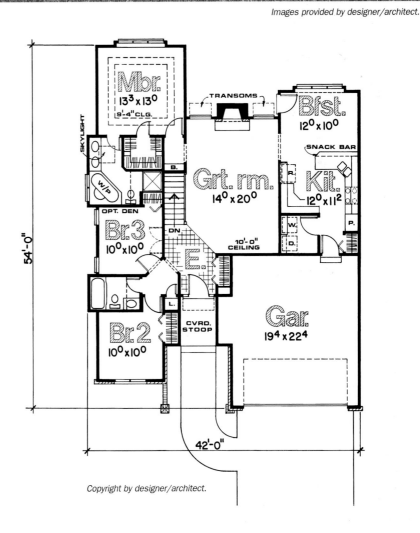

*Copyright by designer/architect.*

porch 12 x 6

living 20 x 20
flat clg

mbr 16 x 13

sto 9x5  sto 9x5

eating 12 x 10
false beams

garage 22 x 22

kit 12x10

dining 12 x 11

entry

br 3 14 x 12

br 2 14 x 12

porch 46 x 6

patio

*Copyright by designer/architect.*

## Plan #211036

**Dimensions:** 80' W x 40' D

**Levels:** 1

**Square Footage:** 1,800

**Bedrooms:** 3

**Bathrooms:** 2

**Foundation:** Slab

**Materials List Available:** Yes

**Price Category:** D

*Images provided by designer/architect.*

SMARTtip

## Dimmer Switches

You can dim lights just slightly to extend lamp life and save energy, and there will be very little perceptible change in light level. For instance, dimming the light to 50 percent will be perceived as though the light were only dimmed to 70 percent. Therefore, there is no dramatic dilation or constriction of the eye due to light level change.

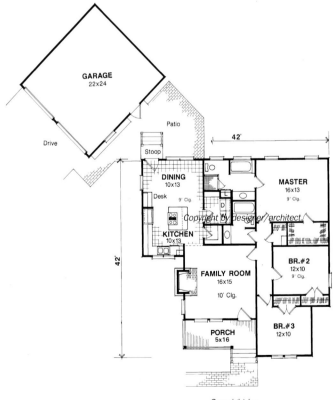

GARAGE 22x24

Drive

Patio

Stoop

DINING 10x13

Desk

9' Clg.

MASTER 16x13 9' Clg.

KITCHEN 10x13

BR.#2 12x10 9' Clg.

FAMILY ROOM 16x15 10' Clg.

PORCH 5x16

BR.#3 12x10

42'

42'

*Copyright by designer/architect.*

## Plan #251003

**Dimensions:** 42' W x 42' D

**Levels:** 1

**Square Footage:** 1,393

**Bedrooms:** 3

**Bathrooms:** 2

**Foundation:** Crawl space, slab

**Materials List Available:** Yes

**Price Category:** B

*Images provided by designer/architect.*

*Copyright by designer/architect.*

## Plan #221016

**Dimensions:** 56' W x 42' D

**Levels:** 1

**Square Footage:** 1,461

**Bedrooms:** 3

**Bathrooms:** 2

**Foundation:** Basement

**Materials List Available:** No

**Price Category:** B

*Images provided by designer/architect.*

Rear Elevation

The interesting roofline and classic siding give this traditional ranch home an instant appeal.

**Features:**

- Ceiling Height: 8 ft.

- Great Room: From the entry, you'll look into this great room, where a handsome fireplace with large flanking windows makes you feel at home.

- Dining Room: Open to the great room, this room features access to the rear deck. An eating island shared with the kitchen allows the whole living area to flow together.

- Kitchen: The step-saving layout and ample counter space will delight the family chef.

- Master Suite: With a large walk-in closet and deluxe bath with a whirlpool tub, separate shower, and two-sink vanity, this private area will become a real retreat at the end of the day.

- Additional Bedrooms: Add the optional door from the entry to transform bedroom #2 into a quiet den, or use it as a bedroom.

*Copyright by designer/architect.*

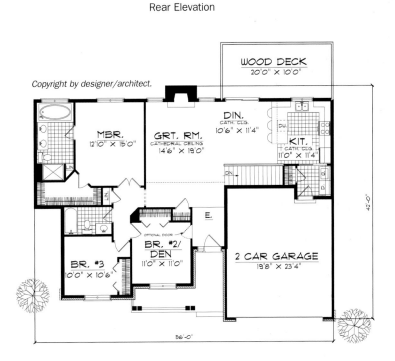

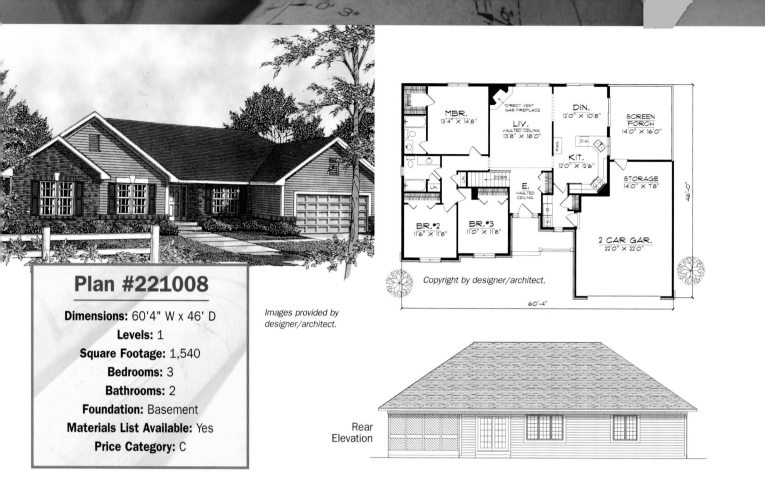

## Plan #221008

**Dimensions:** 60'4" W x 46' D

**Levels:** 1

**Square Footage:** 1,540

**Bedrooms:** 3

**Bathrooms:** 2

**Foundation:** Basement

**Materials List Available:** Yes

**Price Category:** C

*Images provided by designer/architect.*

Copyright by designer/architect.

Rear Elevation

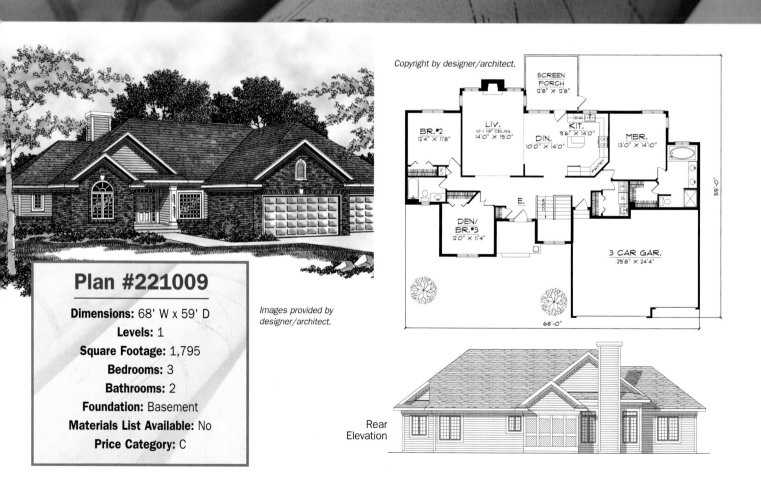

## Plan #221009

**Dimensions:** 68' W x 59' D

**Levels:** 1

**Square Footage:** 1,795

**Bedrooms:** 3

**Bathrooms:** 2

**Foundation:** Basement

**Materials List Available:** No

**Price Category:** C

*Images provided by designer/architect.*

Copyright by designer/architect.

Rear Elevation

Copyright by designer/architect.

## Plan #321010

**Dimensions:** 59' W x 37'8" D
**Levels:** 1
**Square Footage:** 1,787
**Bedrooms:** 3
**Bathrooms:** 2
**Foundation:** Basement
**Materials List Available:** Yes
**Price Category:** C

*Images provided by designer/architect.*

SMARTtip

### Country Décor in Your Bathroom

Collections are often part of a country decor, even in the bathroom. All you need is three or more of anything that have size, shape, or color in common. You can mass them on walls, on shelves, on the windowsills, or even along the edge of the tub.

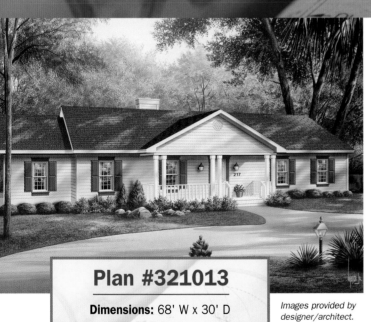

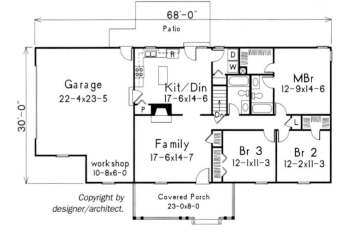

Copyright by designer/architect.

## Plan #321013

**Dimensions:** 68' W x 30' D
**Levels:** 1
**Square Footage:** 1,360
**Bedrooms:** 3
**Bathrooms:** 2
**Foundation:** Basement
**Materials List Available:** Yes
**Price Category:** B

*Images provided by designer/architect.*

SMARTtip

### Glass Doors and Fire Safety

Professionals recommend keeping glass doors open while a fire is burning. When the doors are left completely open, the burning flame has a more realistic appearance and the glass doesn't become soiled by swirling ashes. When the doors are closed, heat from a large hot fire can break the glass.

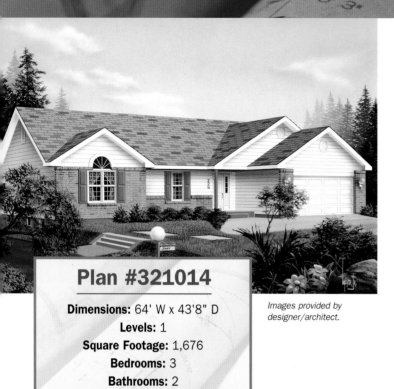

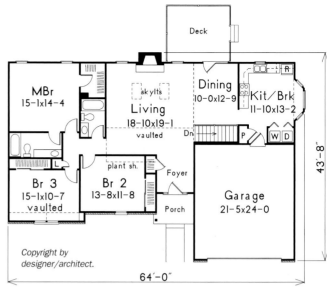

## Plan #321014

**Dimensions:** 64' W x 43'8" D

**Levels:** 1

**Square Footage:** 1,676

**Bedrooms:** 3

**Bathrooms:** 2

**Foundation:** Basement

**Materials List Available:** Yes

**Price Category:** C

*Images provided by designer/architect.*

Copyright by designer/architect.

## SMARTtip

### Blending Architecture

An easy way to blend the new deck with the architecture of a house is with railings. Precut railings and caps come in many styles and sizes.

## Plan #321015

**Dimensions:** 48' W x 64' D

**Levels:** 1

**Square Footage:** 1,501

**Bedrooms:** 3

**Bathrooms:** 2

**Foundation:** Basement

**Materials List Available:** Yes

**Price Category:** C

*Images provided by designer/architect.*

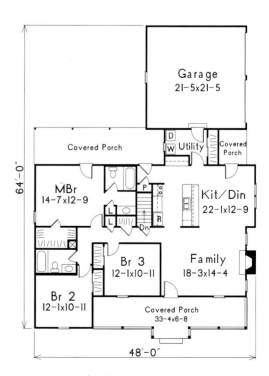

Copyright by designer/architect.

## Plan #321020

**Dimensions:** 58' W x 47'6" D

**Levels:** 1

**Square Footage:** 1,882

**Bedrooms:** 4

**Bathrooms:** 2

**Foundation:** Basement

**Materials List Available:** Yes

**Price Category:** D

*Images provided by designer/architect.*

*Copyright by designer/architect.*

---

## Plan #321021

**Dimensions:** 80' W x 42' D

**Levels:** 1

**Square Footage:** 1,708

**Bedrooms:** 3

**Bathrooms:** 2

**Foundation:** Basement

**Materials List Available:** Yes

**Price Category:** C

*Images provided by designer/architect.*

SMARTtip

### Planning a Safe Children's Room

Keep safety in mind when planning a child's room. Make sure that there are covers on electrical outlets, guard rails on high windows, sturdy screens in front of radiators, and gates blocking any steps. Other suggestions include safety hinges for chests and nonskid backing for rugs.

*Copyright by designer/architect.*

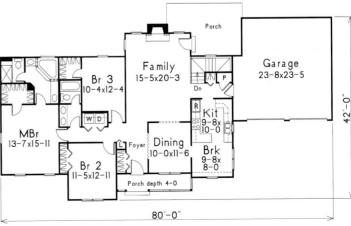

## Plan #211003

**Dimensions:** 62' W x 64'8" D
**Levels:** 1
**Square Footage:** 1,865
**Bedrooms:** 3
**Bathrooms:** 2
**Foundation:** Slab
**Materials List Available:** Yes
**Price Category:** D

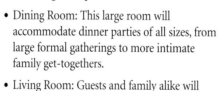

## SMARTtip

### Fire Extinguishers

The word PASS is an easy way to remember the proper way to use a fire extinguisher.

Pull the pin at the top of the extinguisher that keeps the handle from being accidentally pressed.

Aim the nozzle of the extinguisher toward the base of the fire.

Squeeze the handle to discharge the extinguisher. Stand approximately 8 feet away from the fire.

Sweep the nozzle back and forth at the base of the fire. After the fire appears to be out, watch it carefully because it may reignite!

The traditional style of this home is blended with all the amenities required for today's lifestyle.

**Features:**

• Ceiling Height: 8 ft. unless otherwise noted.

• Front Porch: Guests will feel welcome arriving at the front door under this sheltering front porch.

• Dining Room: This large room will accommodate dinner parties of all sizes, from large formal gatherings to more intimate family get-togethers.

• Living Room: Guests and family alike will feel right at home in this inviting room. Sunlight streaming through the skylights in the 12-ft. ceiling, combined with the handsome fireplace, makes the space both airy and warm.

• Back Patio: When warm weather comes around, step out the sliding glass doors in the living room to enjoy entertaining or just relaxing on this patio.

• Kitchen: A cathedral ceiling soars over this efficient modern kitchen. It includes an eating area that is perfect for informal family meals.

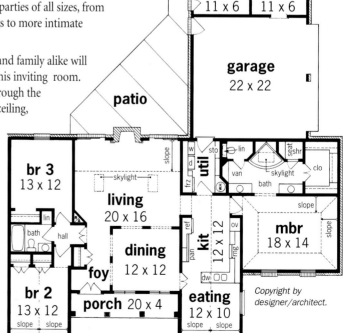

*Copyright by designer/architect.*

## Plan #271050

**Dimensions:** 40' W x 40' D
**Levels:** 2
**Square Footage:** 1,188
**Main Level Sq. Ft.:** 936
**Upper Level Sq. Ft.:** 252
**Bedrooms:** 3
**Bathrooms:** 2
**Foundation:** Daylight basement
**Materials List Available:** Yes
**Price Category:** B

This open and attractive design features multilevel construction and efficient use of living space.

*Images provided by designer/architect.*

**Features:**

- Living Room: A fireplace and a dramatic 15-ft. vaulted ceiling make family and friends gravitate to this area.

- Kitchen/Dining: A U-shaped counter with a snack bar facilitates meals and entertaining. A stacked washer/dryer unit makes weekend chores a breeze.

- Secondary Bedrooms: Five steps up, two sizable bedrooms with vaulted ceilings share

a nice hall bath. One of the bedrooms could serve as a den and features sliding glass doors to a deck.

- Master Suite: On a level of its own, this private space includes a personal bathroom and a romantic deck for stargazing.

- Basement/Garage: The home's lower level offers plenty of space for expansion or storage, plus a tandem, tuck-under garage.

### Main Level Floor Plan

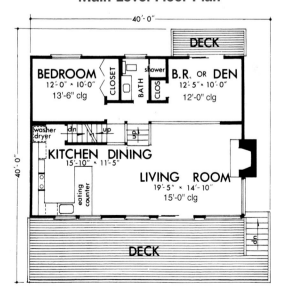

### Basement Level Floor Plan

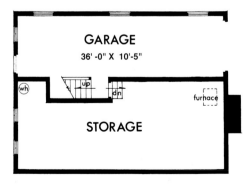

*Copyright by designer/architect.*

### Upper Level Floor Plan

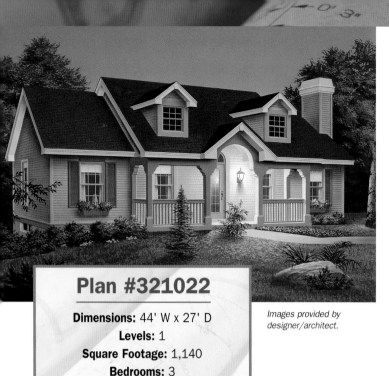

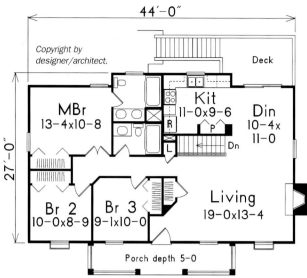

## Plan #321022

**Dimensions:** 44' W x 27' D
**Levels:** 1
**Square Footage:** 1,140
**Bedrooms:** 3
**Bathrooms:** 2
**Foundation:** Basement
**Materials List Available:** Yes
**Price Category:** B

*Images provided by designer/architect.*

MBr
13-4x10-8

Kit
11-0x9-6

Din
10-4x
11-0

Deck

Dn

Br 2
10-0x8-9

Br 3
9-1x10-0

Living
19-0x13-4

44'-0"

27'-0"

Porch depth 5-0

*Copyright by designer/architect.*

## SMARTtip

### Basement Moldings

Keep moldings simple in a basement with lower ceilings. Elaborate moldings around the ceiling or floor can shorten the height of the room.

## Plan #321023

**Dimensions:** 39'8" W x 41' D
**Levels:** 1
**Square Footage:** 1,092
**Bedrooms:** 3
**Bathrooms:** 1½
**Foundation:** Basement
**Materials List Available:** Yes
**Price Category:** B

*Images provided by designer/architect.*

MBr
15-4x12-0

Patio

Kit
11-8x11-9

Br 2
8-7x
10-0

Living
11-8x16-7

Garage
11-4x20-4

Dn

Br 3
12-0x10-0
vaulted

Covered Porch
depth 4-0

41'-0"

39'-8"

*Copyright by designer/architect.*

## Plan #341031

**Dimensions:** 50' W x 50' D

**Levels:** 1

**Square Footage:** 1,400

**Bedrooms:** 3

**Bathrooms:** 2

**Foundation:** Crawl space, slab, or basement

**Materials List Available:** Yes

**Price Category:** B

*Images provided by designer/architect.*

GARAGE
20'-2" X 21'-8"

KITCHEN & DINING
22'-4" X 12'-3"

BEDROOM 3
10'-7" X 10'-0"

GARDEN TUB AND SHWR.

CLOSET

CLOSET

BATH 1

PANTRY

REF.

DW

RANGE

ELEVATED BAR

WASH DRY

BATH 2

BEDROOM 1
13'-6" X 14'-7"

STORAGE

COATS

FAMILY ROOM
15'-10" X 14'-7"

LINENS

BEDROOM 2
10'-7" X 10'-0"

CLOSET

PORCH

50'-0"

50'-0"

*Copyright by designer/architect.*

---

## Plan #341030

**Dimensions:** 52' W x 40' D

**Levels:** 1

**Square Footage:** 1,660

**Bedrooms:** 3

**Bathrooms:** 2

**Foundation:** Crawl space, slab, or basement

**Materials List Available:** Yes

**Price Category:** C

*Images provided by designer/architect.*

52'-0"

PORCH

WASH DRY

UTILITY ROOM

GARDEN TUB

BATH 1

RANGE

BEDROOM 1
13'-5" X 17'-5"

CORNER SHELF

LINENS

TRAY CEILING

KITCHEN/DINING
24'-8" X 11'-5"

SHWR

BATH 2

LINENS

SINK

DW

LINENS

CLOSET

CLOSET

40'-0"

REF.

PANTRY

COATS

GAS LOGS

FAMILY ROOM
21'-5" X 15'-5"

UP TO UNFINISHED SECOND FLOOR

BEDROOM 2
11'-7" X 11'-5"

CLOSET

BEDROOM 3
11'-3" X 11'-5"

CLOSET

PORCH

*Copyright by designer/architect.*

# Plan #131001

**Dimensions:** 72'4" W x 32'4" D
**Levels:** 1
**Square Footage:** 1,615
**Bedrooms:** 3
**Bathrooms:** 2
**Foundation:** Basement, crawl space, or slab
**Materials List Available:** Yes
**Price Category:** D

*Images provided by designer/architect.*

Cathedral ceilings and illuminating skylights add drama and beauty to this practical ranch house.

**Features:**

Ceiling Height: 8 ft.

- **Front Porch:** Watch the rain in comfort from the covered front porch.

- **Foyer:** The stone-tiled foyer flows into the living areas.

- **Living Room:** Oriented towards the front of the house, the living room opens to the dining room and shares a lovely three-sided fireplace with the family room.

- **Family Room:** Conveniently located to share the fireplace with the living room, this room is bright and cheery thanks to its skylights as well as the sliding glass doors that open onto the rear patio.

- **Kitchen:** An island makes this sunny room both efficient and attractive.

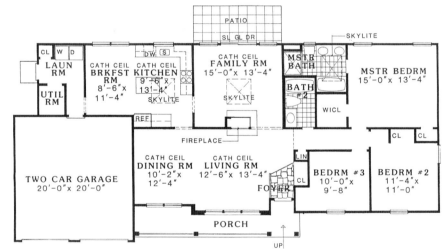

*Copyright by designer/architect.*

- **Breakfast Nook:** Located just off the kitchen, this area can serve double-duty as a spot for kitchen visitors to sit.

- **Dining Room:** The open design between the dining and living rooms adds to the spacious feeling that the cathedral ceiling creates in this area.

- **Laundry Room:** This area opens from the kitchen for convenience.

- **Master Suite:** A walk-in closet makes this room practical, but the master bathroom with a skylight, dual-sink vanity, soaking tub, and separate shower makes it luxurious.

- **Bedrooms:** The two additional bedrooms share a bathroom.

Rear Elevation

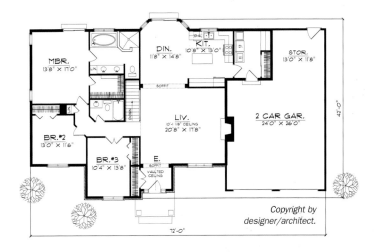

## Plan #221005

**Dimensions:** 72' W x 42' D

**Levels:** 1

**Square Footage:** 1,868

**Bedrooms:** 3

**Bathrooms:** 2

**Foundation:** Basement

**Materials List Available:** No

**Price Category:** D

*Images provided by designer/architect.*

*Copyright by designer/architect.*

---

Rear Elevation

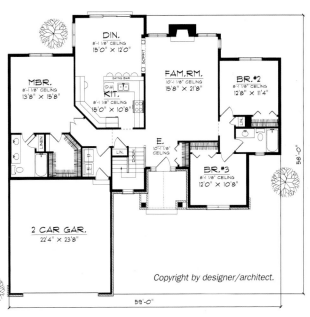

## Plan #221006

**Dimensions:** 59' W x 58' D

**Levels:** 1

**Square Footage:** 1,756

**Bedrooms:** 3

**Bathrooms:** 2

**Foundation:** Basement

**Materials List Available:** No

**Price Category:** C

*Images provided by designer/architect.*

*Copyright by designer/architect.*

Copyright by designer/architect.

*Images provided by designer/architect.*

## Plan #171009

**Dimensions:** 68' W x 50' D
**Levels:** 1
**Square Footage:** 1,771
**Bedrooms:** 3
**Bathrooms:** 2
**Foundation:** Slab, crawl space
**Materials List Available:** Yes
**Price Category:** C

## Plan #201009

**Dimensions:** 65'10" W x 30'10" D
**Levels:** 1
**Square Footage:** 1,263
**Bedrooms:** 3
**Bathrooms:** 2
**Foundation:** Crawl space, slab, or basement
**Materials List Available:** Yes
**Price Category:** B

*Images provided by designer/architect.*

Copyright by designer/architect.

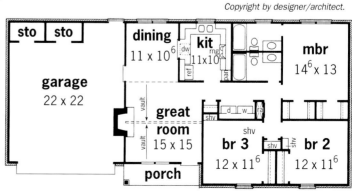

## Plan #151131

**Dimensions:** 28' W x 77' D
**Levels:** 1
**Square Footage:** 1,446
**Bedrooms:** 3
**Bathrooms:** 2
**Foundation:** Crawl space, slab
**Materials List Available:** Yes
**Price Category:** B

*Images provided by designer/architect.*

The 10-in. columns on the lovely front porch make this traditional and gracious home seem a part of the old South.

**Features:**

- **Great Room:** A 10-ft. boxed ceiling gives presence to this spacious room, and an angled corner fireplace lets you create a cozy nook where everyone will gather in chilly weather.

- **Kitchen:** The snack bar and large adjoining breakfast room encourage friends and family to gather here at all times of day. All the household cooks will appreciate the thoughtful layout that makes cooking a delight.

- **Master Suite:** A 10-ft. ceiling emphasizes the luxury you'll find in both the bedroom and private bath, with its two vanities, spacious walk-in closets, and whirlpool tub.

- **Additional Bedrooms:** A deluxe full bath separates bedrooms 2 and 3, and both rooms feature generous closet space.

*Copyright by designer/architect.*

## SMARTtip

## Creating Depth with Wall Frames

Wall frames create an illusion of depth and density because 1) they are three-dimensional and 2) they divide the wall area into smaller, denser segments. The three-dimensional quality of wall frames is fundamentally different from that of the alternative treatment: raised panels. Despite the name, raised panels actually produce a concave-like, or receding, effect whereas wall frames are more convex, protruding outward. In terms of sculpture, concave units create negative space while convex units create positive space. Raised panels, therefore, deliver a uniform sense of volume, mass, and density, while wall frames create a higher level of tension and dramatic interest.

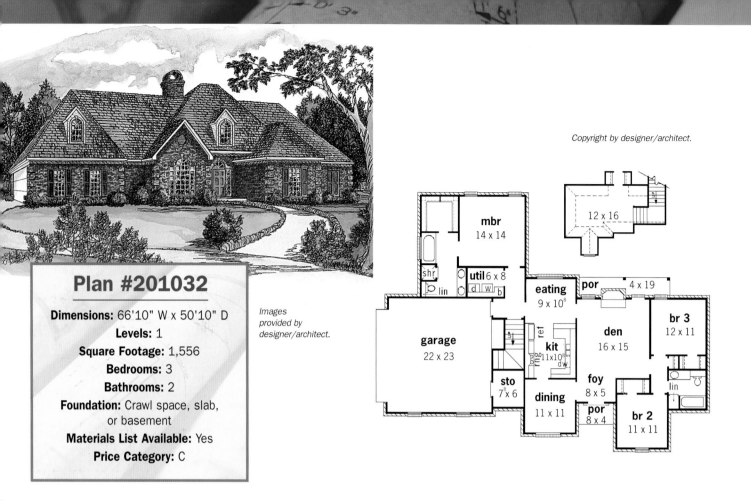

## Plan #201032

**Dimensions:** 66'10" W x 50'10" D

**Levels:** 1

**Square Footage:** 1,556

**Bedrooms:** 3

**Bathrooms:** 2

**Foundation:** Crawl space, slab, or basement

**Materials List Available:** Yes

**Price Category:** C

*Images provided by designer/architect.*

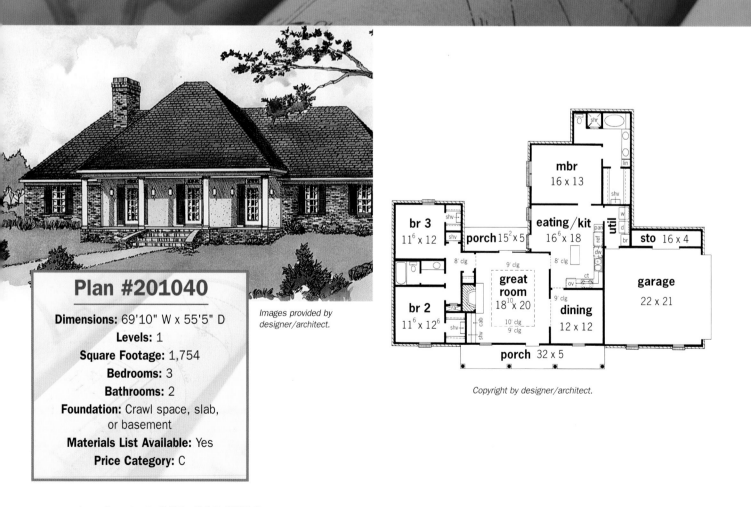

## Plan #201040

**Dimensions:** 69'10" W x 55'5" D

**Levels:** 1

**Square Footage:** 1,754

**Bedrooms:** 3

**Bathrooms:** 2

**Foundation:** Crawl space, slab, or basement

**Materials List Available:** Yes

**Price Category:** C

*Images provided by designer/architect.*

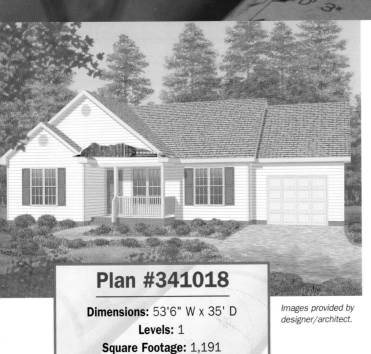

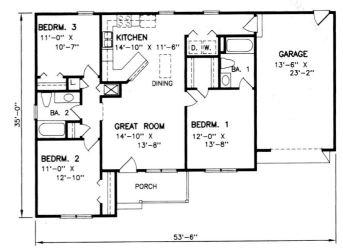

*Images provided by designer/architect.*

## Plan #341018

**Dimensions:** 53'6" W x 35' D

**Levels:** 1

**Square Footage:** 1,191

**Bedrooms:** 3

**Bathrooms:** 2

**Foundation:** Crawl space, slab, or basement

**Materials List Available:** Yes

**Price Category:** B

*Copyright by designer/architect.*

BEDRM. 3
11'-0" X 10'-7"

KITCHEN
14'-10" X 11'-6"

D. W.

DINING

BA. 1

GARAGE
13'-6" X 23'-2"

BA. 2

GREAT ROOM
14'-10" X 13'-8"

BEDRM. 1
12'-0" X 13'-8"

BEDRM. 2
11'-0" X 12'-10"

PORCH

35'-0"

53'-6"

---

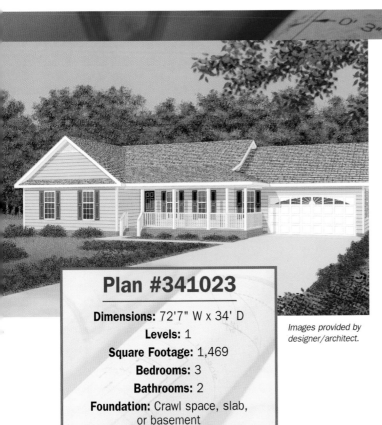

*Copyright by designer/architect.*

## Plan #341023

**Dimensions:** 72'7" W x 34' D

**Levels:** 1

**Square Footage:** 1,469

**Bedrooms:** 3

**Bathrooms:** 2

**Foundation:** Crawl space, slab, or basement

**Materials List Available:** Yes

**Price Category:** B

*Images provided by designer/architect.*

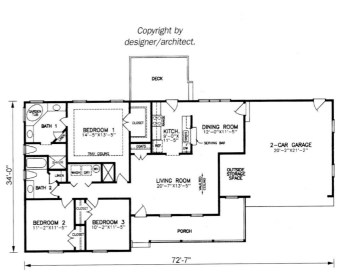

DECK

GARDEN TUB

BATH 1

BEDROOM 1
14'-5"X13'-5"

CLOSET

KITCH.
9'-0"X 11'-5"

DINING ROOM
12'-0"X11'-5"

SERVING BAR

2-CAR GARAGE
20'-2"X21'-2"

REF

COATS

SHWR

LINEN

WASH DRY

LIVING ROOM
20'-7"X13'-5"

OUTSIDE STORAGE SPACE

BATH 2

BEDROOM 2
11'-2"X11'-5"

CLOSET

BEDROOM 3
10'-2"X11'-5"

PORCH

34'-0"

72'-7"

# Creating a Cottage Style

**H**ouses built in the cottage style share design elements with a number of architectural traditions. The typical exterior cottage design shows influences of Country, Arts and Crafts, and Early American designs. The same can be said for the interiors of cottages. Color selections, flooring options, and the size and arrangement of rooms echo these other American design movements.

When selecting furniture for your new home, it is best to stay within the cottage style and select practical and comfortable pieces.

## Furniture "Style"

In choosing furniture, you face a wide menu of traditional styles. America's earliest "Pilgrim" furniture often had a medieval flavor—straight legs and banister-like backs with lively turnings shaped on a lathe. In the mid-1700s, graceful Queen Anne chairs became fashionable, with their curvaceous cabriole legs and backs with carved center splats. This type of furniture overlapped with the heavily carved, robust Chippendale pieces that came into vogue during the second half of the eighteenth century and into the nineteenth century.

This mode was eclipsed by the leaner and straighter Sheraton and Hepplewhite designs of the neoclassic Federal era, which thrived during the early nineteenth century. During the succeeding decades, furniture blossomed into a variety of styles, most notably the ornate furniture of high Victorian. The reaction to over-the-top Victorian design came with the bold straight-line forms of Craftsman furniture and the simple cottage pieces at the dawn of the twentieth century.

**Cottage-style furniture** relies on simple, clean designs for its distinctive look.

**Display pieces,** such as this entertainment center, feature simple molding treatments.

But such arbitrary style divisions often loosen up in cottage as well as country homes. Remember, many of the tables, chairs, benches, stools, and chests used by yesterday's farmers and workers were timeless, simple, and often homemade. Their economically straight, sturdy lines have been remarkably similar across the centuries. Just as in architecture, furniture of a particular style could persist in the country long after its fashionable reign. People rarely discarded anything, and country craftsmen tended to be conservative in adopting new designs. The latest mode

might find interpretation in a simplified form or one that mixed freely with various elements of familiar styles. In essence, country furniture tended toward solid pieces, with nothing too fragile for daily life.

## Informal Styles

Traditional vintage American furniture is noteworthy for its ingenuity—space-saving gateleg and drop-leaf tables, high-back settle benches, and spacious storage cupboards and chests. For example, on t' westward expansion, a "food safe" or —y

cupboard" might have been knocked together from packing crates to furnish a rough kitchen. Food tins decorated w hand-pierced designs often pr ɔd ventilated door panels for a  ɔ .eer's punched-tin food chests.

(In fac    onality-rich storage pieces car ɔ  al to achieving a pleasing design.  ɔ .el-chosen piece can conceal the modern accoutrements that often intrude on vintage-inspired surroundings.)

A prosperous rural house in centuries past might have acquired a few high-style pieces of furniture crafted in mahogany or walnut, frequently in veneers that revealed a wood's figured grain. Less costly country furniture in pine or maple was often painted or faux-grained to protect the wood and to make it more attractive. Today you can rely on the power of paint in the same way to make inexpensive second-hand or unfinished furniture into distinctive pieces.

## A Pair of Furniture Favorites

Two humble stars among America's chairs are the Windsor chair and the rocker. Windsor chairs originated among English farmers: as they cleared back the encroaching woods, they gathered all the thin, flexible branches for stick furniture. Assembled of green or steam-softened wood, the pieces would shrink during drying, making them tight and sturdy. The back of a basic Windsor design has thin spindles that are enclosed by a hooped or straight rail above

**Traditionally formal** Windsor-style chairs work well in a more casual setting, right.

**Cottage and Country** furniture share many qualities of Arts and Crafts furniture, below.

a solid seat. The chair's slightly splayed turned legs are strengthened by stretchers. In American hands the Windsor proliferated in many forms, including a wide settee, a low-back "captain's chair," and a tall "comb-back" version with a curvy top rail.

**Windsor Attributes.** From the 1700s onward, Americans in the city and the country valued Windsors for their lightness, modest price, and graceful durability. In an early example of mass production, apprentices would make and stock-

pile the components to keep the furniture makers busy with a salable staple product between custom commissions. To get the required strength, rigidity, or flexibility, these craftsmen combined different woods in each chair and usually painted them in rich colors, in keeping with the chairs' simple outlines. Furniture authority Wallace Nutting, writing in the 1930s, promoted an appreciation of Windsor chairs as "more suggestive of pleasant reflection than any other article of furniture."

**Rocking Chairs.** The rocking chair's origins are misty, but by the 1700s it was another American favorite—this was a nation that liked motion, even when at leisure! Many early versions were simple standard chairs with the addition of rockers. But the notion soon engendered a variety of friendly styles.

■ The slat-back, or ladder-back, rocker, popular from the 1700s to the late 1800s, when it was perfected by the Shakers
■ A Boston, or Salem, rocker with a wide scooped seat, a spindle back, and a wide top rail, sometimes decoratively painted
■ Windsor rockers, with spindle backs sometimes shaped for an "arrowback" profile

**Wicker porch furniture,** above, contributes to the cottagey feel of this house.

**Choose furniture,** especially pieces for public rooms like dining rooms, that are functional as well as attractive, left.

■ Victorian wicker chairs; curvy, intricate, and light, with a summerhouse air
■ Arts and Crafts or Mission rockers; massive and straight-lined, crafted in oak

Glider rockers might seem modern, but during the nineteenth century, at least a dozen patents set forth platform rockers with inventive arrangements of springs, straps, and pivots.

Luckily in our own era, such soft nests are a standard part of everyday life. For the cottage spirit, sofas and chairs should be of generous proportions, in scale with the room, and usually of simple classic shapes.

■ Camelback sofas have an eighteenth-century flavor. The curved back inspired the name. Characteristic of Hepplewhite and Chippendale styles, the camelback sofa can look more or less formal by the choice of fabrics.

■ Tuxedo sofas feature a boxy frame that is typically associated with contemporary design. But you can soften this sofa's strong geometric lines with floral-print fabrics. If you choose a striped or plaid print, offset the angularity of the sofa's frame with a ruffled skirt and throw pillows.

■ Lawson sofas, with rounded arms that are lower than the back, are classics and can present an invitingly plump form that looks at home in country settings, particularly when paired with a quaint country print.

**Simple designs** for furniture, left, allow you to experiment with the use of strong color combinations.

**Skirted sofas,** such as the one shown to the right, give the room a casual, friendly feeling.

**Comfort is the most** important thing when selecting furniture. The pieces shown below takes advantage of a sunny nook.

## Upholstered Pieces

Our Colonial ancestors made simple wood furniture more comfortable with cushions, perhaps brightened with "turkey work," a type of colorful dense embroidery that suggested a Turkish rug. Early in the 1700s, houses of the well-to-do featured the latest luxury: upholstered wing chairs with high enclosing backs to shield drafts. The earliest examples are inventoried as bedroom furniture, often reserved for the infirm. But by midcentury, such "easie chairs" and settees with curved top lines and gently scrolled arms were company pieces, upholstered in fine, solid-colored wools, embroidered flame-stitch fabrics, damasks, and florals.

**Formal Versus Informal.** A skirted sofa generally seems casual, while carved, exposed legs appear formal. However, pleated or tailored skirts can be formal as well.  Sofas with loose pillows along the back need to be neatly arranged as a regular habit. Loose, informal covers can be a practical addition. Budget permitting, a seasonal change can be a charming notion, with pale linens and ticking for summer, and cozier wools and dark florals for winter.

Padded stools and ottomans invite you to put your feet up and relax, and their presence adds comfort and variety to a country room. They can serve for extra seating in a pinch and double as coffee tables or end tables.

## Cottage-Style Fabrics

Fabrics are the soul of decorating: sensual, soft, and evocative right down to their names—velvet, taffeta, chintz, paisley, muslin, matelassé. Traditional textiles encompass an intriguing range. From the seventeenth to the early nineteenth centuries, one of the basic chores in households was the spinning and weaving of rough homespun fabrics in wool, cotton, or the blended linen and wool of "linsey-woolsy." Often the yarns, tinted with home-brewed dyes, would be woven into simple contrasting stripes, checks, and plaids, staples of Country decorating, whether in Scandinavia, France, or America. In later times, plain-woven cottons would be purchased and home-dyed. Thus you'll find that some simple, inexpensive fabric—plain wools, printed cottons, broadcloth, and rough unbleached muslins—create a warm, inviting effect in a cottage room.

## The Influence of Imported Textiles

Yesterday's homeowners also coveted finer, more-colorful fabrics, with names that betray their exotic origins: bright small-scale calico (named for Calicut, India); delicate gingham checks (from the Malay genggang, meaning "striped"); and glorious flower-decked chintzes (from the Hindi chints, for "bright spots"). From the seventeenth century onward, European producers slavishly imitated exports from Asia. France took the early lead, producing such distinctive eighteenth-century fabrics as the vivid Provençal cottons in small, repetitive prints, and toile de Jouy (named for the French city of Jouy), with finely etched scenic designs in blue or red on linen or cotton. An early country house might blend the utility fabrics of rough wools and home-tanned leather with a few treasured Old World fabrics, such as embroidered, large-scale crewelwork, some bits of velvet, or a brightly painted "tree of life" print from India.

Elegant eighteenth-century furniture demanded damasks, bold designs of Chinese influence, or rococo French swirls. After the American Revolution, sleek Sheraton and Hepplewhite pieces wore rich fabrics in plain colors, narrow stripes, rosettes, and Grecian motifs. French manufacturers even printed toiles with images of patriotic eagles and George Washington in a lion-drawn chariot.

**A Fabric Explosion.** Power looms for weaving, invented later in the eighteenth century, and the increasing ease of importing and transporting goods in the nineteenth century made fabrics of all kinds readily available, right down to the bright bolts of calico at the frontier general store. Honest utility fabrics, such as striped ticking made with a diagonal twilled weave for greater durability, flat-woven heavy sailcloth, and lightweight muslin in sturdy cotton, became workhorse choices. The Victorian era bloomed with floral prints, velvets, satins, and damask weaves.

## Special Fabrics

A sense of tradition accompanies fabrics that suggest hard work. Embroidery's long history ranges from designs as bold as crewel in bright wool on rough linen to finely shaded pictorial needlepoint. Pillows, chair seats, bed linens, and curtain edges and tiebacks offer small, bounded areas that can highlight such rich effects.

Lace is a most romantic textile, a froth of purely decorative impracticality. True handmade lace is created by two techniques.

- Needlepoint lace is stitched over a pattern drawn on fine linen, and the backing fabric is delicately cut away from the finished lacework.
- Bobbin, or pillow, lace is woven with long threads, weighted with hanging bobbins, and pinned over a pattern on a pillow. The lace maker deftly flips and

**Matching pieces,** left, help establish a design theme in this room.

**Wicker provides** a light, airy feeling to the sunporch below.

twists the bobbins over and around each other, moving pins down as the knotted lace takes shape.

## Other Neddlework Techniques.

Similarly delicate openwork results from other widely practiced needlework techniques such as filet netting, knitting, tatting (a form of knotting made with a small shuttle), and crocheting, made popular by Irish immigrants. An 1854 needlework manual touted crochet as "one of those gentle means by which women are kept feminine and ladylike in this fast age." Despite such advantages, it was the era's machine-made products that made lace an affordable country finish for edging shelves and mantels or for trimming curtains and table linens. Antimacassars, lengths of lace laid on the arms and backs of sofas and chairs, defended the upholstery from the dark macassar hair oil used by nineteenth-century beaus. In the modern cottage room, lace is conveniently neutral in the color scheme, yet it has a refreshing lightness, whether with the sun shining through or as a pleasing contrast to dark wood.

## Choosing Fabrics

Because fabric spans such variety, you can match a particular type to the job that makes the most of its qualities. For example, choose a tough linen blend for upholstery, a polished chintz for crisp pleated curtains, or a supple, translucent voile for a lushly draped window scarf. Woven designs generally bear up to more wear than printed fabrics, and midtone colors age more gracefully than very pale or dark fabrics.

The degree of formality is another guide. Informal fabrics are generally plain-woven in cotton or linen with bolder, simpler designs and a matte appearance.

Natural fibers are a logical choice to maintain a cottage mood.

- Cotton offers a good "hand" and durability, though it doesn't bear up to strong sunlight and is subject to staining unless treated or blended with synthetics.
- Linen is one of the most durable fibers. It often appears in mellow tones because it doesn't take dye well.
- Wool is sturdy and abrasion- and stain-resistant. It dyes beautifully but requires mothproofing.

**Different styles of baskets,** above, add a unique texture to a room design.

**Simple patterns** on upholstery, left, usually work best with other patterns in the room.

**Stack baskets,** below, to provide handy storage in bedrooms and guest rooms.

Last, don't dismiss modern synthetics. Especially in blends with natural fibers, they can provide engineered advantages with a reasonably natural look and feel.

Casual rooms appear to mix fabrics with abandon, but a few points will help them harmonize.

- Find links of similar texture and shared colors.
- Vary the scale. Two patterns of the same size can fight for attention.
- Look for simple mixers. Gentle geometric patterns, such as simple plaids, stripes, or checks, can make a harmonious coupling with each other or with florals.

## Accessories

What often pulls together the lively, eclectic look of a cottage room are its delightful details and accessories. Finishing touches, personal possessions, and favorite things transform an impersonal space into an expressive and comfortable dwelling. Laura Ingalls Wilder, author of the Little House books, offers a perfect example of this when she describes how her family made over a rough frontier shanty and turned it into a real home, "with a blue bowl of grass flowers and windflowers on the table and a fashionable whatnot shelf where Ma's china shepherdess stood pink and white and smiling."

## Baskets

Weaving is another ancient craft. Native Americans were skilled basket makers, and each group of immigrants brought its own weaving traditions, such as the fragrant sea-grass baskets from Gullah Islands off the Carolinas, which derive from African inspirations. Even sailors on whaling ships made baskets.

The raw materials can be flexible reeds, tropical rattan palms, ferns, grasses, or flat wood splints to make a particularly sturdy, if usually expensive, hardwood basket. A basket's form follows its function.

For example, market baskets are large and flat-bottomed for generous carrying capacity. Wall baskets are flattened on the back to hang neatly on a hook. Vegetable baskets are big and coarsely woven to allow air to circulate. Berry baskets are smooth and fine to avoid poking or dropping delicate fruits.

**In informal rooms,** such as kids' rooms and playrooms, experiment with mixing different types of furniture together.

# Final Decorating Tips

Continue the fine old tradition of finding fresh possibilities in familiar objects. Furniture doesn't have to be brand new. Something that is comfortably worn is often quite inviting. Wondering how to find new uses for what you already own? Here are a few things you can do.

### Cover Up, Relocate, and Recast.
Loose slipcovers and unusual throw pillows or casually tucked-in quilts can revive a has-been sofa, while a draping of chintz can hide an ugly end table. A tattered kitchen set becomes one-of-a-kind with a sponged or spatter-painted finish.

It seems simple, but just pulling the furniture away from the walls, arranging seating in a cozy grouping, or resettling a piece from another location can give a room a fresh aspect. Shine up the old dresser you've been hiding in the guest room, and move it into the entry hall. Stencil a set of tattered chairs that have been in the attic, and bring them down to brighten the breakfast room.

Sometimes clutter just needs a home to become something more. For instance, bound books scattered around the house or potted flowers make an impression when massed on shelves or a tabletop. Use a big old bowl to hold keys, change, and general junk.

### Establish a Focus.
Highlight the room's most dramatic features and support them with low-key elements. It's tempting to keep adding to a room, but the result can pull the attention in too many directions. One or two focal points are usually all you need to anchor a room and give it drama.

### Slow Down.
Sometimes the first idea you have isn't the best solution. For example, after a move to a new home, you may want to settle everything immediately. But if you live with a room for a while, you can see how the light falls throughout the day, what looks best where, and in what areas people naturally congregate. Let your decorating plans evolve with your lifestyle.

But maintain balance in your caution. It's easy to talk yourself out of bold decorating strokes and into safe but sometimes uninteresting choices. Don't second-guess all the life out of your decorating decisions.

### Aim for Harmony Spiced with a Bit of Variety.
Use the room's overall impression as the organizing principle. Does each addition advance the ambiance of the theme you envision? Dark tartan cushions would enhance an intimate masculine study, for example, but rough muslin curtains would not. However, some contrast or one element of surprise is often appealing—polished brass candlesticks lend just the right drama atop a rustic scrubbed pine table.

**Basket accessories,** bead-board walls, and a claw-and-ball-foot tub combine to give the bathroom at right a cottage look.

**Express yourself** by putting personal items, such as collections and family mementos, on display, below.

Images provided by designer/architect.

Copyright by designer/architect.

## Plan #171002

**Dimensions:** 67' W x 40' D
**Levels:** 1
**Square Footage:** 1,458
**Bedrooms:** 3
**Bathrooms:** 2
**Foundation:** Slab, crawl space
**Materials List Available:** Yes
**Price Category:** B

## Plan #271084

**Dimensions:** 51'9" W x 38'9" D
**Levels:** 1
**Square Footage:** 1,602
**Bedrooms:** 3
**Bathrooms:** 1½
**Foundation:** Daylight
**Materials List Available:** Yes
**Price Category:** C

Images provided by designer/architect.

Copyright by designer/architect.

**Optional Basement Level Floor Plan**

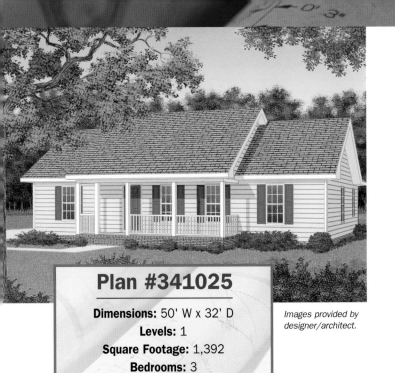

*Images provided by designer/architect.*

## Plan #341025

**Dimensions:** 50' W x 32' D

**Levels:** 1

**Square Footage:** 1,392

**Bedrooms:** 3

**Bathrooms:** 2

**Foundation:** Crawl space, slab, or basement

**Materials List Available:** Yes

**Price Category:** B

*Copyright by designer/architect.*

---

*Images provided by designer/architect.*

## Plan #341032

**Dimensions:** 76' W x 38' D

**Levels:** 1

**Square Footage:** 1,528

**Bedrooms:** 3

**Bathrooms:** 2

**Foundation:** Crawl space, slab, or basement

**Materials List Available:** Yes

**Price Category:** C

*Copyright by designer/architect.*

## Plan #121060

**Dimensions:** 50' W x 46' D

**Levels:** 1

**Square Footage:** 1,339

**Bedrooms:** 3

**Full Bathrooms:** 2

**Foundation:** Basement

**Materials List Available:** Yes

**Price Category:** B

You'll love this compact design if you're looking for either a starter home or a luxurious place to spend your retirement years.

**Features:**

- Foyer: A covered stoop and arched entry open to this gracious foyer, where you'll love to greet guests.

- Great Room: From the foyer, you'll walk into this large area with its 10-ft. ceilings. A fireplace gives you a cozy spot on chilly days and cool evenings.

- Kitchen: This kitchen is truly step-saving and convenient. In addition to plenty of counter and storage space, it features a snack bar and an adjoining breakfast area.

- Master Suite: A 9-ft. ceiling gives a touch of elegance to the bedroom, and the walk-in closet adds practicality. In the bath, you'll find two vanities and a whirlpool tub.

- Garage: There's room for storage, a work bench, and three cars in this huge garage.

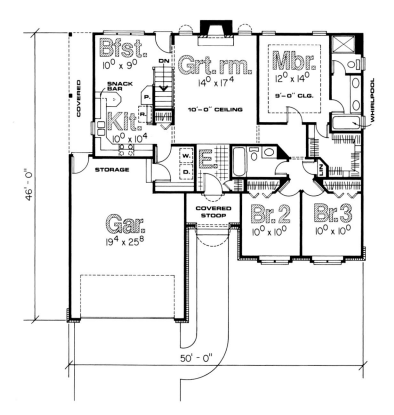

Copyright by designer/architect.

## Plan #211015

**Dimensions:** 38' W x 52' D
**Levels:** 1
**Square Footage:** 1,150
**Bedrooms:** 2
**Bathrooms:** 2
**Foundation:** Slab
**Materials List Available:** Yes
**Price Category:** B

*Images provided by designer/architect.*

Designed for a narrow lot, this home, with its ornate trim, is compact. On the inside, the minimal use of hallways allows the rooms to be large relative to the size of the house.

**Features:**

• Ceiling Height: 9 ft.

• Living Room: The ceiling in the center of this room is 11 ft. tall, adding to the spacious feeling that the well-placed windows and roomy dimensions already create.

• Kitchen: Designed for efficiency, this kitchen is also positioned for sensible traffic flow and easy entertaining. Don't be surprised if family and friends gravitate here to chat and visit with each other.

• Master Suite: You'll love the luxury that you'll find in this gorgeous master suite. The bedroom includes a large sitting area where you can relax or read, a walk-in closet for convenient storage, and a nicely arranged private bath.

*Copyright by designer/architect.*

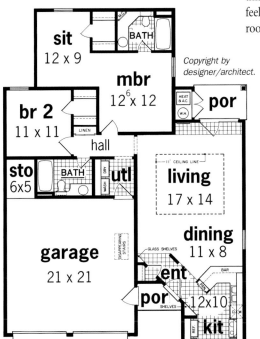

SMARTtip

## Choosing Colors with Color Cards

Choosing specific colors in a multicolor scheme can be a daunting task. To make this process easier, paint manufacturers have created color cards to help the homeowner to select coordinated base and trim colors. Many color cards are also prearranged in color groups that match the typical color schemes of various historical periods. Be aware, however, that colors on sample cards can be deceiving because of the cards limited size or the light in which you view them. Colors tend to look more intense when applied to a home than they do on the card. When in doubt, choose the next lighter shade.

# Plan #211027

**Dimensions:** 54' W x 50' D
**Levels:** 1
**Square Footage:** 1,470
**Bedrooms:** 3
**Bathrooms:** 2
**Foundation:** Slab
**Materials List Available:** Yes
**Price Category:** B

*Images provided by designer/architect.*

You'll be able to tell how lovely this home is just by looking at the exterior, with its attractive roofline, sparkling stucco finish, and elegant window treatments.

**Features:**

- Living Room: Central to the house, this living room features a 10-ft. ceiling and a dramatic fireplace where the family is sure to gather.

- Dining Room: Open to the living room, this area is ideal for comfortable family living or more formal entertaining.

- Kitchen: This U-shaped kitchen has a functional eating bar as well as a pantry for convenience.

- Laundry Area: Tucked into a hallway to the garage are a washer, dryer, and laundry sink.

- Master Suite: Secluded at the back of the home, this master suite has a romantic sitting area and large walk-in closet. Dual sinks and an exciting oval tub make the bath a special place.

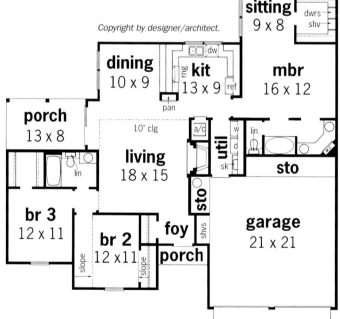

SMARTtip

## Customizing Window Shades

While decorative hems add interest to roller shades, they also increase the cost. If you're handy with a glue gun, choose one of the trims available at fabric and craft stores, and consider attaching it yourself. Give your shades fancy pulls for an inexpensive dash of pizzazz.

## Plan #211028

**Dimensions:** 68' W x 41' D
**Levels:** 1
**Square Footage:** 1,507
**Bedrooms:** 3
**Bathrooms:** 2
**Foundation:** Slab
**Materials List Available:** Yes
**Price Category:** C

Surprise yourself with this ranch-style home, which features every amenity you'll ever need.

**Features:**

- Living Room: A 12-ft. ceiling here adds dimension to the room, and the angled wall blends perfectly with the bay window in the adjoining eating nook. Both rooms overlook the rear covered porch.

- Dining Room: The formality of this room complements the stately entry it adjoins.

- Kitchen: Shaped and positioned as a hub of the home, this kitchen is also designed for efficient work patterns while you cook.

- Master Suite: With a skylight over the dressing room, a walk-in closet, and a private bath, this suite affords privacy and luxury.

- Additional Bedrooms: Each has a walk-in closet, and the larger one has an 11-ft.-high ceiling to accommodate its transom windows.

*Images provided by designer/architect.*

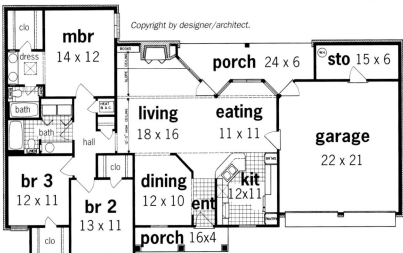

*Copyright by designer/architect.*

## SMARTtip

### Nailing Asphalt Roof Shingles

Shingles are typically fastened with four nails—one at each end of the shingle, and one above each tab slot. In windy areas use six nails to affix the shingles, placing one on each side of the tab slots. Position the nails just beneath the adhesive patch but above the tab slots. Roofing nails should be long enough to penetrate sheathing by 3/4 inch, whether shingling over or replacing existing roofing.

## Plan #211038

**Dimensions:** 72' W x 42' D
**Levels:** 1
**Square Footage:** 1,898
**Bedrooms:** 3
**Bathrooms:** 2
**Foundation:** Slab
**Materials List Available:** Yes
**Price Category:** D

*Images provided by designer/architect.*

A railed front porch, a charming cupola, and stylish shutters add classic flair to this home.

**Features:**

• Ceiling Height: 8 ft. unless otherwise noted.

• Family Room: The welcoming entry flows into this attractive family gathering area. The room features a handsome fireplace and a 14-ft. vaulted ceiling with exposed beams. French doors lead to a backyard patio.

• Formal Dining Room: This elegant room adjoins the living room. You'll usher your guests through a half-wall with decorative spindles.

• Kitchen: Food preparation will be a pleasure working at the wraparound counter.

• Eating Nook: Modern life includes lots of quick, informal meals, and this is the spot to enjoy them. The nook includes a laundry closet, so you can change loads while cooking.

• Master Suite: This private retreat boasts a private bath with a separate dressing area and a roomy walk-in closet.

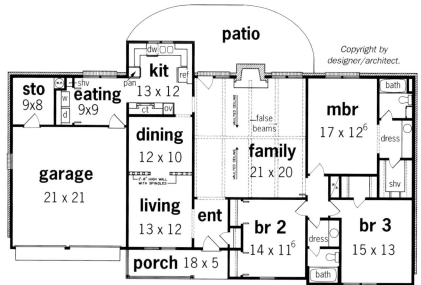

*Copyright by designer/architect.*

## SMARTtip

### Efficient Kitchen Appliances

Appliances that carry the **Energy Star** label — a program of the Department of Energy — are significantly more energy efficient than most other appliances. Dishwashers, for example, must be 25 percent more energy efficient than models that meet minimum federal energy requirements. Energy Star refrigerators must be 10 percent more efficient than the newest standards.

Plan #211039

**Dimensions:** 62' W x 64' D
**Levels:** 1
**Square Footage:** 1,868
**Bedrooms:** 3
**Bathrooms:** 2
**Foundation:** Slab
**Materials List Available:** Yes
**Price Category:** D

*Images provided by designer/architect.*

This home exudes traditional charm, but its layout and amenities are thoroughly modern.

**Features:**

- Formal Dining Room: This elegant room is perfect for dinner parties of any size.

- Kitchen: If you love to cook, you will love this kitchen. It's U-shaped for maximum efficiency, and it boasts a built-in desk for making menus and shopping lists, as well as a handy pantry closet. The kitchen has access to the carport, so groceries make a short trip to the counter.

- Eating Area: Just off the kitchen you'll find this informal eating area designed for quick meals on the go.

- Master Suite: Here is the perfect place to unwind after a long day. This generous bedroom hosts a lavish master bath with a spa tub, separate shower, and his and hers dressing areas.

- Secondary Bedrooms: Located across the home from the master suite, the two secondary bedrooms share another full bath.

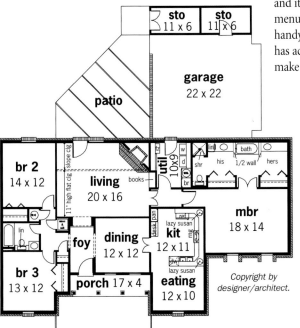

*Copyright by designer/architect.*

## SMARTtip

### Kitchen Wallpapering

For wrapping outside corners, measure from the last piece to the corner, and add ½ inch to the measurement. Cut the paper to size, and place it in position, but before wrapping it around the corner, make small slits in the waste portions of the paper near the ceiling and the baseboard. The cuts will allow you to turn the corner without wrinkling or tearing the paper. Hang the other part of the cut sheet so that it overlaps the first portion.

## Plan #131018

**Dimensions:** 66'4" W x 30'4" D
**Levels:** 1
**Square Footage:** 1,243
**Bedrooms:** 3
**Bathrooms:** 2
**Foundation:** Basement, crawl space, or slab
**Materials List Available:** Yes
**Price Category:** C

*Images provided by designer/architect.*

If you're looking for an easy-care home that makes your family and your guests feel welcome, this charming ranch will delight you.

### Features:

- Living Room: Everyone will gravitate to this central area, not only because of its location but also because it forms the hub of this home.

- Dining Room: Flowing from the living room, this dining room is large enough for a crowd but cozy enough for intimate dinners.

- Kitchen: This well-designed kitchen is a pleasure in which to work, thanks to the ample counter area and good-sized cabinets. It's also large enough that so you can use it as a second eating area.

- Laundry Room: Having a separate space for laundry simplifies this chore.

- Patio: Enjoy the large backyard patio at any time of year, but make it a special place to entertain during the warm months.

*Copyright by designer/architect.*

## SMARTtip

### Fabric for Outdoor Use

For outdoor furnishings, pick a fabric that contains a fade-resistant coating, particularly if you are using dark colors. Sunlight also weakens fibers, so look for sun-resistant coatings as well. But don't be surprised if outdoor fabrics wear faster than those indoors.

## Plan #131013

**Dimensions:** 50' W x 41'8" D
**Levels:** 1
**Square Footage:** 1,489
**Bedrooms:** 3
**Bathrooms:** 2
**Foundation:** Basement, crawl space, or slab
**Materials List Available:** Yes
**Price Category:** C

*Images provided by designer/architect.*

You'll love the Victorian details on the exterior of this charming ranch-style home.

**Features:**

- **Front Porch:** This porch is large enough so that you can sit out on warm summer nights to catch a breeze or create a garden of potted ornamentals.

- **Great Room:** Running from the front of the house to the rear, this great room is bathed in natural light from both directions. The volume ceiling adds a luxurious feeling to it, and the fireplace creates a cozy place on chilly afternoons.

- **Kitchen:** Cooking will be a pleasure in this kitchen, thanks to the thoughtful layout and well-designed work areas.

- **Master Suite:** Enjoy the quiet in this room, where it will be easy to relax and unwind, no matter what the time of day. The walk-in closet gives you plenty of storage space, and you're sure to appreciate both the privacy and large size of the master bath.

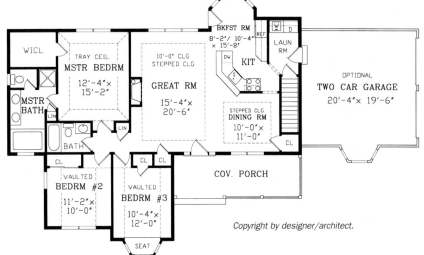

*Copyright by designer/architect.*

Rear Elevation

## Plan #191003

**Dimensions:** 56' W x 42' D
**Levels:** 1
**Square Footage:** 1,785
**Bedrooms:** 3
**Bathrooms:** 3
**Foundation:** Crawl space, slab, or basement
**Materials List Available:** No
**Price Category:** C

Enjoy the amenities you'll find in this gracious home, with its traditional Southern appearance.

**Features:**

- Great Room: This expansive room is so versatile that everyone will gather here. A built-in entertainment area with desk makes a great lounging spot, and the French doors topped by transoms open onto the lovely rear porch.

- Dining Room: An arched entry to this room helps to create the open feeling in this home.

- Kitchen: Another arched entryway leads to this fabulous kitchen, which has been designed with the cook's comfort in mind. It features a downdraft range, many cabinets, a snack bar, and a sunny breakfast area, where the family is sure to gather.

- Laundry: A sink, shower, toilet area, and cabinets galore give total convenience in this room.

- Master Suite: Enjoy the walk-in closet and bath with toilet room, whirlpool tub, and shower.

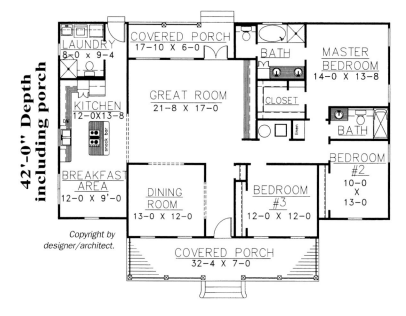

*Copyright by designer/architect.*

**56'-0" Width**

## Plan #131017

**Dimensions:** 69'8" W x 39'4" D
**Levels:** 1
**Square Footage:** 1,480
**Bedrooms:** 3
**Bathrooms:** 2
**Foundation:** Basement, crawl space, or slab
**Materials List Available:** Yes
**Price Category:** C

This fully accessible home is designed for wheelchair access to every area, giving everyone true enjoyment and freedom of movement.

**Features:**

- Great Room: Facing towards the rear, this great room features a volume ceiling that adds to the spacious feeling of the room.

- Kitchen: Designed for total convenience and easy work patterns, this kitchen also offers a view out to the covered front porch.

- Master Bedroom: Enjoy the quiet in this room which is sure to become your favorite place to relax at the end of the day.

- Additional Bedrooms: Both rooms have easy access to a full bath and feature nicely sized closet spaces.

- Garage: Use the extra space in this attached garage for storage..

*Images provided by designer/architect.*

Copyright by designer/architect.

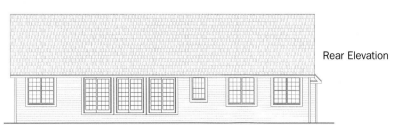

Rear Elevation

## Plan #131010

**Dimensions:** 70' W x 34'4" D
**Levels:** 1
**Square Footage:** 1,667
**Bedrooms:** 3
**Bathrooms:** 2
**Foundation:** Basement, crawl space, or slab
**Materials List Available:** Yes
**Price Category:** D

*Images provided by designer/architect.*

You'll love this affordable ranch house, with its open floor plan that gives so much usable space, and its graceful layout.

**Features:**

- **Living Room:** Adjacent to the dining room, this living room features a pass-through fireplace that is open to the family room beyond.

- **Family Room:** A vaulted ceiling with a sky light gives character to this room, where everyone will gather on weekend afternoons and in the evening, to relax.

- **Kitchen:** Also lit from above by a skylight, this kitchen features an island work space.

- **Breakfast Room:** Just off the kitchen, this breakfast room is sure to be a popular spot at any time of day.

- **Master Bedroom:** Get away from it all in this lovely room, with space to spread out and relax in private.

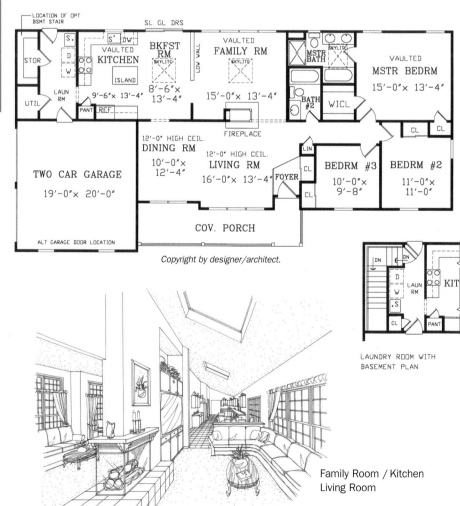

*Copyright by designer/architect.*

LAUNDRY ROOM WITH
BASEMENT PLAN

Family Room / Kitchen
Living Room

## Plan #131012

**Dimensions:** 71'4" W x 35'10" D
**Levels:** 1
**Square Footage:** 1,366
**Bedrooms:** 3
**Bathrooms:** 2
**Foundation:** Basement, crawl space, or slab
**Materials List Available:** Yes
**Price Category:** C

*Images provided by designer/architect.*

You're sure to love this home, with its covered front porch and gabled roofline.

**Features:**

- Entry: The 11-ft. ceiling height makes an impressive entryway.

- Living Room: A pair of French doors frames the fireplace in this room, and a central sky light provides natural lighting during the day and drama at night.

- Dining Room: Open to the living room, this area also features an 11-ft.-high ceiling.

- Kitchen: A laundry closet, ample counter space, and dinette opening to the expansive backyard terrace add up to convenience in this room.

- Master Suite: Enjoy the dressing area, two closets, and bath with whirlpool tub and shower.

- Additional Bedrooms: An arched window and 11-ft. ceiling mark the larger of these two rooms.

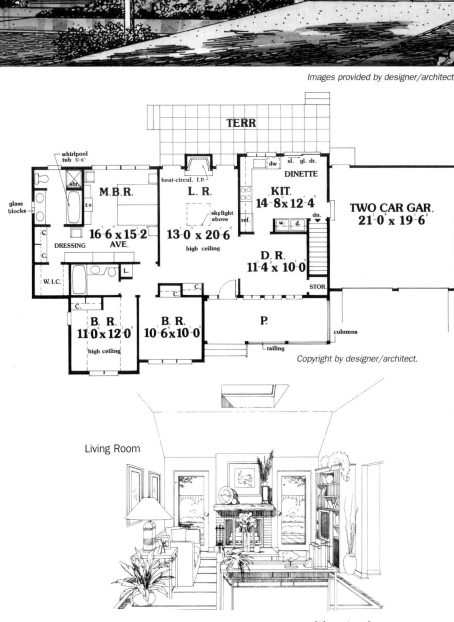

Living Room

*Copyright by designer/architect.*

## Plan #161003

**Dimensions:** 60' W x 47' D

**Levels:** 1

**Square Footage:** 1,508

**Bedrooms:** 3

**Bathrooms:** 2

**Foundation:** Basement

**Materials List Available:** Yes

**Price Category:** C

Multiple gables and a cozy front porch invite you to this enchanting one-story home.

### Features:

- **Great Room:** This bright and cheery room features a sloped ceiling and fireplace. The great room is designed for convenience, with easy access to the foyer and dining area, creating the look and feel of a home much larger than its actual size.

- **Dining Area:** Adjacent to the great room, this dining area has multiple windows and angles that add light and dimension.

- **Kitchen:** This spacious kitchen is designed for easy work patterns with an abundance of counter and cabinet space. It also features a snack bar.

- **Master Bedroom:** Designed for step-saving convenience, this master bedroom includes a compartmented bath, double-bowl vanity, and large walk-in closet.

*Images provided by designer/architect.*

*Copyright by designer/architect.*

Rear Elevation

## Plan #131047

**Dimensions:** 69'10" W x 51'8" D
**Levels:** 1
**Square Footage:** 1,793
**Bedrooms:** 3
**Bathrooms:** 2
**Foundation:** Basement, crawl space, or slab
**Materials List Available:** Yes
**Price Category:** E

*Images provided by designer/architect.*

The country charm of this well-designed home is mixed with the convenience and luxury normally reserved for more contemporary plans.

**Features:**

- Great Room: The spaciousness of this great room is enhanced by the 11-ft. stepped ceiling. A fireplace makes it cozy on cool evenings or on chilly winter days, and two sets of French sliding glass doors open to the back porch.

- Kitchen: In addition to the convenient layout of this design, you'll also love its bright, airy position. It includes an old-fashioned pantry,

a sink under a window, and a sunny breakfast area that opens to the wraparound porch.

- Master Suite: You'll find 11-ft. ceilings in both the master bedroom and the bayed sitting area that the suite includes. In the bath, the circular spa tub is surrounded by a glass-block wall.

- Bonus Space: A permanent staircase leads to an unfinished bonus space on the upper level.

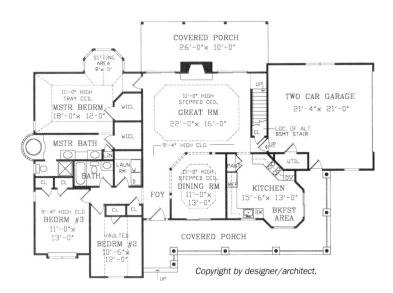

*Copyright by designer/architect.*

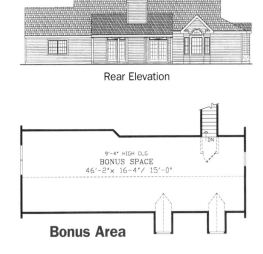

Rear Elevation

Bonus Area

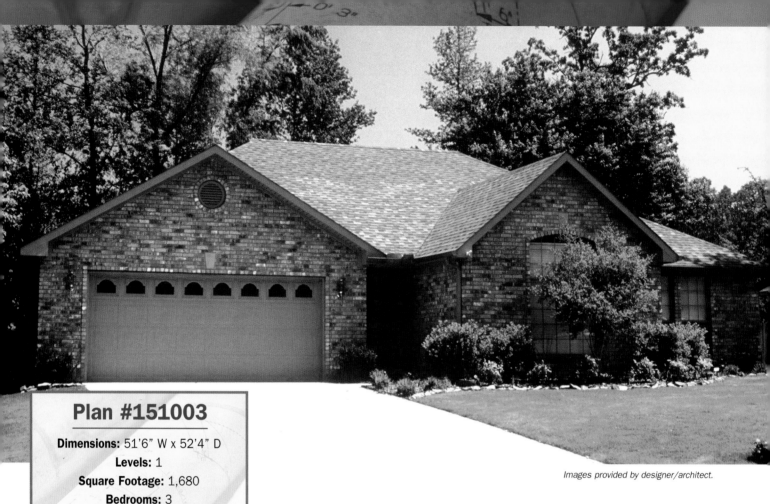

## Plan #151003

**Dimensions:** 51'6" W x 52'4" D
**Levels:** 1
**Square Footage:** 1,680
**Bedrooms:** 3
**Bathrooms:** 2
**Foundation:** Basement, slab, or daylight basement.
**Materials List Available:** Yes
**Price Category:** C

A lovely front porch, bay windows, and dormers add sparkle to this country-style home.

**Features:**

- Great Room: Perfect for entertaining, this room features a tray ceiling, wet bar, and a quiet screened porch nearby.

- Dining Room: This bayed dining room facing the front porch is cozy yet roomy enough for family parties during the holidays.

- Kitchen: This eat-in kitchen also faces the front and is ideal for preparing meals for any occasion.

- Master Suite: The tray ceiling here gives an added feeling of space, while the distance from the other bedrooms allows for all the privacy you'll need.

Images provided by designer/architect.

# Plan #151007

**Dimensions:** 54'2" W x 56'2" D

**Levels:** 1

**Square Footage:** 1,787

**Bedrooms:** 3

**Bathrooms:** 2

**Foundation:** Basement, crawl space, or slab

**Materials List Available:** Yes

**Price Category:** C

This compact, well-designed home is graced with amenities usually reserved for larger houses.

## Features:

- Foyer: A 10-ft. ceiling creates unity between the foyer and the dining room just beyond it.

- Dining Room: 8-in. boxed columns welcome you to this dining room, with its 10-ft. ceilings.

- Great Room: The 9-ft. boxed ceiling suits the spacious design. Enjoy the fireplace in the winter and the rear-grilling porch in the summer.

- Breakfast Room: This bright room is a lovely spot for any time of day.

- Master Suite: Double vanities and a large walk-in closet add practicality to this quiet room with a 9-ft. pan ceiling. The master bath includes whirlpool tub with glass block and a separate shower.

- Bedrooms: Bedroom 2 features a bay window, and both rooms are convenient to the bathroom.

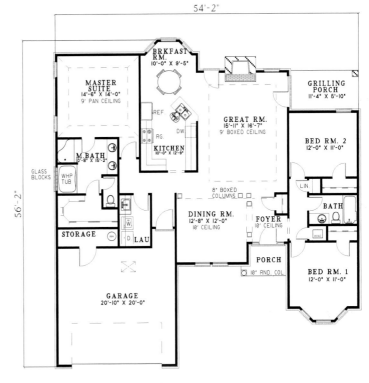

Copyright by designer/architect.

## Plan #101004

**Dimensions:** 55'8" W x 56'6" D
**Levels:** 1
**Square Footage:** 1,787
**Bedrooms:** 3
**Bathrooms:** 2
**Foundation:** Slab, crawl space, basement
**Materials List Available:** No
**Price Category:** C

This carefully designed ranch provides the feel and features of a much larger home.

**Features:**

• **Ceiling Height:** 9 ft. unless otherwise noted.

• **Foyer:** Guests will step up onto the inviting front porch and into this foyer, with its impressive 11-ft. ceiling.

• **Dining Room:** Open to the entry and to its left is this elegant dining room, perfect for entertaining or informal family gatherings.

• **Family Room:** This family gathering place features an 11-ft. ceiling to enhance its sense of spaciousness.

• **Kitchen:** This intelligently designed kitchen has an open plan. A breakfast bar and a serving bar are features that add to its convenience.

• **Master Suite:** This suite is loaded with amenities, including a double-step tray ceiling, direct access to the screened porch, a sitting room, deluxe bath, and his and her walk-in closets.

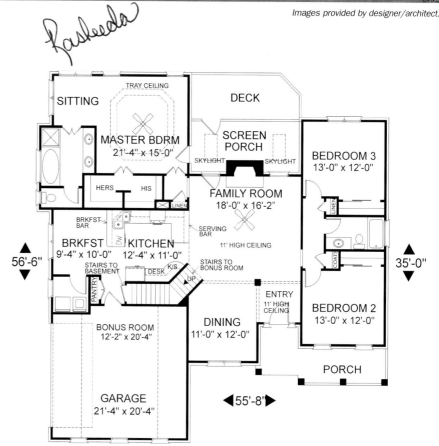

Copyright by designer/architect.

## Plan #161005

**Dimensions:** 60' W x 48'10" D
**Levels:** 1
**Square Footage:** 1,593
**Bedrooms:** 3
**Bathrooms:** 2
**Foundation:** Basement
**Materials List Available:** Yes
**Price Category:** C

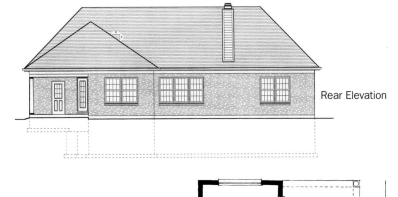

Rear Elevation

This delightful ranch home includes many thoughtful conveniences and a full basement to expand your living enjoyment.

**Features:**

- Great Room: Take pleasure in welcoming guests through a spacious foyer into the warm and friendly confines of this great room with corner fireplace, sloped ceiling, and view to the rear yard.

- Kitchen: Experience the convenience of enjoying meals while seated at the large island that separates the dining area from this well-designed kitchen. Also included is an over-sized pantry with an abundance of storage.

- Master Suite: This master suite features a compartmented bath, large walk-in closet, and master bedroom that has a tray ceiling with 9-ft. center height.

- Porch: Retreat to this delightful rear porch to enjoy a relaxing evening.

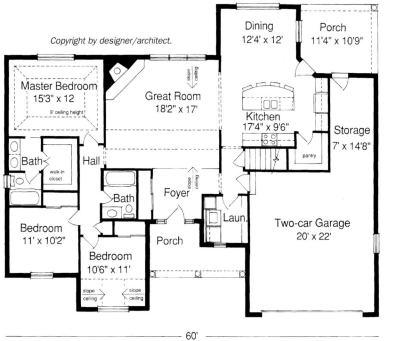

Copyright by designer/architect.

## Plan #161006

**Dimensions:** 78'6" W x 47'7" D

**Levels:** 1

**Square Footage:** 1,755

**Bedrooms:** 3

**Bathrooms:** 2

**Foundation:** Basement

**Materials List Available:** Yes

**Price Category:** C

*Images provided by designer/architect.*

This enchanting, family-friendly home combines a solid brick exterior with an arched window, front porch, and three-car garage.

**Features:**

- Great Room: The 10-ft. ceiling complements the grand first impression created by the warm and friendly fireplace, which is flanked by matching French doors.

- Kitchen: In this functional kitchen, you can enjoy sitting at the bar or in the spacious dining area, with its angled bay and view of a delightful rear porch.

- Master Bedroom: Whether beginning your day or relaxing at its end, enjoy the comfort and luxury of the lavishly equipped bath and large walk-in closet.

- Additional Bedrooms: A full bath is easily accessible from both rooms which feature ample closet space.

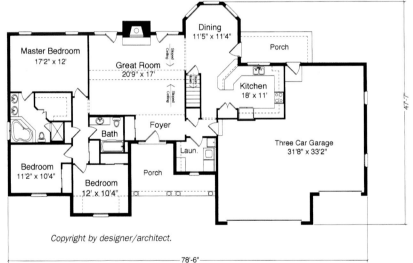

*Copyright by designer/architect.*

Rear Elevation

## Plan #161007

**Dimensions:** 66'4" W x 43'10" D
**Levels:** 1
**Square Footage:** 1,611
**Bedrooms:** 3
**Bathrooms:** 2
**Foundation:** Basement
**Materials List Available:** Yes
**Price Category:** C

A lovely front porch and an entry with side-lights invite you to experience the impressive amenities offered in this exceptional ranch home.

**Features:**

- Great Room: Grand openings, featuring columns from the foyer to this great room and continuing to the bayed dining area, convey an open, spacious feel. The fireplace and matching windows on the rear wall of the great room enhance this effect.

- Kitchen: This well-designed kitchen offers convenient access to the laundry and garage. It also features an angled counter with ample space and an abundance of cabinets.

- Master Suite: This deluxe master suite contains many exciting amenities, including a lavishly appointed dressing room and a large walk-in closet.

- Porch: Sliding doors lead to this delightful screened porch for relaxing summer interludes.

*Images provided by designer/architect.*

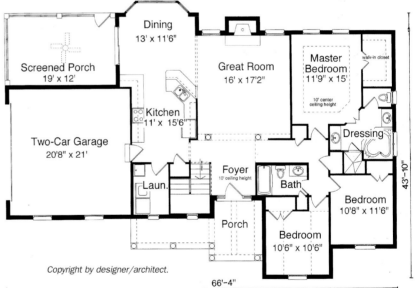

*Copyright by designer/architect.*

Rear Elevation

## Plan #161010

**Dimensions:** 50'8" W x 44'2" D
**Levels:** 1
**Square Footage:** 1,544
**Bedrooms:** 3
**Bathrooms:** 2
**Foundation:** Basement
**Materials List Available:** Yes
**Price Category:** C

*Images provided by designer/architect.*

This one-story home's many distinctive and elegant features—including arched openings and sloped ceilings—will surprise and excite you at every turn.

**Features:**

- Great Room: Decorative columns frame the entrance from the foyer to this great room and are repeated at the opening to the formal dining area.

- Kitchen: Designed for quick meals or to accommodate an oversized crowd, this kitchen features a curved countertop with seating that functions as a delightful bar.

- Master Bedroom: This master bedroom is split to afford you more privacy and features a compartmented bath that forms a separate vanity area.

- Additional Bedrooms: Take advantage of the double doors off the foyer to allow one bedroom to function as a library.

Right Side Elevation

Left Side Elevation

Rear Elevation

*Copyright by designer/architect.*

# Plan #161011

**Dimensions:** 66' W x 69' D
**Levels:** 1
**Square Footage:** 1,788
**Bedrooms:** 3
**Bathrooms:** 2
**Foundation:** Basement
**Materials List Available:** Yes
**Price Category:** C

A beautiful facade, an exciting interior, and step-saving convenience combine to make this lovely home appealing to a variety of discriminating tastes.

## Features:

- **Great Room:** This great room provides easy access to the formal dining area and breakfast area. You will enjoy the openness of the sloped ceiling and the warmth of the corner fireplace.

- **Kitchen:** This well-designed, spacious kitchen offers the convenience of island seating, the charm of a boxed window at the sink, and the luxury of a large breakfast area that opens to a spectacular screened porch.

- **Master Suite:** Pamper yourself and relax at the end of the day in the luxurious bath that this master suite provides.

- **Laundry Room:** You will appreciate the convenience of a separate area to simplify the chore of wash days.

*Images provided by designer/architect.*

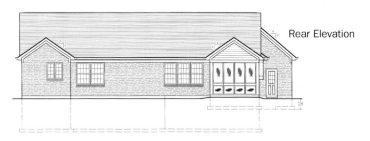

**Screened Porch** 11'5" x 11'8"

**Breakfast** 10'8" x 11'8"

**Great Room** 17'6" x 16'12"

**Master Bedroom** 15' x 13'

**Dress.**

**WALK-IN CLOSET**

**Kitchen** 12' x 13'

**Dining Room** 10'8" x 8'7"

**Foyer**

**Hall**

**Bath**

**Laun.**

**Hall**

**Porch**

**Library/ Bedroom** 11' x 12'6"

**Bedroom** 12'6" x 11'4"

SLOPED  SLOPED

**Garage** 22'4" x 24'4"

63'4"

69'-0"

66'-0"

*Copyright by designer/architect.*

**Rear Elevation**

## Plan #161001

**Dimensions:** 67'2" W x 47' D

**Levels:** 1

**Square Footage:** 1,782

**Bedrooms:** 3

**Bathrooms:** 2

**Foundation:** Basement

**Materials List Available:** Yes

**Price Category:** C

An all-brick exterior displays the solid strength that characterizes this gracious home.

### Features:

- **Gathering Area:** A feeling of spaciousness permeates this gathering area, created by the foyer, great room, and dining room. Multiple windows provide natural light that dances along a sloped ceiling, spilling onto decorative columns and a fireplace.

- **Breakfast Area:** A continuation of the sloped ceiling leads to this breakfast area, where French doors open to a screened porch.

- **Kitchen:** An abundance of cabinets and counter space are the hallmarks of this large kitchen, with its easy access to a spacious laundry room and storage area.

- **Master Suite:** A tray ceiling and spacious walk-in closet in the master bedroom, along with a whirlpool tub and double-bowl vanity in the bathroom, enable you to pamper yourself.

*Images provided by designer/architect.*

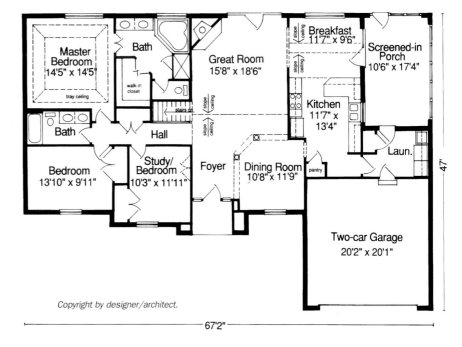

*Copyright by designer/architect.*

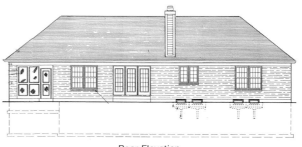

Rear Elevation

### Left Side Elevation

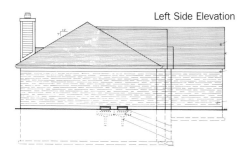

### Right Side Elevation

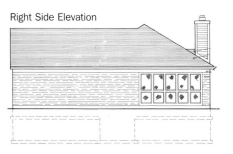

Front View

Great Room / Foyer

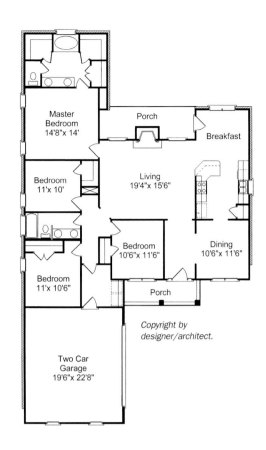

## Plan #111014

**Dimensions:** 78' W x 47' D

**Levels:** 1

**Square Footage:** 1,865

**Bedrooms:** 4

**Bathrooms:** 2

**Foundation:** Crawl space

**Materials List Available:** No

**Price Category:** D

*Images provided by designer/architect.*

*Copyright by designer/architect.*

Master Bedroom 14'8"x 14'

Porch

Breakfast

Bedroom 11'x 10'

Living 19'4"x 15'6"

Bedroom 10'6"x 11'6"

Dining 10'6"x 11'6"

Bedroom 11'x 10'6"

Porch

Two Car Garage 19'6"x 22'8"

## Plan #111013

**Dimensions:** 33' W x 59' D

**Levels:** 1

**Square Footage:** 1,606

**Bedrooms:** 3

**Bathrooms:** 2

**Foundation:** Slab

**Materials List Available:** No

**Price Category:** C

*Images provided by designer/architect.*

*Copyright by designer/architect.*

Porch

Stor.

Master Bedroom 13'x 15'2"

Breakfast

Bedroom 12'x 10'4"

Living 13'8"x 17'

Bedroom 12'x 11'6"

Porch

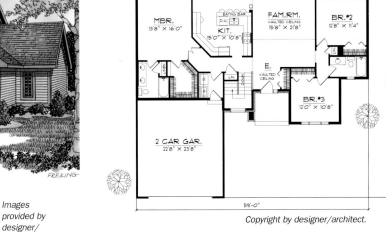

Images provided by designer/architect.

## Plan #221011

**Dimensions:** 59' W x 58' D

**Levels:** 1

**Square Footage:** 1,756

**Bedrooms:** 3

**Bathrooms:** 2

**Foundation:** Basement

**Materials List Available:** No

**Price Category:** C

Rear Elevation

Images provided by designer/architect.

## Plan #271059

**Dimensions:** 67' W x 57' D

**Levels:** 1

**Square Footage:** 1,790

**Bedrooms:** 1-3

**Bathrooms:** 1½-2½

**Foundation:** Daylight basement

**Materials List Available:** No

**Price Category:** C

**Optional Basement Level Floor Plan**

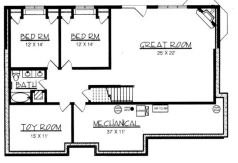

# Cottage Kitchens and Baths

Of all the rooms in a house, kitchens present unique decorating challenges because so much tends to happen in these spaces. In addition to preparing meals, most families use kitchens as gathering and entertaining areas. Kitchens need to be functional, comfortable, and inviting.

Who can't relate to this scenario: you turn on the oven to preheat it, but wait, did you take out the large roasting pan first?

How about the lasagna dish, muffin tins, pizza stone, and cookie sheets that are in there, too? Now where can you put everything that was in the oven while the casserole is baking and the countertop is laden with the rest of tonight's dinner ingredients? Good cabinetry outfitted with an assortment of organizing options can help you there. It can make your kitchen more efficient and a whole lot neater while establishing a style, or "look," for the room.

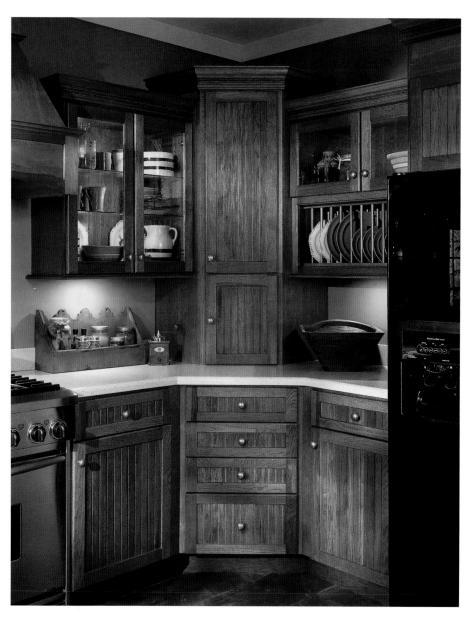

## Cabinet Construction

Basically, cabinets are constructed in one of two ways: framed or frameless. Framed cabinets have a traditional look, with a full frame across the face of the cabinet box that may show between closed doors, that fits a Cottage decor. This secures adjacent cabinets and strengthens wider cabinet boxes with a center rail. Hinges on framed cabinets may or may not be visible around doors when they are closed. The door's face may be ornamented with raised or recessed panels, trimmed or framed panels, or a framed-glass panel with or without muntins (the narrow vertical and horizontal strips of wood that divide panes of glass).

**Frameless cabinets.** These are also known as European-style cabinets, although American manufacturers also make them—are built without a face frame and sport a clean, contemporary look, often not befitting a Cottage style. There's no trim or molding with this simple design. Close-fitting doors cover the entire front of the box, no ornamentation appears on the face of the doors, and hinges are typically hidden inside the cabinet box.

## Selecting Cabinets

Choosing one type over another is generally a matter of taste, although framed units offer slightly less interior space. But the quality of construction is a factor that always should be taken into consideration. How do you judge it? Solid wood is too expensive for most of today's budgets, but it might be used on just the doors and frames. More typical is plywood box construction, which offers good structural support and solid wood on the doors and frames. To save money, cabinetmakers sometimes use strong plywood for support elements, such as the box and frame, and medium-density fiberboard for other parts, such as doors and drawer fronts. In yet

another alternative, good-quality laminate cabinets can be made with high-quality, thick particleboard underneath the laminate finish.

**Quality Points.** There are other things to look for in cabinet construction. They include dovetail or mortise-and-tenon joinery and solidly mortised hinges. Also, make sure that the interior of every cabinet is well finished, with adjustable shelves that are a minimum ⅜ inch thick to prevent bowing.

**Bead-board paneled doors,** opposite, are at home in cottage-style kitchens.

**Framed cabinets,** above, offer a traditional look to an otherwise modern kitchen.

**Cottage-style designs** have many of the attributes of Country decor, right.

Unless you have the time and skill to build the cabinets yourself or can hire someone else to do it, you'll have to purchase them in one of four ways. **Knockdown cabinetry** (also known as RTA, ready to assemble) is shipped flat and, sometimes, unfinished because you put the pieces together. **Stock cabinetry** comes in standard sizes but limited styles and colors; it is often available on the spot or can be delivered quickly. Like stock, **semi-custom cabinetry** comes in standard styles, but it is manufactured to fit a homeowner's specific size and finish needs. **Custom cabinetry** is not limited in terms of style or size because it is built to the designer's specifications.

## The Decorative Role of Cabinets

The look you create in your kitchen will be largely influenced by the cabinetry you select. Finding a style that suits you and how you will use your new kitchen is similar to shopping for furniture. In fact, don't be surprised to see many furniture details dressing up the cabinets on view in showrooms and home centers today.

**Details That Stand Out.** Besides architectural elements such as fluted pilasters, corbels, moldings, and bull's-eye panels, look for details such as fretwork, rope motifs, gingerbread trim, balusters, composition ornamentation (it looks like carving), even footed cabinets that mimic separate furniture pieces. If your taste runs toward less fussy design, you'll also find handsome door and drawer styles that feature minimal decoration, if any. Woods and finishes are just as varied, and range from informal looks in birch, oak, ash, and maple to rich mahogany and cherry. Laminate finishes, though less popular than they were a decade ago, haven't completely disappeared from the marketplace, but an array of colors has replaced the once-ubiquitous almond and white finishes.

## Color

Color is coming on strong on wood cabinetry, too. Accents in one, two, or more hues are pairing with natural wood tones. White-painted cabinets take on a warmer glow with tinted shades of this always pop-ular neutral. Special "vintage" finishes, such as translucent color glazes, continue to grow in popularity, as do distressed finishing techniques such as wire brushing and rubbed-through color that add both another dimension and the appeal of handcraftmanship, even on mass-produced items.

If you're shy about using color on such a high-ticket item as cabinetry, try it as an accent on molding, door trim, or island cabinetry. Just as matched furniture suites have become passé in other rooms of the house, the same is true for the kitchen, where mixing several looks can add sophistication and visual interest.

## Cabinet Hardware

Another way to emphasize your kitchen's Cottage style is with hardware. From exquisite reproductions in brass, pewter, wrought iron, or ceramic to handsome bronze, chrome, nickel, glass, steel, plastic, rubber, wood, or stone creations, a smorgasbord of shapes and designs is available. Some pieces are highly polished; others are matte-finished, smooth, or hammered. Some are abstract or geometrical; others are simple,

elegant shapes. Whimsical designs take on the forms of animals or teapots, vegetables or flowers. Even just one or two great-looking door or drawer pulls can be showstoppers in a kitchen that may otherwise be devoid of much personality. Like mixing cabinet finishes, a combination of two hardware styles—perhaps picked up from other materials in the room—makes a big design statement. As the famed architect Mies Van der Rohe once stated, "God is in the details," and the most perfect detail in your new kitchen may be the artistic hardware that you select.

**Cabinet style** will set the tone for the design of the entire kitchen. The simple door styles keeps the room at left airy and casual.

**The rustic look** of the cabinets above is tailored made for any Country or cottage-style kitchen.

**Color accents,** such as the splash of color on the kitchen island shown right, can customize any simple cabinet design.

**Cabinet hardware** should complement the cabinet door and drawer designs, but it should also be easy for everyone in the household to grasp, above.

**Kitchen storage** comes in a variety of forms, including cabinets, drawers, pullout extensions, and the glass-front bins shown to the right.

Besides looks, consider the function of a pull or knob. You have to be able to grip it easily and comfortably. If your fingers or hands get stiff easily, or if you have arthritis, select C- or U-shaped pulls. If you like a knob, try it out in the showroom to make sure it isn't slippery or awkward when you grab it. Knobs and pulls can be inexpensive if you can stick to unfinished ones that you can paint in an accent color picked up from the tile or wallpaper. If you don't plan to buy new cabinets, changing the hardware on old ones can redefine their style. The right knob or pull can suggest any one of a number of vintage looks or decorative styles, from Colonial to Victorian, and reinforce your cottage decor.

## Types of Storage

Storage facilities can make or break a kitchen, so choose the places you'll put things with care. Here's a look at a few alternatives:

**Pantries.** How often you shop and how many groceries you typically bring home determine the amount of food storage space your family needs. If you like to stock up or take advantage of sales, add a pantry

to your kitchen. To maximize a pantry's convenience, plan shallow, 6-inch-deep shelves so that cans and packages will never be stored more than two deep. This way, you'll easily be able to see what you've got on hand. Pantries range in size from floor-to-ceiling models to narrow units designed to fit between two standard-size cabinets.

**Appliance Garages.** Appliance garages make use of dead space in a corner, but they can be installed anywhere in the vertical space between wall-mounted cabinets and the countertop. A tambour (rolltop) door hides small appliances like a food processor or anything else you want within reach but hidden from view.

**Lazy Susans and Carousel Shelves.** Rotating shelves like lazy Susans and carousels maximize dead corner storage and put items like dishes or pots and pans within easy reach. A lazy Susan rotates 360 degrees, so just spin it to find what you're looking for. Carousel shelves, which attach to two right-angled doors, rotate 270 degrees; open the doors, and the shelves swing out allowing you to reach items easily.

**Pivoting Shelves.** Door-mounted shelves and in-cabinet swiveling shelf units offer easy access to kitchen supplies. Taller units serve as pantries that hold a great deal in minimal space.

**Pullout Tables and Trays.** In tight kitchens, pullout tables and trays are excellent ways to gain eating space or an extra work surface. Pullout cutting boards come in handy near cooktops, microwaves, and food prep areas. Pullout tea carts are also available.

**Customized Organizers.** If you decide to use value-priced cabinets or choose to forego the storage accessories offered by manufacturers, consider refitting their interiors with cabinet organizers you purchase yourself. These plastic, plastic-coated wire, or enameled-steel racks and hangers are widely available at department stores, hardware stores, and home centers.

Some of these units slide in and out of base cabinets, similar to the racks in a dishwasher. Others let you mount shallow drawers to the undersides of wall cabinets.

Still others consist of stackable plastic bins with plenty of room to hold kitchen sundries.

Beware of the temptation to overspecialize your kitchen storage facilities. Sizes and needs for certain items change, so be sure to allot at least 50 percent of your kitchen's storage to standard cabinets with one or more movable shelves. And don't forget to allow for storing recyclable items.

**Today's cabinets** can be customized with storage accessories, right.

**Full-height pantries,** above, provide a number of different types of storage near where you need the items. This pantry is next to the food-prep area.

**Base cabinets** can be outfitted with accessories for kitchen storage or for wet bar storage as is shown in the cabinet below.

## Storage Checklist

Here's a guide to help you get your storage needs in order.

■ **Do you like kitchen gadgets?**
Plan drawer space, countertop sorters, wall magnets, or hooks to keep these items handy near where you often use them.

■ **Do you own a food processor, blender, mixer, toaster oven, electric can opener, knife sharpener, juicer, coffee maker, or coffee mill?**
If you're particularly tidy, you may want small appliances like these tucked away in an appliance garage or cupboard to be taken out only when needed. If you pre-fer to have frequently used machines sitting on the counter, ready to go, plan enough space, along with conveniently located electrical outlets.

■ **Do you plan to store large quantities of food?**
Be sure to allow plenty of freezer, bin, and shelf space for the kind of food shopping you do.

■ **Do you intend to do a lot of freezing or canning?**
Allow a work space and place to stow equipment. Also plan adequate storage for the fruits of your labor—an extra stand-alone freezer, a good-sized food safe in the kitchen, or a separate pantry or cellar.

■ **Do you bake often?**
Consider a baking center that can house your equipment and serve as a separate baking-ingredients pantry.

■ **Do you collect pottery, tinware, or anything else that might be displayed in the kitchen?**
Soffits provide an obvious place to hang small objects like collectible plates. Eliminating soffits provides a shelf on top of the wall cabinets for larger light-weight objects like baskets. Open shelving, glass-front cupboards, and display cabinets are other options.

■ **Do you collect cookbooks?**
If so, you'll need expandable shelf space and perhaps a bookstand.

## Personal Profile of You and Your Family

■ **How tall are you and everyone else who will use your kitchen?**
Adjust your counter and wall-cabinet heights to suit. Multilevel work surfaces for special tasks are a necessity for good kitchen design.

■ **Do you or any of your family members use a walker, leg braces, or a wheelchair?**
Plan a good work height, knee space, grab bars, secure seating, slide-out work

**Fold-down ironing boards,** above left, are a true luxury. If you have the space, install one near the kitchen or laundry room.

**Corner cabinets** often contain storage space you can't reach. Make it accessible by installing swing-out shelves, above right, or a lazy Susan.

**Glass doors** put your kitchen items on display. The owners of the kitchen below chose distinctive pottery and glassware for their glass-door cabinets.

boards, and other convenience features to make your kitchen comfortable for all who will use it.

■ **Are you left- or right-handed?**
Think about your natural motion when you choose whether to open cupboards or refrigerator doors from the left or right side, whether to locate your dishwasher to the left or right of the sink, and so on.

■ **How high can you comfortably reach?**
If you're tall, hang your wall cabinets high. If you're petite, you may want to hang the cabinets lower and plan a spot to keep a step stool handy.

■ **Can you comfortably bend and reach for something in a base cabinet? Can you lift heavy objects easily and without strain or pain?**
If your range is limited in these areas, be sure to plan roll-out shelving on both upper and lower tiers of your base cabinets. Also, look into spring-up shelves designed to lift mixer bases or other heavy appliances to counter height.

■ **Do you frequently share cooking tasks with another family member?**
If so, you may each prefer to have your own work area.

ous plan demands this kind of attention. Even if you are designing a modest bath, you can greatly increase its performance and your ultimate comfort by thoughtfully planning out every square inch of floor and wall space. In fact, small spaces require more attention to details than larger spaces.

## Types of bathrooms

The most-common-size American bathroom measures 60 x 84 inches or 60 x 96 inches. The most common complaint about it is the lack of space. The arrangement may have suited families 50 years ago, but times and habits have changed. If it's the only bathroom in the house, making it work better becomes even more important.

When planning the layout, try angling a sink or shower unit in a corner to free up some floor space. Unlike a traditional door, which swings into the room and takes up wall space when it is open, a pocket door slides into the wall. Another smart way to add function to a small bathroom is to remove the drywall and install shelves between the studs.

**The Importance of Lighting.** You can also make a small bathroom feel roomier by bringing in natural light with a skylight or roof window or by replacing one small standard window with several small casement units that can be installed high on the wall to maintain privacy while admitting light.

## Cottage Bath Design

Many professionals believe that bathrooms may be the most difficult rooms in the house to design properly. The space is often small, yet it must be able to accommodate a variety of large fixtures. In addition, many homeowners tend to focus, at least initially, on the way the bathroom looks. They fall in love with the whirlpool tub that is really too large for the space or the exquisite hand-painted sink that, while beautiful, demands too much effort to keep it

looking that way. Design your cottage-style bath to be functional as well as beautiful.

Architect Louis Sullivan said, "Form follows function." That does not mean that style has to be subservient to function, but there must be a balance between the two. So even if you have a clear picture about how you want the new bathroom to look, put that thought on hold—temporarily—and think about how it will work.

**Thorough Planning.** Don't mislead yourself into believing that only a luxuri-

## The Master Bath

The concept of the master bath has come of age in the past decade. It is one of the most popular rooms for splurging on high-end items and gives one of the highest returns on investment upon resale. It's where you can create that sought-after getaway—the home version of a European spa.

**Latest Trends.** Some popular amenities to include in your plan are a sauna, greenhouse, exercise studio, fireplace, audio and video systems, faucets and sprayers with full massaging options, steam room,

**Windows placed high** on the wall let in light while maintaining privacy, opposite.

**Mater baths,** above, often contain an attached dressing area.

**Traditional designs** do not prevent you from using the latest shower products, right.

**Cottage baths** tend to be bright and airy, such as the one shown to the left.

**A simple floral** design decorates the border of the medicine cabinet above.

**Cottage bathroom cabinetry** should be simple and traditional in design, below.

whirlpool tub, and dressing table. You are only limited by size and imagination.

**Planning for Extras.** Extras can be tempting but may require special planning. For example, you may need additional support in the floor, as well as supplemental heating and ventilation. You would not want to slip into a tub and have it fall two floors to the middle of the living room.

Some of the best floor plans for the modern adult bath also include a separate room for the toilet and bidet, a detached tub and shower, and dual sinks on opposite sides of the room with adjacent dressing rooms and walk-in closets. Modern couples

want to share a master bed and bath, but they also want to have privacy and the ease of getting ready in the morning without tripping over their mates. The only way to do this harmoniously is to mingle the parts of the room that invite sharing and separate those elements that are always private. Such items as a sauna, exercise area, and a whirlpool tub would be part of shared space. Dressing tables and clothes closets would be private spaces.

## The Powder Room

The guest bath. The half bath. It has a lot of names, and it may be the most efficient room in the house, providing just what you

need often in tight quarters. A powder room normally includes nothing more than a lavatory and a toilet. You can find small-scale fixtures specifically designed for the powder room, from the tiniest lavs to unusually narrow toilets.

Keep a small powder room as light and open as possible. Plan to install good lighting because the powder room is often used for touching up makeup.

**Focal Points.** In the powder room, the vanity is often the focal point. The room offers the best opportunity to showcase a decorative piece, such as a hand-painted pedestal sink or a custom-made vanity.

Because the powder room is often for guests and is normally located on the ground floor near the living area, take extra care to ensure privacy. If possible, the best location is in a hallway, away from the living room, kitchen, and dining area. This room can also handle stronger wall colors—either dark or bright ones—as well as larger, bolder wallpaper patterns because it is a short-stay room.

## The Family Bath

Compartmentalizing is the best way to start planning the family bath. But remember, when you separate the bathroom into smaller, distinct areas, you run the risk of making the room feel cramped. Try to alleviate this with extra natural light, good artificial lighting, and translucent partitions made of glass blocks or etched glass. Anything that divides with privacy while also allowing light to enter will help ease the closed-in feeling.

**Separate Areas.** If separating the fixtures is not possible because of the size of the room, include a sink in the dressing area within the master bedroom to provide a second place for applying makeup or shaving. It will help relieve bottlenecks when everyone is dressing in the morning.

Investigate building a back-to-back bath in lieu of one large shared room. Another popular option is to locate the bathing fixtures, both the tub and separate shower, in the center of the room; install the bidet, a toilet, and sink on either side in their own separate areas. To make the arrangement work, keep each side of the room accessible to the door.

There are other options you can use. It is important to remember that you don't need to do them all at once; you can do some remodeling once you've moved into your house.

**Ceramic-tile** counters for cottage vanities are easy to clean and can stand up to abuse.

# Plan #161012

**Dimensions:** 69' W x 50'10" D
**Levels:** 1
**Square Footage:** 1,648
**Bedrooms:** 3
**Bathrooms:** 2
**Foundation:** Basement
**Materials List Available:** Yes
**Price Category:** C

*Images provided by designer/architect.*

Right Side Elevation

Left Side Elevation

Rear Elevation

This delightful brick home, with multiple gables and an inviting front porch, offers an exciting interior with varied ceiling heights and an open floor plan.

**Features:**

- Great Room: This great room showcases an 11-ft. ceiling and a gas fireplace. Enjoy a beverage seated at the convenient bar, and move freely through a generous opening to the relaxed dining area.

- Kitchen: This galley kitchen is expanded by easy access to the garage and laundry room.

- Master Bedroom: You will appreciate the openness of this large master bedroom, which features an 11-ft. ceiling. You can also retreat to the privacy of an adjoining covered porch.

- Library: Thoughtful design allows you to exercise the option of converting the bedroom off the foyer into a library.

Covered Porch
14' X 12'

Dining
8' CEILING HT
13'6" x 11'

Master Bedroom
11' CEILING HT
16' x 15'8"

Great Room
11' CEILING HT
17'8" x 16'2"

Two-Car Garage
22'6" x 22'

Kitchen
8' CEILING HT

PANTRY

WALK-IN CLOSET

Bath

STAIRS UP

Library/Bedroom
10' X 11'6"

Bath

Bedroom
10' X 11'6"

Laun.

Foyer

Porch

*Copyright by designer/architect.*

69'-0"

50'-10"

## Plan #121058

**Dimensions:** 50' W x 52'8" D
**Levels:** 1
**Square Footage:** 1,554
**Bedrooms:** 3
**Bathrooms:** 2
**Foundation:** Basement
**Materials List Available:** Yes
**Price Category:** C

*Images provided by designer/architect.*

The high ceilings and well-placed windows make this home bright and airy.

**Features:**

- **Great Room:** A soaring cathedral ceiling sets the tone for this gracious room. Enjoy the fireplace that's framed by views to the outside.

- **Dining Room:** A 10-ft. ceiling highlights formality, while a built-in display cabinet and picturesque window give it even more character.

- **Kitchen:** This well-designed kitchen shares a snack bar with the breakfast area.

- **Breakfast Area:** Natural light streams into this room, and the door to the backyard lets everyone move outside for a meal or drink in fine weather.

- **Master Suite:** A tray ceiling gives elegance to the bedroom, with its practical walk-in closet. The bath features a sunlit whirlpool tub, double vanity, and separate shower.

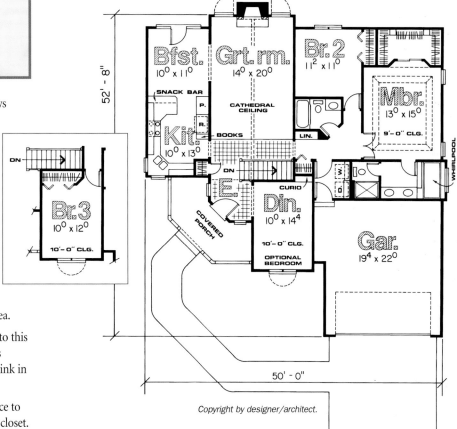

*Copyright by designer/architect.*

## Plan #101003

**Dimensions:** 50' W x 54'10" D
**Levels:** 1
**Square Footage:** 1,593
**Bedrooms:** 3
**Bathrooms:** 2
**Foundation:** Slab, crawl space, basement
**Materials List Available:** Yes
**Price Category:** C

*Images provided by designer/architect.*

The brick-and-siding exterior is accented with multilevel wood trim and copper roofing returns.

**Features:**

- Ceiling Height: 9 ft. unless otherwise noted.
- Covered Porch: The inviting covered porch is the perfect place for a swing or old-fashioned rockers. Rediscover the old-fashioned pleasure of relaxing on the porch.
  - Kitchen: This large, carefully designed kitchen makes cooking a pleasure.

- Laundry Room: In addition to housing the washer and dryer, this laundry room provides a place to sort and fold.
- Family Room: The 12-ft. ceiling gives this family gathering place a sense of spaciousness.
- Dining Room: The tray ceiling makes this room a dramatic and elegant place in which to entertain.
- Master Suite: This luxurious retreat features a sitting area and a 6-ft x 10-ft. walk-in closet. The bathroom has a garden tub, shower, and enormous 8-ft. double vanity.

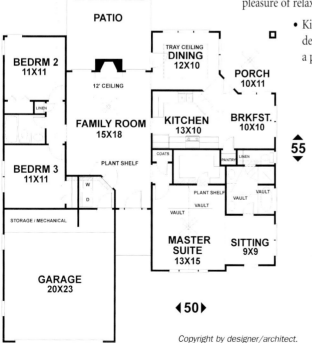

*Copyright by designer/architect.*

## Plan #191030

**Dimensions:** 33' W x 36' D

**Levels:** 1

**Square Footage:** 864

**Bedrooms:** 2

**Bathrooms:** 1

**Foundation:** Crawl space or slab

**Materials List Available:** No

**Price Category:** A

*Images provided by designer/architect.*

Enjoy the view from the spacious front porch of this cozy cottage, which is ideal for a retirement home, vacation retreat, or starter home.

**Features:**

- **Porch:** This 6-ft.-wide porch, which runs the length of the home, gives you plenty of space to set up a couple of rockers next to a potted herb garden.

- **Living/Dining Room:** This huge living and dining area gives you many options for design. The snack bar that it shares with the kitchen is a practical touch.

- **Kitchen:** The first thing you'll notice in this well-planned kitchen is how much counter and storage space it offers.

- **Laundry Room:** Opening to the backyard, this room also features ample storage space.

- **Bedrooms:** Both rooms have good closet space and easy access to the large, luxurious bath.

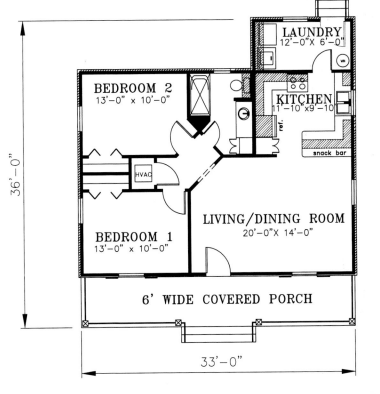

*Copyright by designer/architect.*

## Plan #141001

**Dimensions:** 48' W x 29' D
**Levels:** 1
**Square Footage:** 1,208
**Bedrooms:** 3
**Bathrooms:** 2
**Foundation:** Basement
**Materials List Available:** Yes
**Price Category:** B

*Images provided by designer/architect.*

The spacious feel of this raised ranch belies its compact floor plan.

**Features:**

- Ceiling Height: 8 ft. unless otherwise noted.

- Porch: This country-style porch lends character and lots of curb appeal.

- Drive-Under Garage: The garage is tucked below for a more attractive facade but can also be built with a front entry if lot restrictions dictate.

- Living Room: The cathedral ceiling in the living room creates a dramatic fireplace wall.

- Kitchen: You'll love cooking in this super-efficient U-shaped kitchen, with its generous counter space and storage.

- Laundry: The laundry closet is conveniently located in the hall bath.

- Master Suite: A cathedral ceiling makes this bedroom seem spacious. The oversize tub has a showerhead so that you can enjoy an oversize shower as well.

*Copyright by designer/architect.*

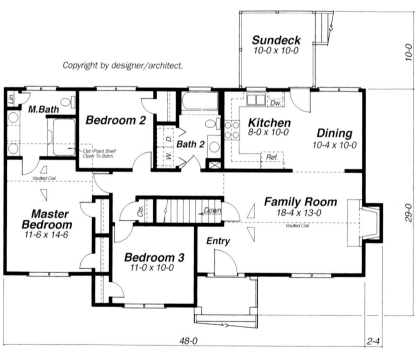

## SMARTtip

### Hydro-seeding

An alternative to traditional seeding is hydro-seeding. In this process, a slurry of grass seed, wood fibers, and fertilizer is spray-applied in one step. Hydro-seeding is relatively inexpensive. Compared with seeding by hand, hydro-seeding is also very fast.

## Plan #141005

**Dimensions:** 38' W x 66' D

**Levels:** 1

**Square Footage:** 1,532

**Bedrooms:** 3

**Bathrooms:** 2

**Foundation:** Slab, basement

**Materials List Available:** No

**Price Category:** C

Board and batten combine with shake siding to give this cottage an appealing Tudor style.

**Features:**

- Ceiling Height: 8 ft. unless otherwise noted.

- Entry: This front entry is highlighted by a dormer that opens to the cathedral ceiling of the spacious open great room.

- Open Floor Plan: The living room, dining areas, and kitchen all flow together to create the feeling of a much larger home.

- Kitchen: This kitchen is defined by a curved bar, which can house a bench seat to service a small cafe-style table.

- Master Suite: This private suite is separated from the rest of the bedrooms. It features a volume ceiling and separate sitting area.

- Basement Option: The house is designed primarily for a slab on a narrow lot but can also be built over a basement.

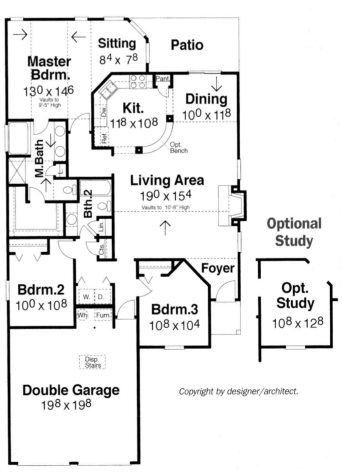

*Copyright by designer/architect.*

## Plan #241005

**Dimensions:** 53' W x 55'9" D
**Levels:** 1
**Square Footage:** 1,670
**Bedrooms:** 3
**Bathrooms:** 2
**Foundation:** Slab
**Materials List Available:** No
**Price Category:** C

*Images provided by designer/architect.*

This charming starter home, in split-bedroom format, combines big-house features in a compact design.

**Features:**

- **Great Room:** With easy access to the formal dining room, kitchen, and breakfast area, this great room features a cozy fireplace.

- **Kitchen:** This big kitchen, with easy access to a walk-in pantry, features an island for added work space and a lovely plant shelf that separates it from the great room.

- **Master Suite:** Separated for privacy, this master suite offers a roomy bath with whirlpool tub, dual vanities, a separate shower, and a large walk-in closet.

- **Additional Rooms:** Additional rooms include a laundry/utility room—with space for a washer, dryer, and freezer—a large area above the garage, well-suited for a media or game room, and two secondary bedrooms.

*Copyright by designer/architect.*

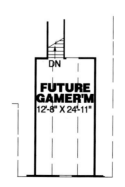

## Plan #141006

**Dimensions:** 64' W x 52' D

**Levels:** 1

**Square Footage:** 1,787

**Bedrooms:** 3

**Bathrooms:** 2½

**Foundation:** Basement

**Materials List Available:** No

**Price Category:** C

This stately and traditional ranch has a well-designed floor plan that makes it seem larger.

### Features:

- Ceiling Height: 9 ft. unless otherwise noted:

- Tall Main Ceilings: The main part of the house has an elegant look, with 12-ft. ceilings in the foyer, living area, and dining room. The taller windows allow room for transom windows that fill the rooms with sunlight.

- Fireplace: The handsome fireplace is designed to vent directly to the outside. Without the need for a chimney, a television niche can be installed above the fireplace, maximizing the use of space in the room.

- Kitchen: This kitchen gains light from the breakfast room and the living area. The sink is angled to allow the cook to participate in living-area conversation.

- Master Suite: This elegant private suite has its own access off the rear entry hall.

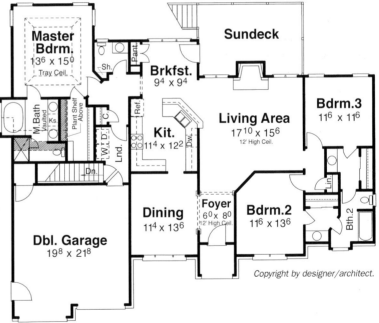

Copyright by designer/architect.

## SMARTtip

### Arts and Crafts Style in Your Kitchen

The heart of this style lies in its earthy connection. The more you can bring nature into it, the more authentic it will appear. An easy way to do this is with plants. Open the space up to nature with glass doors that provide a view to a green garden.

## Plan #141007

**Dimensions:** 65' W x 56'5" D

**Levels:** 1

**Square Footage:** 1,854

**Bedrooms:** 3

**Bathrooms:** 2½

**Foundation:** Basement

**Materials List Available:** No

**Price Category:** D

This home offers a spacious layout, all on one level for convenient modern living.

**Features:**

- Ceiling Height: 8 ft. unless otherwise noted.

- Dining Room: The 12-ft. ceiling makes this the perfect dining room for the most elegant of dinner parties.

- Living Room: The elegant 12-ft. ceiling continues into this living room. Its handsome fireplace will make it the focal point for all gatherings.

- Kitchen: This well-designed kitchen will make cooking a pleasure. It features a pantry and an island for food preparation.

- Breakfast Area: The breakfast area is just off the kitchen. Measuring 11 ft. x 11 ft., it offers plenty of room for the whole family to enjoy informal meals.

- Master Suite: Located away from the other bedrooms, this luxurious retreat has a tray ceiling. The master bath has separate vanities, a jet tub, and a separate shower.

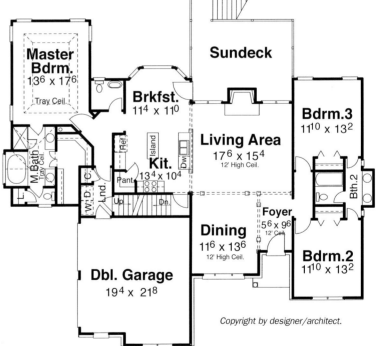

## SMARTtip

### Painting Walls

Paint won't hide imperfections. Rather, it will make them stand out. So shine a bright light at a low angle across the surface to spot problem areas before painting.

## Plan #141011

**Dimensions:** 54' W x 60'6" D

**Levels:** 1

**Square Footage:** 1,869

**Bedrooms:** 3

**Bathrooms:** 2

**Foundation:** Basement, crawl space, or slab

**Materials List Available:** Yes

**Price Category:** D

*Images provided by designer/architect.*

The blending of brick and stone on this plan gives the home an old-world appeal.

**Features:**

• Ceiling Height: 8 ft. unless otherwise noted.

• Tall Ceilings: The main living areas feature dramatic 12-ft. ceilings.

• Open Plan: This home's open floor plan maximizes the use of space and makes it flexible. The main living area has plenty of room for large gatherings.

• Kitchen: This kitchen is integrated into the main living area. It features a breakfast room that is ideal for informal family meals.

• Master Suite: You'll enjoy unwinding at the end of the day in this luxurious space. It's located away from the rest of the house for maximum privacy.

• Secondary Bedrooms: You have the option of adding extra style to the secondary bedrooms by including volume ceilings.

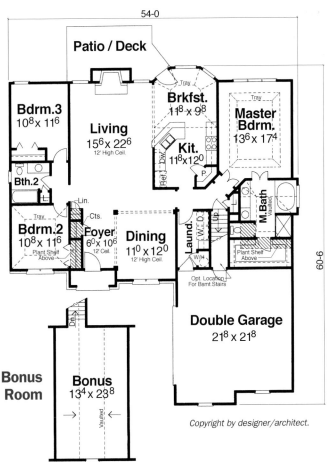

*Copyright by designer/architect.*

Images provided by designer/architect.

# Plan #171001

**Dimensions:** 44' W x 41' D
**Levels:** 1
**Square Footage:** 1,277
**Bedrooms:** 3
**Bathrooms:** 2
**Foundation:** Crawl space, slab, or basement
**Materials List Available:** Yes
**Price Category:** B

You'll love this design if you're looking for a compact ranch with rustic, country styling and plenty of well designed family areas.

**Features:**

- **Porch:** Set a couple of rockers and containers of blooming plants and fragrant herbs on this lovely front porch.

- **Great Room:** A substantial fireplace is the focal point of this large room. Fill it with a dried floral bouquet in summer, and gather chairs around its warmth in winter.

- **Dining Room:** This room adjoins the great room for easy entertaining in any season and opens to the large screened porch for summer parties.

- **Kitchen:** With good counter space and an open layout, this kitchen is built for efficiency.

- **Master Bedroom:** Split from the other two bedrooms for privacy, this quiet retreat features a large walk-in closet and lovely window area.

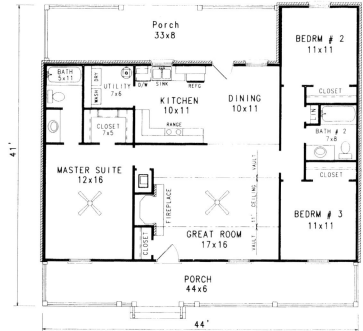

Copyright by designer/architect.

## Plan #101002

**Dimensions:** 46' W x 42' D
**Levels:** 1
**Square Footage:** 1,296
**Bedrooms:** 3
**Bathrooms:** 2
**Foundation:** Crawl space, slab, basement
**Materials List Available:** No
**Price Category:** B

This affordable compact home is also strikingly attractive.

**Features:**

- Ceiling Height: 8 ft.

- Foyer: Beveled glass front provides a luxurious entry.

- Family Room: This spacious 16-ft. x 20-ft. room has a vaulted ceiling.

- Laundry Room: Here is ample space to fold clothes—and a convenient sink.

- Master Bedroom Suite: Split from other bedrooms, this suite has many his and her features.

- Kitchen: This galley kitchen offers open traffic patterns with a breakfast bar.

- Breakfast Eating Area: A growing family will find additional seating space that leads to a covered porch providing a pleasant retreat

*Images provided by designer/architect.*

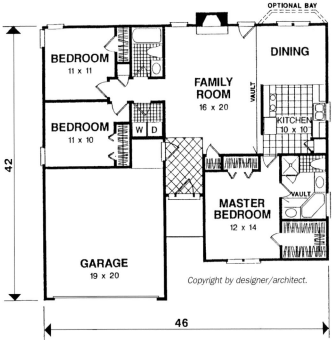

*Copyright by designer/architect.*

## SMARTtip

### Preparing Walls for Paint

Poor surface preparation is the number-one cause of paint failure. Preparing surfaces properly—including removing loose paint and thoroughly sanding—may be tedious, but it's important for a good-looking and long-lasting finish.

## Plan #321002

**Dimensions:** 72' W x 28' D
**Levels:** 1
**Square Footage:** 1,400
**Bedrooms:** 3
**Bathrooms:** 2
**Foundation:** Basement, crawl space
**Materials List Available:** Yes
**Price Category:** B

*Images provided by designer/architect.*

If you're looking for a well-designed compact home with contemporary amenities, this could be the home of your dreams.

**Features:**

• Porch: Just the right size for some rockers and a swing, this porch could become your outdoor living area when the weather is fine.

• Living Room: A vaulted ceiling adds to the spacious feeling in this room, where friends and family are sure to gather.

• Kitchen: This space-saving design, in combination with the ample counter and cabinet space, makes cooking a pleasure.

• Utility Room: This large room is fitted with cabinets for extra storage space. You'll find storage space in the large garage, too.

• Master Bedroom: This room is somewhat secluded for privacy, making it an ideal place for some quiet time at the end of the day.

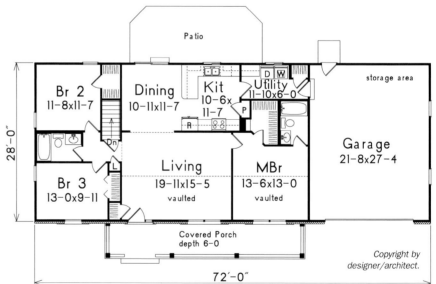

## SMARTtip

### Fabric Draping Ability

Test a fabric's draping ability by looking at a large piece in a fabric store. Gather at least two to three yards of material, holding one end in your hand. Check how it drapes. Does it fall into folds easily? Also look at the pattern when it is gathered. Does the design become lost in the folds? Ask a salesclerk or a friend to hold the fabric, and look at it from a few feet away.

## Plan #201006

**Dimensions:** 69'10" W x 25'10" D
**Levels:** 1
**Square Footage:** 1,172
**Bedrooms:** 3
**Bathrooms:** 2
**Foundation:** Crawl space, slab, or basement
**Materials List Available:** Yes
**Price Category:** B

*Images provided by designer/architect.*

The traditional style of this gracious home is complemented by its contemporary amenities.

**Features:**

- Great Room: A vaulted ceiling adds a majestic feeling to this large room. The fireplace makes a cozy focal point at any time of year, and the doorway to the rear covered porch balances the matching window area.

- Dining Room: Open to both the great room and the kitchen, this dining room is a natural hub of the home.

- Kitchen: This well-planned kitchen features ample counter and cabinet space and opens to the large laundry area with its extra storage space.

- Master Suite: A walk-in closet adds a practical touch to this large suite, and a private bath imparts luxury.

- Storage Room: Use the storage room in the carport for out-of-season gear.

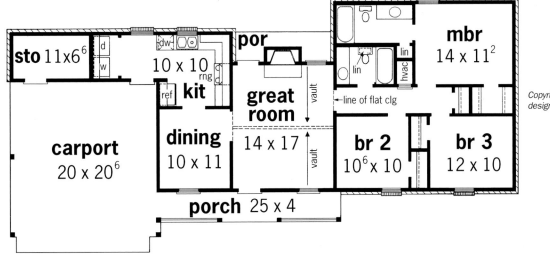

*Copyright by designer/architect.*

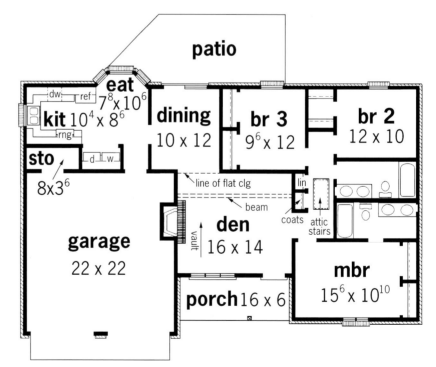

Images provided by designer/architect.

## Plan #201007

**Dimensions:** 56'10" W x 34'10" D
**Levels:** 1
**Square Footage:** 1,239
**Bedrooms:** 3
**Bathrooms:** 2
**Foundation:** Crawl space, slab, or basement
**Materials List Available:** Yes
**Price Category:** B

Traditional good looks, combined with a well-designed interior and a large rear patio, welcome your guests to this gracious family home.

### Features:

• **Den:** A beam across the vaulted ceiling adds interest to this spacious room, while the fire place gives it a cozy feeling at any time of year.

• **Dining Room:** Open to both the den and kitchen, this room also leads to the rear patio, where you're sure to entertain when the weather's fine.

• **Kitchen:** Designed for efficiency, this kitchen has great counter and storage space as well as a lovely bayed area ideal for casual meals and kitchen visitors. An alcove off the room is fitted with a washer and dryer.

• **Master Suite:** Two large closets and a private bath add special touches to this large area.

• **Additional Bedrooms:** Both bedrooms have large closets and easy access to a lovely bath.

Copyright by designer/architect.

# Plan #201027

**Dimensions:** 58'10" W x 46'10" D

**Levels:** 1

**Square Footage:** 1,494

**Bedrooms:** 3

**Bathrooms:** 2

**Foundation:** Crawl space, slab, or basement

**Materials List Available:** Yes

**Price Category:** B

*Images provided by designer/architect.*

The exterior styling is timelessly charming, but the interior features give contemporary comfort.

**Features:**

- Foyer: This formal foyer features a coat closet for everyone's convenience.

- Great Room: The hub of this home, the great room has a lovely vaulted ceiling, a handsome fireplace with built-in shelves on one side, and a door leading to the covered patio in the rear.

- Dining Room: This large room with spectacular windows is perfect for formal dinner parties.

- Dining Area: Adjoining the kitchen and opening from the dining room, this casual area is ideal for family meals at any time of day.

- Kitchen: This spacious U-shaped room has plenty of counter and cabinet space.

- Master Bedroom: Enjoy the walk-in closet and private bath you'll find in this cozy retreat.

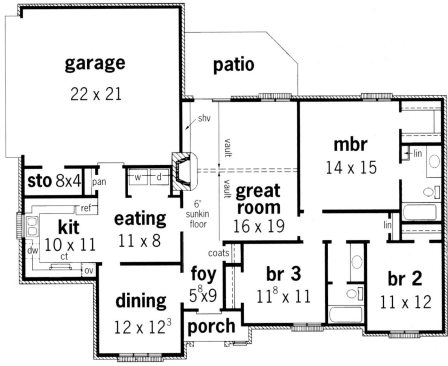

*Copyright by designer/architect.*

## Plan #201031

**Dimensions:** 60'10" W x 41'5" D

**Levels:** 1

**Square Footage:** 1,531

**Bedrooms:** 3

**Bathrooms:** 2

**Foundation:** Crawl space, slab, or basement

**Materials List Available:** Yes

**Price Category:** C

The stylish exterior of this home tells you how beautiful it is on the inside, but you may be surprised by its many contemporary amenities.

**Features:**

• Den: Just off the foyer, this room features a raised ceiling and a handsome fireplace flanked by built-in shelves for books or a media center.

• Dining Room: This gracious room has a vaulted ceiling and is naturally lit thanks to an expansive window area.

• Breakfast Nook: The bay window here gives a cheery feeling in the morning and a cozy one at night.

• Kitchen: Designed to delight any cook, this kitchen features ample counter space, cabinets galore, a pantry, and an angled snack bar.

• Master Bedroom: A raised ceiling in combination with a huge walk-in closet and private bath make this area a true retreat where you'll love to relax.

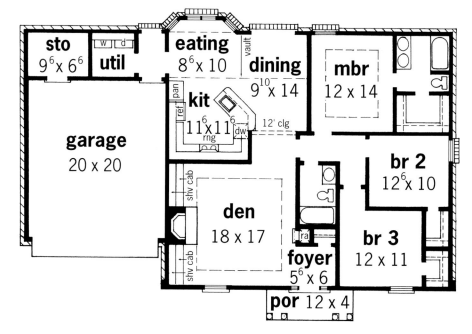

# Plan #201038

**Dimensions:** 71'10" W x 51'5" D
**Levels:** 1
**Square Footage:** 1,789
**Bedrooms:** 3
**Bathrooms:** 2
**Foundation:** Crawl space, slab, or basement
**Materials List Available:** Yes
**Price Category:** C

*Images provided by designer/architect.*

Elegant European styling announces the interior charm of this lovely family home.

**Features:**

- **Ceiling Height:** 9-ft. ceilings add to the spacious interior feeling.

- **Great Room:** Everyone will love this room, with its Palladian windows, 11-ft. ceiling, and cozy fireplace surrounded by built-in shelves.

- **Dining Room:** This formal room is ideal for serving both friends and family.

- **Kitchen:** For convenience, this well-designed U-shaped kitchen is positioned between the dining room and the breakfast nook.

- **Breakfast Nook:** Nestle a table in this bayed area to make an ideal dining spot at any time of day.

- **Master Suite:** Two walk-in closets and a double vanity in the bath spell luxury in this suite, which is spacious enough for a private sitting area, too.

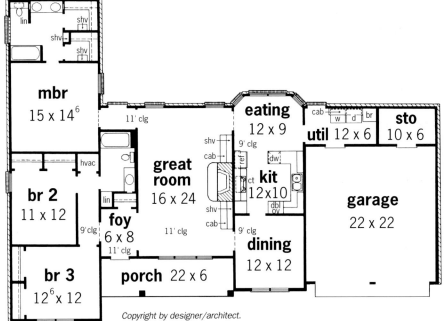

*Copyright by designer/architect.*

# Plan #201039

**Dimensions:** 46'10" W x 62'5" D

**Levels:** 1

**Square Footage:** 1,775

**Bedrooms:** 3

**Bathrooms:** 2

**Foundation:** Crawl space, slab, or basement

**Materials List Available:** Yes

**Price Category:** C

You'll love the elegant feeling in this spacious home that's ideal for an active family.

**Features:**

- Ceiling Height: 9-ft. ceilings emphasize the airy feeling inside this home.

- Living Room: The 11-ft. raised ceiling and fireplace flanked by doors leading to the rear covered porch give elegance to this room.

- Dining Room: Decorate this room for formal dinners, or serve everyday meals here.

- Breakfast Nook: Open to the kitchen, this area is ideal for entertaining or casual dining.

- Kitchen: This spacious room features ample counter and cabinet space and even has a pantry for extra storage space.

- Master Suite: A vaulted ceiling in the bath and a raised, 10-ft. ceiling in the bedroom create an understated elegance in this quiet suite.

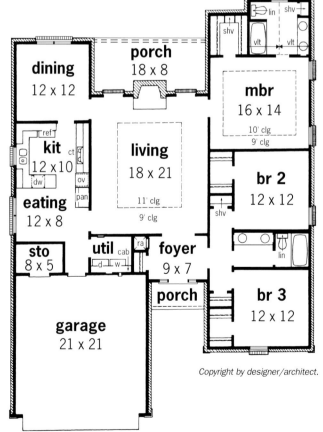

## Plan #131048

**Dimensions:** 67'6" W x 53'2" D
**Levels:** 1
**Square Footage:** 1,579
**Bedrooms:** 3
**Bathrooms:** 2
**Foundation:** Basement, crawl space, or slab
**Materials List Available:** Yes
**Price Category:** D

*Images provided by designer/architect.*

You'll love the country appearance of this expandable ranch, with its covered porch and shuttered windows.

**Features:**

- Foyer: This foyer flows into the great room but gives you a gracious space to welcome guests.
- Great Room: Enjoy the 9-ft. ceiling, fireplace, and tall windows in this room, which gives you a view of the front porch.
- Dining Room: Adjoining the great room, this dining room opens through French doors to the backyard terrace, making this area ideal

for hosting a party or grilling a family meal.

- Kitchen: The dinette in this kitchen area opens to the terrace, and an angled pass-through to the dining room makes entertaining a pleasure.
- Mudroom: With access to the garage and terrace, this mudroom also includes laundry facilities.

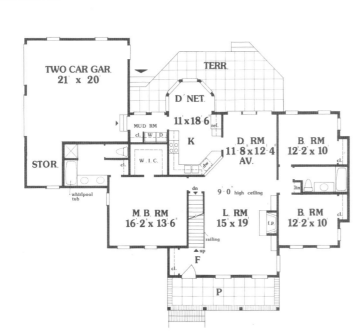

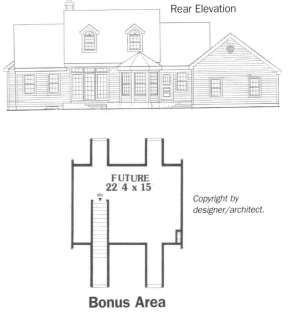

*Copyright by designer/architect.*

## Plan #281011

**Dimensions:** 50' W x 54' D
**Levels:** 1
**Square Footage:** 1,314
**Bedrooms:** 3
**Bathrooms:** 2
**Foundation:** Basement
**Materials List Available:** Yes
**Price Category:** B

*Images provided by designer/architect.*

This attractive ranch home takes advantage of views at both the front and rear.

**Features:**

- Ceiling Height: 8 ft.
- Porch: This large, inviting porch welcomes your guests and provides shade for the big living-room window on hot summer days.
- Living Room: This large main living area has plenty of room for entertaining and family activities.

- Dining Room: This room can accommodate large dinner parties. It's located near the living room and the kitchen for convenient entertaining.
- Deck: Family and friends will enjoy stepping out on this large covered sun deck that is accessible from the living room, dining room, and kitchen.
- Master Suite: You'll enjoy retiring at the end of the day to this luxurious master suite, which features its own walk-in closet and bathroom.

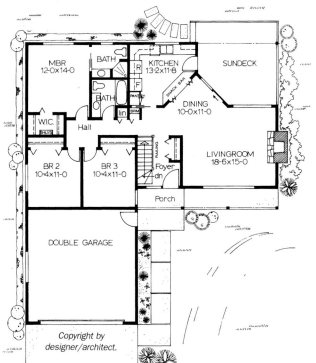

*Copyright by designer/architect.*

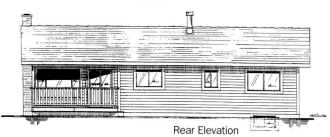

Rear Elevation

## SMARTtip

### Rag-Rolling Off

Paint Tip: Work with a partner. One person can roll on the glaze while the other lifts it off with the rag in a rhythmic pattern of even, steady strokes.

## Plan #201002

**Dimensions:** 54'10" W x 33'10" D

**Levels:** 1

**Square Footage:** 1,191

**Bedrooms:** 3

**Bathrooms:** 2

**Foundation:** Crawl space, slab, or basement

**Materials List Available:** No

**Price Category:** B

Varying rooflines will attract your eye, and an inviting, covered front porch will draw you to this lovely single-level home.

**Features:**

- **Great Room:** The foyer introduces you to this warm vaulted-ceiling great room, which features a handsome fireplace.

- **Kitchen:** This kitchen, large enough to be used as a second eating area, is designed for convenience and easy work flow, with ample counter space and immediate access to the dining room.

- **Master Bedroom:** This master bedroom features large closets and has easy access to the great room and its cozy fireplace.

- **Additional Bedrooms:** Two secondary bedrooms share a full bath.

- **Garage:** The garage features a convenient storage room.

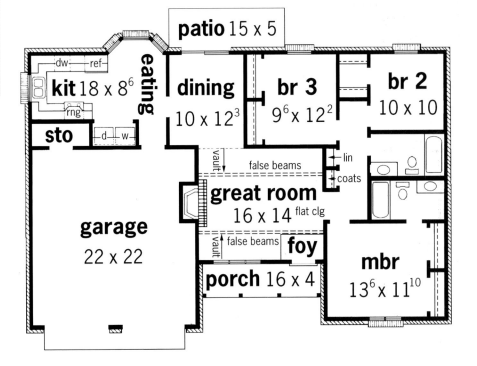

# Plan #151008

**Dimensions:** 42' W x 67'10" D
**Square Footage:** 1,892
**Bedrooms:** 3
**Bathrooms:** 2
**Foundation:** Crawl space, slab, basement, or daylight basement
**Materials List Available:** Yes
**Price Category:** D

*Images provided by designer/architect.*

This cozy home features a foyer with 8-in. columns and a wide-open welcoming great room and kitchen.

**Features:**

- Great Room/Kitchen: Enjoy the fireplace in the great room while seated at the kitchen island or in the breakfast room. Access to the rear patio and covered porch makes this room a natural spot for family as well as for entertaining.

- Dining Room: For a formal evening, entertain in this dining room, with its grand entrance through elegant 8-in. columns.

- Master Suite: Luxuriate in the privacy of this master suite, with its 10-ft. ceiling and private access to the covered porch. The master bath pampers you with a whirlpool tub, separate vanities, a shower, and a walk-in closet.

- Bedrooms: A bedroom with walk-in closet and private access to full bath is a cozy retreat, while the other bedroom makes room for one more!

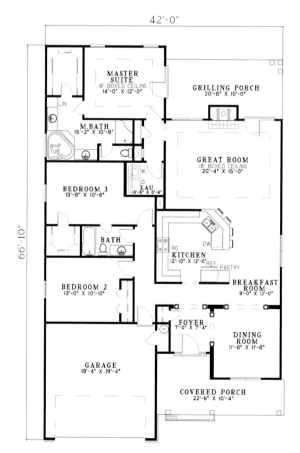

*Copyright by designer/architect.*

## Plan #151009

**Dimensions:** 44' W x 86'2" D
**Levels:** 1
**Square Footage:** 1,601
**Bedrooms:** 3
**Bathrooms:** 2
**Foundation:** Crawl, slab
**Materials List Available:** Yes
**Price Category:** C

This can be the perfect home for a site with views you can enjoy in all seasons and at all times.

**Features:**

- Porches: Enjoy the front porch with its 10-ft. ceiling and the more private back porch where you can set up a grill or just get away from it all.

- Foyer: With a 10-ft. ceiling, this foyer opens to the great room for a warm welcome.

- Great Room: Your family will love the media center and the easy access to the rear porch.

- Kitchen: This well-designed kitchen is open to the dining room and the breakfast nook, which also opens to the rear porch.

- Master Suite: The bedroom has a 10-ft. boxed ceiling and a door to the rear. The bath includes a corner whirlpool tub with glass block windows.

- Bedrooms: Bedroom 2 has a vaulted ceiling, while bedroom 3 features a built-in desk.

*Images provided by designer/architect.*

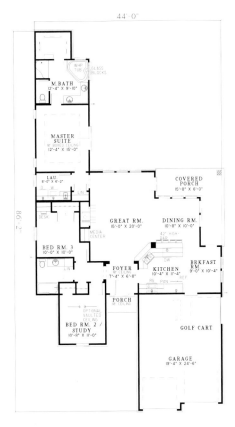

*Copyright by designer/architect.*

*Images provided by designer/architect.*

## Plan #201019

**Dimensions:** 65'2" W x 37'6" D
**Levels:** 1
**Square Footage:** 1,362
**Bedrooms:** 3
**Bathrooms:** 2
**Foundation:** Crawl space or slab
**Materials List Available:** No
**Price Category:** B

With country styling on the exterior and contemporary features inside, this cozy home is sure to please the most discriminating family.

**Features:**

- Foyer: Opening to the spacious den, this foyer features a coat closet for your convenience.

- Den: A vaulted ceiling, false beams, and handsome fireplace make this room the heart of the home.

- Dining Room: Use this room for formal parties or family dinners if you wish.

- Breakfast Nook: The bay window here makes this space a treat at any time of day.

- Kitchen: The U-shaped layout means efficiency in this room, and its position between the breakfast nook and the dining room make it convenient.

- Master Suite: Enjoy the large walk-in closet and private bath that make this suite a special place.

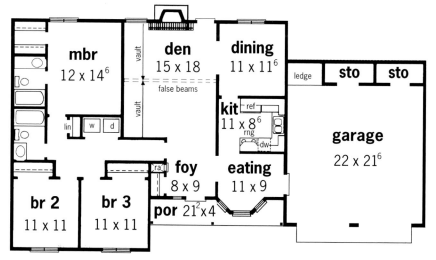

*Copyright by designer/architect.*

# Plan #321003

**Dimensions:** 67'4" W x 48' D
**Levels:** 1
**Square Footage:** 1,791
**Bedrooms:** 4
**Bathrooms:** 2
**Foundation:** Basement
**Materials List Available:** Yes
**Price Category:** C

The traditional good looks of the exterior of this home are complemented by the stunning contemporary design of the interior.

## Features:

- Great Room: With a vaulted ceiling to highlight its spacious dimensions, this room is certain to be the central gathering spot for friends and family.

- Dining Room: Also with a vaulted ceiling, this room has an octagonal shape for added interest. Windows here and in the great room look out to the covered patio.

- Kitchen: A center island gives a convenient work space in this well-designed kitchen, which features a pass-through to the dining room for easy serving, and large, walk-in pantry for storage.

- Breakfast Room: A bay window lets sunshine pour in to start your morning with a smile.

- Master Bedroom: A vaulted ceiling and a sitting area make you feel truly pampered in this room.

*Images provided by designer/architect.*

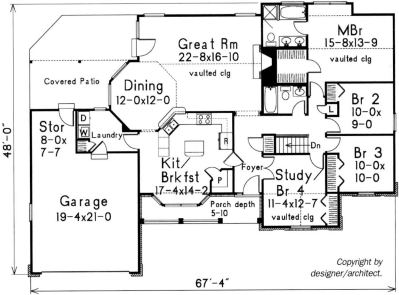

*Copyright by designer/architect.*

## SMARTtip

### Bay & Bow Windows

Occasionally too little room exists between the window frame (if there is one) and the ceiling. In this situation you might be able to use ceiling-mounted hardware. Alternatively, a cornice across the top and a rod mounted inside the cornice will give you the dual benefit of visually lowering the top of the window and concealing the hardware.

## Plan #151010

**Dimensions:** 38'4" W x 68'6" D
**Levels:** 1
**Square Footage:** 1,379
**Bedrooms:** 3
**Bathrooms:** 2
**Foundation:** Crawl, slab
**Materials List Available:** Yes
**Price Category:** B

This French Country home has a spacious great room for friends and family to gather, but you can sneak away to the covered rear porch or patio off the master suite for cozy tête-à-têtes.

**Features:**

• Entry: Take advantage of the marvelous 10-ft. ceilings to hang groups of potted flowering plants.

• Great Room: This spacious room, with an optional 10-ft. boxed ceiling, is the place to curl up by the gas fireplace on a cold winter night.

• Kitchen: The kitchen includes a bar for casual meals, and is open to the breakfast room.

• Rear Porch: Enjoy leisurely meals on the covered rear porch that you can access from both the master suite and the breakfast room.

• Master Suite: The 10-ft. boxed ceiling in the bedroom and the master bath with a whirlpool tub and separate shower make this suite a luxurious place to end a long day.

## Plan #271002

**Dimensions:** 45' W x 51' D
**Levels:** 1
**Square Footage:** 1,252
**Bedrooms:** 3
**Bathrooms:** 2
**Foundation:** Basement
**Materials List Available:** Yes
**Price Category:** B

*Images provided by designer/architect.*

This traditional home combines a modest square footage with stylish extras.

**Features:**

- Living Room: Spacious and inviting, this gathering spot is brightened by a Palladian window arrangement, warmed by a fireplace, and topped by a vaulted ceiling.

- Dining Room: The vaulted ceiling also crowns this room, which shares the living room's fireplace. Sliding doors lead to a backyard deck.

- Kitchen: Smart design ensures a place for everything.

- Master Suite: The master bedroom boasts a vaulted ceiling, cheery windows, and a private bath.

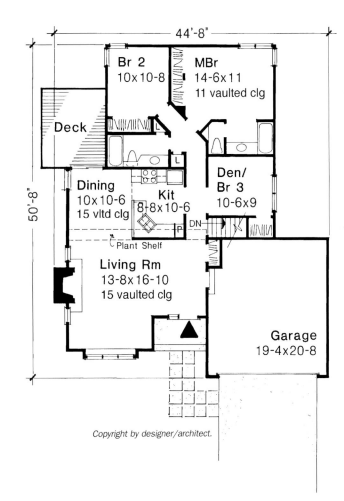

*Copyright by designer/architect.*

## Plan #211001

**Dimensions:** 52' W x 66' D
**Levels:** 1
**Square Footage:** 1,655
**Bedrooms:** 3
**Bathrooms:** 2
**Foundation:** Slab
**Materials List Available:** Yes
**Price Category:** C

You'll love this elegant one-story home, both practical and gorgeous, with its many amenities.

**Features:**

- Entry: A covered porch and three glass doors with transoms announce this home.
- Living Room: At the center of the house, this living room has a 15-ft. ceiling and a fireplace. A glass door flanked by windows opens to a skylighted porch at the rear of the home.
- Dining Room: This elegant octagonal room, which is shaped by columns and cased openings, overlooks both backyard porches.
- Kitchen: A 14-ft. sloped ceiling with a skylight adds drama.
- Master Suite: Enjoy the seclusion of this area at the rear of the home, as well as its private access to a rear porch. The bath features an oval spa tub, separate shower, dual vanities, and huge walk-in closet.

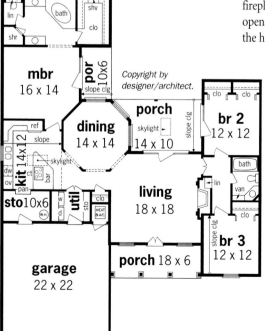

Copyright by designer/architect.

## SMARTtip

### Plotting a Potting Space

Whether you opt for a simple corner potting bench or a multipurpose shed or greenhouse, organization is key. You'll need a work surface — a counter or table that's a convenient height for standing while at work — plus storage accommodations for hand tools, long-handled tools, watering cans, extra lengths of hose, hose nozzles, flowerpots, bags of fertilizer and potting soil, gardening books, and notebooks. Plastic garbage cans (with lids) are good for soil and seeds. Most of these spaces are small, so use hooks and stacking bins, which keep items neat and at hand's reach. High shelves free up floor space while holding least-used things.

## Plan #321008

**Dimensions:** 57' W x 52'2" D
**Levels:** 1
**Square Footage:** 1,761
**Bedrooms:** 4
**Bathrooms:** 2
**Foundation:** Basement
**Materials List Available:** Yes
**Price Category:** C

One look at the roof dormers and planter boxes that grace the outside of this ranch, and you'll know that the interior is planned for comfortable family living.

**Features:**

- **Great Room:** A vaulted ceiling in this room points up its generous dimensions. Put a grouping of chairs near the fireplace to take advantage of the cozy spot it creates in chilly weather.

- **Kitchen:** Open to the great room, this kitchen has been planned for convenience. It features a pass-through to the dining area for easy serving when you've got a crowd to feed.

- **Master Bedroom:** A vaulted ceiling here makes you feel especially pampered, and the walk-in closet and amenity-filled bath add to that feeling.

- **Additional Bedrooms:** Great closet space characterizes all the rooms in this home, making it easy for children of any age to keep it organized and tidy.

*Images provided by designer/architect.*

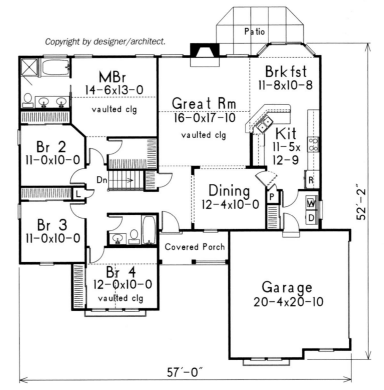

Copyright by designer/architect.

MBr
14-6x13-0
vaulted clg

Br 2
11-0x10-0

Dn

Br 3
11-0x10-0

Br 4
12-0x10-0
vaulted clg

Great Rm
16-0x17-10
vaulted clg

Brk fst
11-8x10-8

Kit
11-5x
12-9

Dining
12-4x10-0

Covered Porch

Garage
20-4x20-10

Patio

52'-2"

57'-0"

## SMARTtip

### Hanging Wallpaper

Use liner paper to smooth out a damaged wall and to provide uniform support for expensive paper.

# Accessorizing Your Landscape

Your new cottage home won't be complete until the lawns and plants in the landscape are established. That takes time, but one way to move the design along and to provide some design punch in the established garden is to include landscape accessories, such as trellises, arbors, distinctive planters, and landscape lighting.

## Trellises

Trellises were a key element in Renaissance gardens and continued in popularity through the eighteenth century. Trellises enjoyed a resurgence of popularity in the late-nineteenth century, but never to the extent of earlier times.

Trellises can lend an air of magic and mystery to a cottage garden. Generally we think of trellises in terms of the prefabricated sheets of diamond- or square-grid lattice and the fan-shaped supports for training climbers, both of which are readily available at home and garden centers in both wood and plastic. Lacking a pattern book, most gardeners are unaware of the incredible variety of designs, patterns, and optical illusions that can be created with trellises.

### Uses for Trellises

A trellis screen is a wonderfully airy way to achieve privacy or to partition off a space. The lath slats of lattice interrupt the view without totally obscuring it, creating the effect of a transparent curtain. Left bare, the pretty design of diamonds or squares makes an attractive effect. Covered in vines a trellis screen is enchanting.

**Cover a Wall with a Trellis.** The art of treillage, as the French call it, is not limited to screens. You can cover a bare wall or unattractive fence with a trellis pattern. Arrange the trellis pieces to create an optical illusion of an archway in the wall. Use a trellis for the walls of a gazebo to provide enclosure without being claustrophobic. Put a trellis screen with a pleasing, intricate

**A metal trellis** adorns a blank brick wall.

**This stand-alone trellis** provides interest even without plants.

**Installing a ready-made trellises** is a good way to jump-start your cottage landscape design.

## Arbors and Pergolas

Arbors and pergolas can play a vital role in elevating the design and use of space from the ordinary to something special. The differences between an arbor and a pergola are somewhat technical, and you'll find people using the terms interchangeably. An arbor is a sheltered spot in which to sit. A pergola is generally a tunnel-like walkway or seating area created with columns or posts that support an open "roof" of beams or trelliswork. An arch (whether or not it has a curved top) is a structure through which you can walk. Usually all three structures are covered with vines.

## Designing with Arbors and Pergolas

Because they stand tall, they add drama and importance to the scenery, especially if the rest of the garden features are predominantly horizontal. Take advantage of the upright supports to indulge in vertical gardening, growing climbing vines—preferably ones that flower profusely—up and over the structure. In addition, an arbor or pergola creates a shady, private retreat.

**Create Transitions.** Arches, arbors, and pergolas are stylish ways to mark the transition from one part of the cottage garden to another. Place an arch or arbor around the gate into the garden, or to mark the entrance from one garden room to another. Design the garden with reference to the arch or arbor so that it works like a picture window, framing a vista or a pretty vignette. Another idea is to nestle an arbor on the edge of the property to give the illusion that there is a passageway to another section. Place a bench beneath the arch for a protected, private place to sit. Design it so there is an appealing view from the arbor seat into the rest of the garden.

The English language is rich with synonyms for garden structures. Pergolas are also known as colonnades, galleries, piazzas, or porticos. Whatever you call them, these structures play a valuable role in the landscape design. In addition to being a walkway leading from one place to another, a pergola or gallery also can function as a garden wall, dividing two spaces. Instead of using a pergola as a walkway, you might place one across the far side of a patio so it serves as a partition, dividing the paved space from the planted area beyond. In addition to being a handsome architectural feature, the vine-covered structure will provide a shady retreat where people can comfortably sit, and if the central support posts are spaced properly, they can frame the view into the rest of the garden.

## Integrate Arbors into the Cottage Landscape

Proper siting of an arbor or pergola is essential to its success in the design. All too often people plunk down an arbor in the middle of a lawn or garden space with no reference to the rest of the environment. Instead of being a beautiful feature, such an oddly placed structure is a curious anomaly, looking uncomfortably out of place.

Arches, arbors, and pergolas must be

**An arbor or pergola** placed along a path anchors the path and creates a destination for someone walking in the garden. It allows you to engage in vertical gardening.

connected to the overall design. For example, a path should lead to an arch or arbor. Place an arbor on the edge of the property, and then enhance the illusion that it is leading to additional grounds by camouflaging the property boundary with shrubs. Be sure to have a path leading to the arbor to anchor its position and to encourage people to stroll over and enjoy it.

**Position Pergolas Over Paths.** The best location for a pergola is over an important path. Ideally a pergola should not lead to a dead end. Even a small garden can have room for a pergola. Instead of running it down the center of the property, set it along the property line. Plant shade-loving plants under its protected canopy, and place a bench underneath to create a shady retreat. A vine-covered pergola gives much-valued privacy from the upper stories of adjacent houses.

Although a pergola often covers a straight walkway, there is no rule that says a pergola cannot cover a curving path. In such a case, the curve prompts curiosity.

**The curving top** of an arbor is a good shape to copy for other structures, such as the fence above, in a cottage garden.

**A pergola and trellis** combine to provide shade and a certain level of privacy to the patio shown below.

**A pergola-like structure,** right, supported by a deck railing provides dappled shade for the benches below it.

Near the house it is wise to choose a design for your arbor or pergola that complements the design of the building. For a traditional-style house like a cottage you may want to support your arbor or pergola with classical columns made of concrete, fiberglass, or stone. Augment a brick house with brick support posts. Cast-iron or aluminum posts could echo other wrought-iron features, such as a balcony, railing, or gate. Farther from the house, you can have more leeway.

## Scale Pergolas to Garden Size.
In a small cottage garden, make a pergola less architecturally domineering by building the support posts and rafters out of thinner material such as metal or finer-cut lumber. In a large garden where you need the extra mass, opt for columns built of brick, stone, or substantial pieces of lumber.

**Place arbors and pergolas** so that they become a destination in the yard, left.

**An unusual shape** draws attention to this arbor and the property beyond, above.

## Plants for Arches, Arbors, and Pergolas

| BOTANICAL NAME | COMMON NAME | ZONE |
|---|---|---|
| *Aristolochia macrophylla* | Dutchman's pipe | 4–8 |
| *Bignonia capreolata* | cross vine | 6–9 |
| *Bougainvillea cultivars* | | 10 |
| *Campsis radians* | trumpet creeper | 4–9 |
| *Clematis species and cultivars* | | |
| | 'Comtesse de Bouchard' | 4–9 |
| | 'Duchess of Albany' | 4–9 |
| | 'Ernest Markham' | 4–9 |
| | 'Gypsy Queen' | 4–9 |
| | 'Gravetye Beauty' | 4–9 |
| | 'Hagley Hybrid' | 4–9 |
| | 'Henryi' | 4–9 |
| | 'Horn of Plenty', | 4–9 |
| | C. x jackmanii 'Superba' | 3–9 |
| | C. montana | 6–9 |
| | C. tangutica 'Bill MacKenzie' | 5–7 |
| | C. terniflora sweet autumn clematis | 5–9 |
| *Hydrangea petiolaris* | climbing hydrangea | 4–9, 4–10 in west |
| *Lonicera species* | honeysuckle | zones vary with species |
| *Parthenocissus tricuspidata* | Boston ivy | 4–9 |
| *Rosa cultivars* | climbing rose | |
| | 'Alberic Barbier' | 4–10 |
| | 'Albertine' | 4–10 |
| | 'Blaze' | 4–10 |
| | 'Chaplin's Pink Companion' | 4–10 |
| | 'Felicite Perpetue' | 4–10 |
| | R. filipes 'Kiftsgate' | 5–10 |
| | 'Mme. Gregoire Staechelin' | 4–10 |
| | 'New Dawn' | 4–10 |
| | 'Veilchenblau' | 4–10 |
| *Schizophragma hydrangeoides* | Japanese hydrangea vine | 5–9 |
| *Trachelospermum jasminoïdes* | star jasmine | 8–10 |
| *Vitis coignetiae* | crimson glory vine | 6–9 |
| *Vitis vinifera 'Purpurea'* | purpleleaf grape | 6–9 |
| *Wisteria species* | wisteria | 5–10 |

Pergolas should always be somewhat higher than they are wide. A minimum width of about 5 feet allows two people to walk through the pergola abreast. The structure should be high enough to allow a tall adult to walk underneath comfortably. The upright support posts also need to be in proportion to the roof. If the supports are hefty, the overhead beams also should be substantial. How far apart you space the roof beams depends on the final effect you want. Wide spacing creates a skylight. Close spacing of the beams makes the pergola more tunnel-like.

Bear in mind that an arbor or pergola covered in vines must bear a lot of weight. The upright posts should be strong and properly rooted in a solid foundation, and the roof structure should be well built.

You can build your own or purchase ready-made units from a home center or garden-supply outlet. In most cases, large trellises, arbors, and pergolas come unassembled. Check with the local building department (or your house builder may know) for code requirements for foundations and construction.

## Tips for Containers and Hanging Baskets

- To keep down the weight of containers filled with soil, fill the lower half of large pots with foam peanuts, perlite, or any other lightweight material that will not compact over time. Put potting mix in the remaining space, and plant as usual.

- To keep up with the heavy feeding most container-grown plants need, add compost to the planting mix or add liquid seaweed or a fish emulsion/liquid seaweed combination to the water every few weeks to ensure a well-balanced supply of all essential micronutrients.

- To remoisten peat moss if it becomes dry, fill a tub with water and add a drop of liquid detergent to help the water stick to the peat moss. Set the basket in the water, and leave it for several hours until the potting soil and peat moss mix is saturated with water.

- Pinch off dead blossoms regularly to keep container plants bushy and full of flowers.

- Cluster your pots together in a sheltered spot if you will be away for several days. The plants will need watering less frequently, and it will be easier to water if the containers are all in one place.

- To automatically water containers, bury one end of a long wick (such as those sold with oil-fueled lanterns) near the plant's roots. Insert the other end in a bucket of water. The wick will gradually soak up the water and provide a slow, continuous source of water for the plant.

- If a plant is root-bound, prune the roots by cutting back the outer edges of the root ball instead of transplanting it to a larger container. Then repot it in the same container with fresh soil.

- Consider watering many containers with an automatic drip irrigation system; install a line to each container.

- To reduce moisture loss, top the soil in your containers with mulch.

## Containers for Plants

People have been gardening in containers at least since King Nebuchadnezzar built the Hanging Gardens of Babylon in 600 BC. While most people do not attempt container gardening on the massive scale achieved by Nebuchadnezzar, containers still play an important role in enhancing a garden. There are many advantages to container gardening.

### Container Gardens are Versatile.

Container gardens can be moved when they are past their prime. You can grow tropical plants in containers by keeping them outside in the summer and moving them indoors to overwinter where winters are harsh. If your soil is alkaline, you can grow acid-loving plants in pots. Containers add color and excitement to patios. Cluster a group of containers to create a pleasing composition of shapes, sizes, and colors.

Attach baskets of cascading plants to pergolas, arbors, and eaves to bring color up high.

### Designing with Containers

Choose your containers with the same care as you would a sculpture or any other garden ornament. In addition to finding pots that complement your garden style, think about which plants to put in them.

**Match Plants to Containers.** Showy plants such as palms, Dracaena, and shrubs pruned as standards look best in traditionally designed planters such as classic urns or white planter boxes. Rustic barrels or half barrels are inexpensive and unpretentious containers in an informal setting.

**Try Unusual Containers.** Fill an old wheelbarrow with potted plants, or give new life to a leaky metal watering can by turning it into a planter. Or plant an old shoe with shallow-rooted succuclents.

Use your imagination and have fun. Whatever container you use, however, make sure it has drainage holes in the bottom. Unless you're growing bog plants, they'll be short-lived if their roots are sitting permanently in water.

## Plan #181152

**Dimensions:** 43' W x 34' D
**Levels:** 1
**Square Footage:** 1,339
**Bedrooms:** 3
**Bathrooms:** 1
**Foundation:** Basement
**Materials List Available:** Yes
**Price Category:** B

*Images provided by designer/architect.*

This gracious cottage has ample space for a busy family life or entertaining friends and family.

**Features:**

- Ceiling Height: 9-ft. ceilings enhance the airy feeling that the many windows create in this well-planned home.

- Foyer: This foyer adds an elegant touch.

- Family Room: Open to the central hall and adjacent dining area, this family room features a 10-ft. ceiling and is large enough to host a crowd.

- Dining Area: Open to the kitchen, this room also features a door leading to the backyard where you're sure to entertain.

- Master Bedroom: A walk-in closet gives a practical touch to this large room, which has space for a sitting area.

- Bathroom: Enjoy the luxury of a corner shower, double vanity, and corner shower.

*Copyright by designer/architect.*

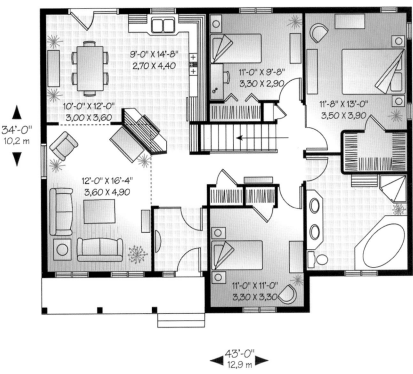

# Plan #341004

**Dimensions:** 56'10" W x 28'6" D

**Levels:** 1

**Square Footage:** 1,101

**Bedrooms:** 3

**Bathrooms:** 2

**Foundation:** Crawl space, slab, or basement

**Materials List Available:** Yes

**Price Category:** B

*Images provided by designer/architect.*

You'll love the romantic feeling that the gables and front porch give to this well designed home, with its family-oriented layout.

**Features:**

• Living Room: The open design between this spacious room and the kitchen/dining area makes this home as ideal for family activities as it is for entertaining.

• Outdoor Living Space: French doors open to the back deck, where you're sure to host alfresco dinners or easy summer brunches.

• Kitchen: Designed for the cook's convenience, this kitchen features ample work area as well as excellent storage space in the nearby pantry.

• Laundry Area: Located behind closed doors to shut out the noise, this laundry closet is conveniently placed.

• Master Suite: With triple windows, a wide closet, and a private bath, this is a luxurious suite.

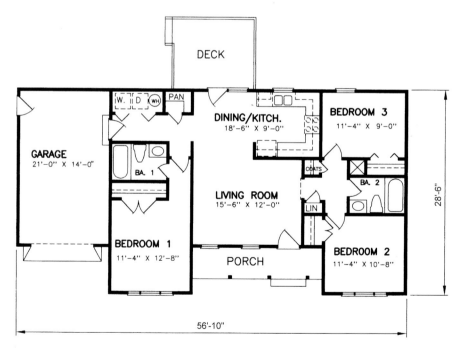

*Copyright by designer/architect.*

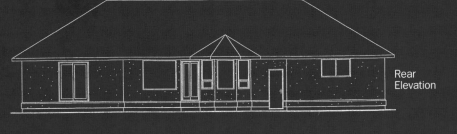

Rear Elevation

*Images provided by designer/architect.*

## Plan #281008

**Dimensions:** 74' W x 45' D
**Levels:** 1
**Square Footage:** 1,731
**Bedrooms:** 3
**Bathrooms:** 2½
**Foundation:** Basement, crawl space
**Materials List Available:** Yes
**Price Category:** C

Here is a cheery ranch home characterized by lots of windows and an open, airy plan.

**Features:**

• Ceiling Height: 8 ft.

• Foyer: This home was originally designed to sit on the edge of a golf course with panoramic vistas in every direction, hence the open design. As you step into the spacious foyer, your eye travels across the great room out the view at the rear.

• Great Room: This room seems even larger than it is, thanks to the open plan and the great views that seem to bring the outdoors in.

• Kitchen: This open, airy kitchen is a pleasure in which to work. It features an unusual octagonal breakfast nook that's the perfect place to enjoy informal meals with the family or pause with a morning cup of coffee.

• Laundry: This laundry facility is located on the main floor, so you won't have to carry clothing up and down stairs to the basement.

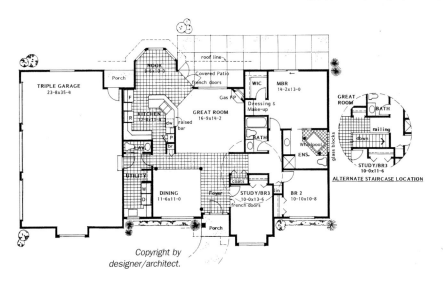

*Copyright by designer/architect.*

## SMARTtip

### The Provençal Style in Your Kitchen

No French country kitchen would be complete without a massive harvest table. If you can't find an affordable antique, create your own. Buy a long, unfinished pine table, and stain it a rich walnut color. Because pine is a softwood, you won't have to add "authentic" distress marks because normal wear and tear will do that for you. Pair the table with an assortment of unmatched chairs to add casual ambiance.

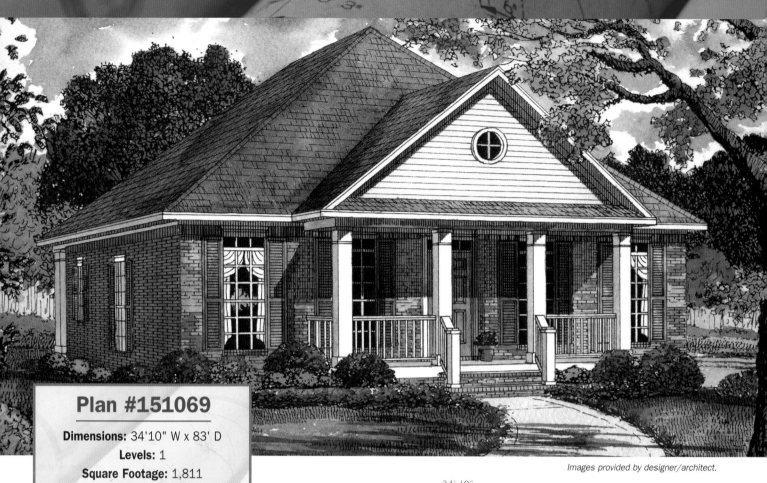

# Plan #151069

**Dimensions:** 34'10" W x 83' D
**Levels:** 1
**Square Footage:** 1,811
**Bedrooms:** 3
**Bathrooms:** 2
**Foundation:** Crawl space or slab
**Materials List Available:** Yes
**Price Category:** D

*Images provided by designer/architect.*

The open design of this home gives it an airy, spacious feeling, and its many amenities will delight everyone in the family.

**Features:**

- **Great Room:** A 10-ft. boxed ceiling here and in the adjoining dining room sets an elegant tone. The fireplace makes an excellent focal point, no matter what the season.

- **Dining Room:** In addition to having its own boxed ceiling, this dining room is defined by boxed columns.

- **Kitchen:** Also part of the open design, this large kitchen is designed for easy work patterns. You'll love the pantry closet, ample counter space, and snack bar that can double as a serving bar.

- **Master Suite:** A 10-ft. boxed ceiling in the bedroom complements the large dimensions of the room. A huge walk-in closet and bath with two separate vanities and both whirlpool and standard tubs give it a luxurious feeling.

*Copyright by designer/architect.*

# Plan #251001

**Dimensions:** 61'3" W x 40'6" D
**Levels:** 1
**Square Footage:** 1,253
**Bedrooms:** 3
**Bathrooms:** 2
**Foundation:** Crawl space, basement
**Materials List Available:** Yes
**Price Category:** B

*Images provided by designer/architect.*

• **Master Bedroom:** This master bedroom features a large walk-in closet. It has its own master bath with a single vanity, a tub, and a walk-in shower.

• **Garage:** This attached garage provides plenty of extra storage space, as well as parking for two cars.

This charming country home has a classic full front porch for enjoying summertime breezes.

**Features:**

• Ceiling Height: 8 ft.

• Foyer: Guests will walk through the front porch into this foyer, which opens to the family room.

• Screened Porch: A second porch is screened and is located at the rear of the home off the dining room, so your guests can step t for a bit of fresh air after dinner.

• Family Room: Family and friends will drawn to this large open space, with i handsome fireplace and sloped ceiling

• Kitchen: This open and airy kitchen is pleasure in which to work. It has amp counter space and a pantry.

Copyright by designer/architect.

Rear Porch 16 x 5/9

Master 14 x 12 · 8' Clg.

Dining 10/9 x 11 · 8' clg.

Kitchen 9 x 11

Pant.

Pass Thru

Garage 20 x 22

Bedroom #3 10/4 x 10/7 · 8' Clg.

W D

Stor.

Family Room 14 x 16/8 · 11'-4" Clg.

Bedroom #2 10 x 10/8 · 8' Clg.

Sloped Ceiling

Foyer

Porch 34/8 x 6

*Images provided by designer/architect.*

## Plan #251002

**Dimensions:** 55'6" W x 64'3" D
**Levels:** 1
**Square Footage:** 1,333
**Bedrooms:** 3
**Bathrooms:** 2
**Foundation:** Crawl space, slab
**Materials List Available:** Yes
**Price Category:** B

Although compact, this farmhouse has all the amenities for comfortable modern living.

**Features:**

- Ceiling Height: 8 ft. unless otherwise noted.

- Foyer: This gracious and welcoming foyer opens to the family room.

- Family Room: This inviting family room is designed to accommodate all kinds of family activities. It features a 9-ft. ceiling and a handsome, warming fireplace.

- Kitchen: Cooking in this kitchen is a real pleasure. It includes a center island, so you'll never run out of counter space for food preparation.

- Master Bedroom: This master bedroom features a large walk-in closet and an elegant 9-ft. recessed ceiling.

- Master Bath: This master bath offers a double vanity, a tub, and a walk-in shower.

- Garage: This attached garage provides plenty of extra storage space, as well as parking for two cars.

SMARTtip

## Arts and Crafts Style

The heart of this style rests in its earthy connection. The more you can bring nature into it, the more authentic it will be. An easy way to do this is with plants. A bonus is that plants naturally thrive in the bathroom, where they enjoy the humid environment.

*Copyright by designer/architect.*

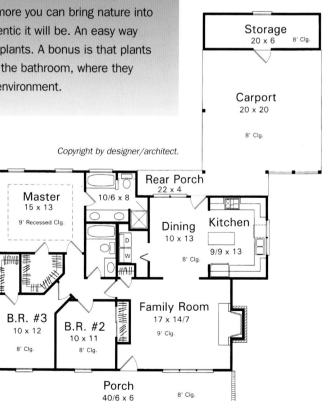

# Plan #251004

**Dimensions:** 50'9" W x 42'1" D
**Levels:** 1
**Square Footage:** 1,500
**Bedrooms:** 3
**Bathrooms:** 2
**Foundation:** Crawl space, slab
**Materials List Available:** Yes
**Price Category:** C

Combine the old-fashioned appeal of a country farmhouse with all the comforts of modern living.

*Images provided by designer/architect.*

**Features:**

• Ceiling Height: 9 ft.

• Foyer: When guests enter this inviting foyer, they will be greeted by a view of the lovely family room.

• Family Room: Usher family and friends into this welcoming family room, where they can warm up in front of the fireplace. The room's 12-ft. ceiling enhances its sense of spaciousness.

• Kitchen: Gather around and keep the cook company at the snack bar in this roomy kitchen. There's still plenty of counter space for food preparation, thanks to the kitchen island.

• Master Bedroom: This elegant master bedroom features a large walk-in closet and a 9-ft. recessed ceiling.

• Master Bath. This master bath includes a double vanity, a tub, and a walk-in shower.

• Garage: This attached garage provides plenty of extra storage space, as well as parking for two cars.

*Copyright by designer/architect.*

## SMARTtip

### Shaker Style in Your Bathroom

This warm, likable style fits in perfectly with a country home because of its old-fashioned values. But it blends in well with contemporary interiors, too, because of its clean lines and plain geometric shapes. In fact, adding a few Shaker elements can warm up the sometimes cold look of a thoroughly modern room.

## Plan #221002

**Dimensions:** 52' W x 46' D

**Levels:** 1

**Square Footage:** 1,508

**Bedrooms:** 3

**Bathrooms:** 2

**Foundation:** Basement

**Materials List Available:** No

**Price Category:** C

*Images provided by designer/architect.*

The classic brick-and-siding exterior of this ranch allows you to choose landscaping plants of any size, shape, or color.

**Features:**

• Ceiling Height: 8 ft.

• Entry: A vaulted ceiling announces the distinction of this design.

• Living Room: Also with a vaulted ceiling for a feeling of spaciousness, this living room features well-positioned windows that look out to the backyard.

• Dining Room: Sliding glass doors in this room open to the outside.

• Kitchen: This thoughtfully designed kitchen will please even the most discerning cook. For serving ease, the bright and cheery room is open to the dining room.

• Master Bedroom: You can look out to the backyard from the windows in this private retreat or relax in the charming, fully equipped bath.

Rear Elevation

*Copyright by designer/architect.*

## Plan #221003

**Dimensions:** 69' W x 51'4" D

**Levels:** 1

**Square Footage:** 1,802

**Bedrooms:** 3

**Bathrooms:** 2

**Foundation:** Basement

**Materials List Available:** No

**Price Category:** D

*Images provided by designer/architect.*

If you'd love to enjoy the evening breeze from a rocker on your own front porch, this stylish ranch design could be the home of your dreams.

### Features:

- Ceiling Height: 8 ft.

- Great Room: A cathedral ceiling in this room gives it grandeur as well as a spacious feeling. Large windows that look out to the backyard flank the classic fireplace here.

- Kitchen: This step-saving layout will delight the cooks in the family. Everyone will gather in the dining nook here, and when there's a party, you'll appreciate the open design between the kitchen/nook area and the great room.

- Master Suite: You'll love the storage space in the bedroom's walk-in closet and revel in the luxury of the fully equipped private bath.

- Garage: You can park two cars in this garage and still have room to store a mower, tools and equipment, and even off-season clothing.

Rear Elevation

*Copyright by designer/architect.*

## Plan #221004

**Dimensions:** 67'8" W x 43' D

**Levels:** 1

**Square Footage:** 1,763

**Bedrooms:** 3

**Bathrooms:** 2

**Foundation:** Basement

**Materials List Available:** No

**Price Category:** C

*Images provided by designer/architect.*

You'll love the spacious feeling provided by the open design of this traditional ranch.

**Features:**

- Ceiling Height: 8 ft.

- Dining Room: This formal room is perfect for entertaining groups both large and small, and the open design makes it easy to serve.

- Living Room: The vaulted ceiling here and in the dining room adds to the elegance of these rooms. Use window treatments that emphasize these ceilings for a truly sumptuous look.

- Kitchen: Designed for practicality and efficiency, this kitchen will thrill all the cooks in the family. An attached dining nook makes a natural gathering place for friends and family.

- Master Suite: The private bath in this suite features a double vanity and whirlpool tub. You'll find a walk-in closet in the bedroom.

- Garage: You'll love the extra storage space in this two-car garage.

Rear Elevation

*Copyright by designer/architect.*

## Plan #201005

**Dimensions:** 61'10" W x 30'5" D

**Levels:** 1

**Square Footage:** 1,128

**Bedrooms:** 3

**Bathrooms:** 2

**Foundation:** Crawl space, slab, or basement

**Materials List Available:** Yes

**Price Category:** B

*Images provided by designer/architect.*

The appearance, layout, and features of this charming home make it ideal for a busy family with an active social life.

**Features:**

- Den: Use this large room for family times or entertaining. Everyone will admire the vaulted ceiling and cozy up to the fireplace when the weather's chilly.

- Dining Room: Open to both the den and the kitchen, this room is flooded with natural light during the daytime.

- Kitchen: The step-saving design and large convenient counter area in this kitchen promote efficient work patterns.

- Master Suite: Two large closets and a private bath make this area a practical space and a wonderful retreat at the end of the day.

- Utility Area: Roomy enough for extra storage, this room makes it easy for anyone to do the laundry.

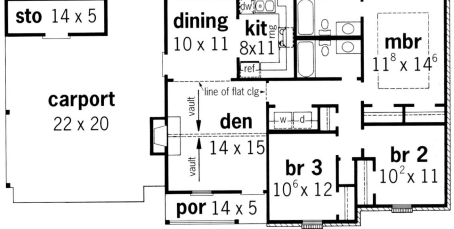

*Copyright by designer/architect.*

## Plan #151058

**Dimensions:** 58'8" W x 58'6" D
**Levels:** 1
**Square Footage:** 1,854
**Bedrooms:** 4
**Bathrooms:** 2
**Foundation:** Crawl space or slab; basement with fee
**Materials List Available:** Yes
**Price Category:** D

If you love traditional styling but crave modern amenities, this could be your dream home.

**Features:**

- **Great Room:** A 10-ft. ceiling and the fireplace flanked by French doors opening to the rear covered porch set a gracious tone.

- **Dining Room:** Columns delineate this room, which is as perfect for parties as it is for family dinners.

- **Breakfast Room:** Ideal for casual meals, this room is open to the kitchen.

- **Kitchen:** With a step-saving layout and angled snack bar that it shares with the breakfast room, this practical kitchen is a treat for the eyes.

- **Master Suite:** This spacious suite includes a bath with two large walk-in closets, a whirlpool tub, separate shower, and double-sink vanity.

- **Additional Bedrooms:** Each of these rooms has a walk-in closet and easy access to a shared bath.

*Images provided by designer/architect.*

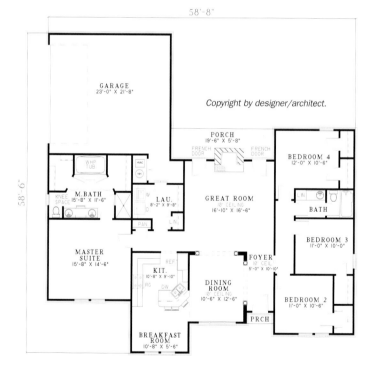

*Copyright by designer/architect.*

## Plan #201003

**Dimensions:** 55'10" W x 45'4" D
**Levels:** 1
**Square Footage:** 1,144
**Bedrooms:** 2
**Bathrooms:** 1
**Foundation:** Crawl space, slab, or basement
**Materials List Available:** Yes
**Price Category:** B

The fieldstone fireplace and false dormers on the roof emphasize the charm of this lovely rustic-looking home.

**Features:**

- **Great Room:** A vaulted ceiling adds elegance to this large room, where windows flanking the fireplace add a gracious feeling.

- **Dining Room:** Just off the foyer, this room looks out onto the spacious front porch and opens to the kitchen.

- **Kitchen:** This well-designed space features ample counter and cabinet space as well as a dining area and a door into the garage.

- **Patio:** You'll use this covered area at the rear of the house for entertaining or just relaxing at the end of the day.

- **Master Bedroom:** The two large closets and doorway to the bathroom are sure to pamper you in this spacious room.

*Images provided by designer/architect.*

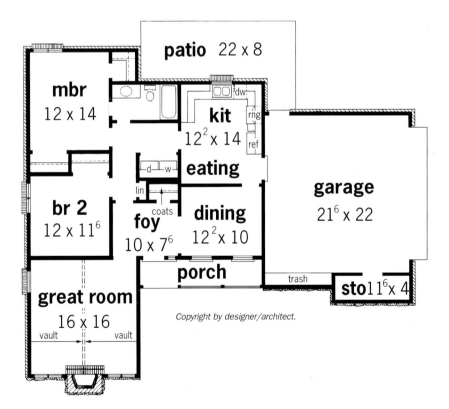

*Copyright by designer/architect.*

## Plan #151071

**Dimensions:** 27' W x 75'10" D
**Levels:** 1
**Square Footage:** 1,370
**Bedrooms:** 3
**Bathrooms:** 2
**Foundation:** Crawl space or slab
**Materials List Available:** Yes
**Price Category:** B

You'll love the elegant touches and spacious feeling of this comfortable family home, which has been designed to suit a narrow lot.

**Features:**

- Ceiling Height: 9-ft. ceilings add to the airy feeling of the home.

- Great Room: A 10-ft. boxed ceiling and cozy fireplace make this room a natural gathering place for both friends and family.

- Dining Room: Located in the rear of the home, this spacious room features a bank of windows for natural lighting and a door to the attached garage for convenience in any weather.

- Kitchen: This large room is laid out in a step-saving U-shape. In addition to the many cabinets and good counter space, you'll appreciate the washer and dryer hidden behind cabinet doors.

- Master Suite: A 10-ft. boxed ceiling, enormous closet, and amenity-filled bath make this area a treat.

Copyright by designer/architect.

## Plan #151053

**Dimensions:** 44' W x 71'2" D

**Levels:** 1

**Square Footage:** 1,449

**Bedrooms:** 3

**Bathrooms:** 2

**Foundation:** Crawl space or slab

**Materials List Available:** Yes

**Price Category:** B

This well-designed home is compact but feels airy and spacious, thanks to the open design and generously sized rooms.

**Features:**

- Great Room: A 10-ft. boxed ceiling sets the tone for this large room with cozy fireplace.

- Office/Bedroom: Separated by columns from the great room, this room could make a lovely dining room as well as an office or a third bedroom.

- Kitchen: Designed with ample counter and cabinet space, this kitchen also features a washer and dryer closet and a snack bar that's open to the breakfast room beyond.

- Breakfast Room: A large window area floods this room with natural light, giving it a cheery feeling. It opens to the grilling porch beyond.

- Master Suite: This suite features a 10-ft.-high boxed ceiling, door to the grilling porch, walk-in closet, and bath with whirlpool tub.

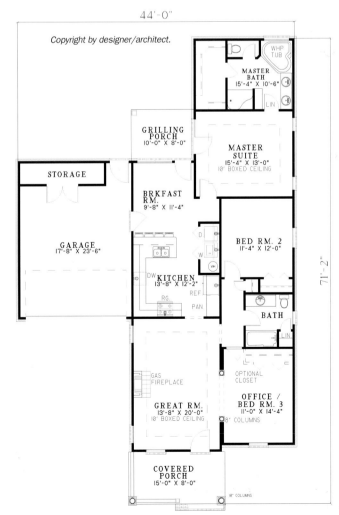

## Plan #151037

**Dimensions:** 50' W x 56' D

**Levels:** 1

**Square Footage:** 1,538

**Bedrooms:** 3

**Bathrooms:** 2

**Foundation:** Crawl space, slab, or basement

**Materials List Available:** Yes

**Price Category:** C

You'll love this traditional-looking home, with its covered porch and interesting front windows.

**Features:**

- Ceiling Height: 8 ft.

- Great Room: This large room has a boxed window that emphasizes its dimensions and a fireplace where everyone will gather on chilly evenings. A door opens to the backyard.

- Dining Room: A bay window overlooking the front porch makes this room easy to decorate.

- Kitchen: This well-planned kitchen features ample counter space, a full pantry, and an eating bar that it shares with the dining room.

- Master Suite: A pan ceiling in this lovely room gives an elegant touch. The huge private bath includes two walk-in closets, a whirlpool tub, a dual-sink vanity, and a skylight in the ceiling.

- Additional Bedrooms: On the opposite side of the house, these bedrooms share a large bath, and both feature excellent closet space.

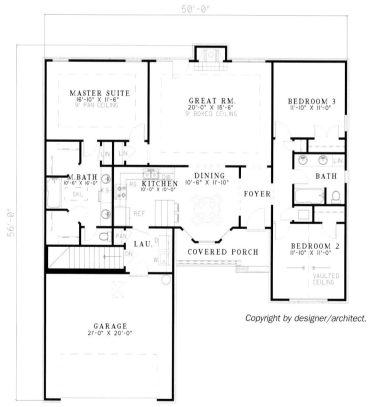

*Copyright by designer/architect.*

## Plan #181015

**Dimensions:** 58' W x 28'4" D
**Levels:** 1
**Square Footage:** 1,776
**Bedrooms:** 3
**Bathrooms:** 1
**Foundation:** Basement
**Materials List Available:** Yes
**Price Category:** B

*Images provided by designer/architect.*

A pillared front porch and beautifully arched windows enhance the stucco exterior.

**Features:**

- Ceiling Height: 8 ft.

- Kitchen: Cooking will be a pleasure in this bright and spacious kitchen. There is ample counter space for food preparation, in addition to a center island. The kitchen is flooded with light from sliding glass doors that provide access to the outdoors.

- Family Room: Nothing warms you on a cold winter day quite like the radiant heat from the cozy wood-burning fireplace/stove you will find in this family gathering room.

- Front Porch: Step directly out of the living room onto this spacious front porch. Relax in a porch rocker, and enjoy a summer breeze with your favorite book or just rock and watch the sun set.

- Bedrooms: Three family bedrooms share a full bathroom complete with dual vanities and laundry facilities.

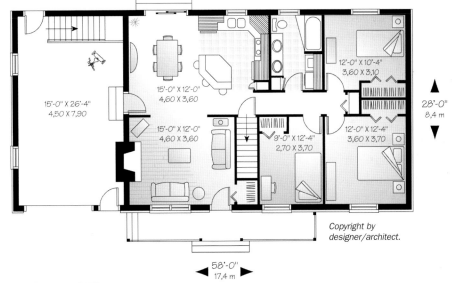

*Copyright by designer/architect.*

## SMARTtip

### Electrical Safety in the Kitchen

Sometimes the special needs of the disabled may seem to conflict with those of the very young. A case in point is accessible switch placement, which is lower on a wall. The NKBA recommends locating outlets and switches inside the front of an adult-accessible tilt-down drawer to conceal them from children. Alternatively, an outlet strip can be kept out of a child's reach and at a convenient adult location while lessening the reach to outlets and switches installed in the backsplash.

## Plan #221020

**Dimensions:** 69'8" W x 43' D

**Levels:** 1

**Square Footage:** 1,859

**Bedrooms:** 3

**Bathrooms:** 2½

**Foundation:** Basement

**Materials List Available:** No

**Price Category:** D

*Images provided by designer/architect.*

You'll love this design if you're looking for a compact home with amenities usually found in much larger designs.

**Features:**

- Ceiling Height: 8 ft.

- Living Room: A vaulted ceiling gives an elegant feeling, and a bank of windows lets natural light pour in during the daytime.

- Dining Room: Located just off the entry for the convenience of your guests, this room is ideal for intimate family meals or formal dinner parties.

- Kitchen: Just across from the dining room, this kitchen is distinguished by its ample counter space. The adjacent nook is large enough to use as a casual dining area, and it features access to the backyard.

- Master Suite: The large bay window lends interest to this room, and you'll love the walk-in closet and private bath, with its whirlpool tub, standing shower, and dual-sink vanity.

Rear Elevation

*Copyright by designer/architect.*

Images provided by designer/architect.

## Plan #121013

**Dimensions:** 40' W x 55'8" D
**Levels:** 1
**Square Footage:** 1,375
**Bedrooms:** 1
**Bathrooms:** 2
**Foundation:** Basement
**Materials List Available:** Yes
**Price Category:** B

This convenient open plan is well-suited to retirement or as a starter home.

**Features:**

- Ceiling Height: 8 ft., unless otherwise noted.

- Den: To the left of the entry, French doors lead to a den that can convert to a second bedroom.

- Kitchen: A center island doubles as a snack bar while the breakfast area includes a pantry and a desk for compiling shopping lists and menus.

- Open Plan: The sense of spaciousness is enhanced by the large open area that includes the family room, kitchen, and breakfast area.

- Family Room: A handsome fireplace invites family and friends to gather in this area.

- Porch: Step through the breakfast area to enjoy the fresh air on this secluded porch.

- Master Bedroom: This distinctive bedroom features a boxed ceiling. It's served by a private bath with a walk-in closet.

### SMARTtip
## Paint Color Choices for Your Home

Earth tones are easy to decorate with because they are neutral colors. Use neutral or muted tones, such as light grays, browns, or greens with either lighter or darker shades for accenting.

Use bright colors sparingly, to catch the eye. Painting the front door a bright color creates a cheerful entryway.

Investigate home shows, magazines, and houses in your area for color ideas. Paint suppliers can also give you valuable tips on appropriate color schemes.

Colors that look just right on a color card may need to be toned down for painting large areas. If in doubt, buy a quart of paint and test it.

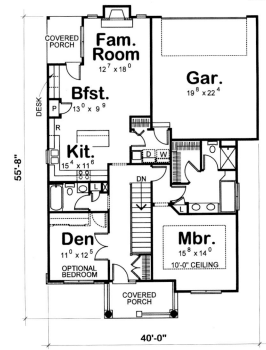

Copyright by designer/architect.

## Plan #121012

**Dimensions:** 40' W x 48'8" D
**Levels:** 1
**Square Footage:** 1,195
**Bedrooms:** 3
**Bathrooms:** 2
**Foundation:** Basement
**Materials List Available:** Yes
**Price Category:** B

*Images provided by designer/architect.*

This compact one-level home uses an open plan to make the most of its square footage.

**Features:**

- Ceiling Height: 8 ft.

- Covered Porch: This delightful area, located off the kitchen, provides a private spot to enjoy some fresh air.

- Open Plan: The family room, dining area and kitchen share a big open space to provide a sense of spaciousness. Moving so easily between these interrelated areas provides the convenience demanded by a busy lifestyle.

- Master Suite: An open plan is convenient, but it is still important for everyone to have their private space. The master suite enjoys its own bath and walk-in closet. The secondary bedrooms share a nearby bath.

- Garage: Here you will find parking for two cars and plenty of extra storage space as well.

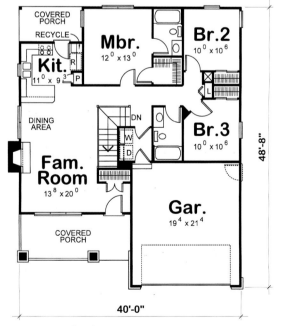

*Copyright by designer/architect.*

## SMARTtip

### Painting Doors

To protect the door finish while working, cover the sawhorses with towels or carpet scraps. Be sure to allow sufficient time for the door to dry before flipping it over.

To paint both sides of the door at one time, drive a pair of 16d nails into the top and bottom edges of the door, and then rest the door on the sawhorses, as shown below. After painting one side, simply flip the door over to paint the other side. (Note: This method may not work quite as well with very heavy wood or steel doors.)

## Plan #121011

**Dimensions:** 50' W x 50' D
**Levels:** 1
**Square Footage:** 1,724
**Bedrooms:** 3
**Bathrooms:** 2
**Foundation:** Basement
**Materials List Available:** Yes
**Price Category:** C

*Images provided by designer/architect.*

This one-level home is perfect for retirement or for convenient living for the growing family.

**Features:**

• Ceiling Height: 8 ft.

• Master Suite: For privacy and quiet, the master suite is segregated from the other bedrooms.

• Family Room: Sit by the fire and read as light streams through the windows flanking the fireplace. Or enjoy the built-in entertainment center.

• Breakfast Area: Located just off the family room, the sunny breakfast area will lure you to linger over impromptu family meals. Here you will find a built-in desk for compiling shopping lists and menus.

• Private Porch: Step out of the breakfast area to enjoy a breeze on this porch.

• Kitchen: Efficient and attractive, this kitchen offers an angled pantry and an island that doubles as a snack bar.

## SMARTtip

### Measuring for Kitchen Countertops

Custom cabinetmakers will sometimes come to your house to measure for a countertop, but home centers and kitchen stores may require that you come to them with the dimensions already in hand. Be sure to double-check measurements carefully. Being off by only ½ in. can be quite upsetting.

To ensure accuracy, sketch out the countertop on a sheet of graph paper. Include all the essential dimensions. To be on the safe side, have someone else double-check your numbers.

*Copyright by designer/architect.*

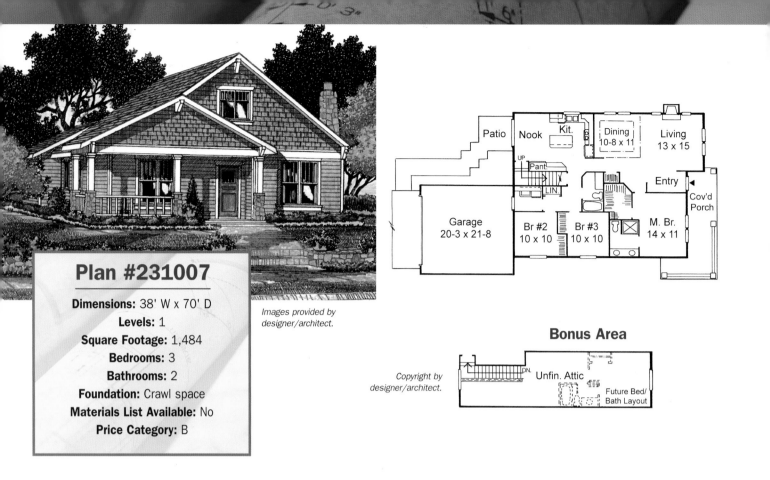

## Plan #231007

**Dimensions:** 38' W x 70' D
**Levels:** 1
**Square Footage:** 1,484
**Bedrooms:** 3
**Bathrooms:** 2
**Foundation:** Crawl space
**Materials List Available:** No
**Price Category:** B

*Images provided by designer/architect.*

Patio · Nook · Kit. · Dining 10-8 x 11 · Living 13 x 15

UP · Pant · Entry · Cov'd Porch · LIN

Garage 20-3 x 21-8 · Br #2 10 x 10 · Br #3 10 x 10 · M. Br. 14 x 11

### Bonus Area

*Copyright by designer/architect.*

DN. · Unfin. Attic · Future Bed/Bath Layout

---

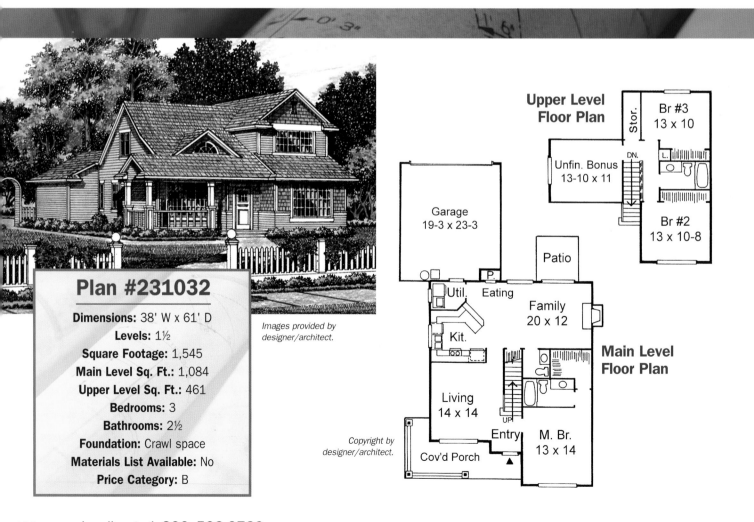

## Plan #231032

**Dimensions:** 38' W x 61' D
**Levels:** 1½
**Square Footage:** 1,545
**Main Level Sq. Ft.:** 1,084
**Upper Level Sq. Ft.:** 461
**Bedrooms:** 3
**Bathrooms:** 2½
**Foundation:** Crawl space
**Materials List Available:** No
**Price Category:** B

*Images provided by designer/architect.*

**Upper Level Floor Plan**

Stor. · Br #3 13 x 10 · Unfin. Bonus 13-10 x 11 · DN. · Br #2 13 x 10-8

Garage 19-3 x 23-3 · Patio · P. · Util. · Eating · Family 20 x 12 · Kit. · Living 14 x 14 · Entry · M. Br. 13 x 14 · UP · Cov'd Porch

**Main Level Floor Plan**

*Copyright by designer/architect.*

## Plan #231035

**Dimensions:** 50' W x 50' D

**Levels:** 2

**Square Footage:** 1,954

**Main Level Sq. Ft.:** 1,508

**Upper Level Sq. Ft.:** 446

**Bedrooms:** 3

**Bathrooms:** 3

**Foundation:** Crawl space, slab

**Materials List Available:** No

**Price Category:** D

*Images provided by designer/architect.*

**Main Level Floor Plan**

- Patio
- Kit. 11-6x9
- Dining 12x10
- M.Br. 14x11
- Family 14x12
- VAULTED CEILING
- Util
- Br. 13-6x10
- Parlor 11-6x13
- Den 9x10
- Garage 19-6x21-6
- Cov.Porch

**Upper Level Floor Plan**

*Copyright by designer/architect.*

- OPEN TO BELOW
- DN
- Loft
- Br. 11x12-4

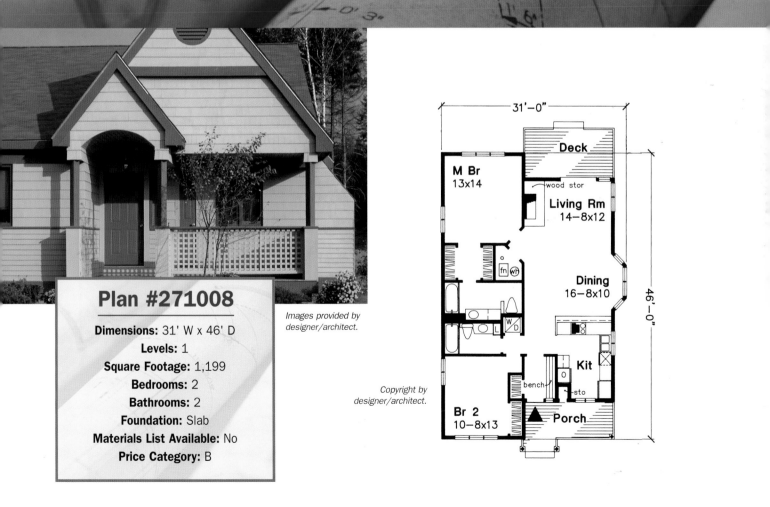

## Plan #271008

**Dimensions:** 31' W x 46' D

**Levels:** 1

**Square Footage:** 1,199

**Bedrooms:** 2

**Bathrooms:** 2

**Foundation:** Slab

**Materials List Available:** No

**Price Category:** B

*Images provided by designer/architect.*

*Copyright by designer/architect.*

- 31'-0"
- 46'-0"
- Deck
- M Br 13x14
- wood stor
- Living Rm 14-8x12
- fn / wh
- Dining 16-8x10
- W/D
- Kit
- bench
- sto
- Br 2 10-8x13
- Porch

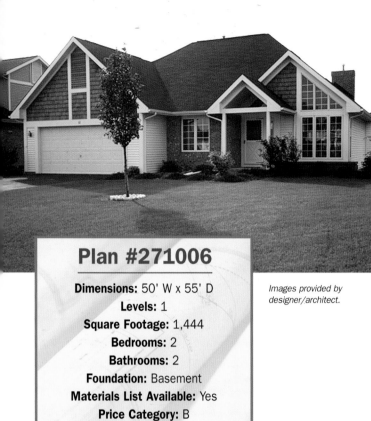

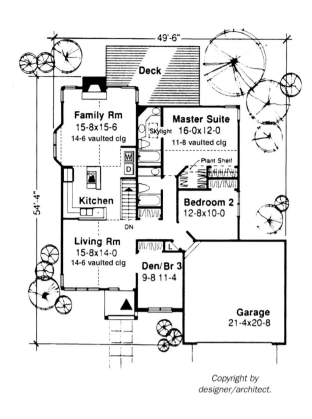

## Plan #271006

**Dimensions:** 50' W x 55' D
**Levels:** 1
**Square Footage:** 1,444
**Bedrooms:** 2
**Bathrooms:** 2
**Foundation:** Basement
**Materials List Available:** Yes
**Price Category:** B

*Images provided by designer/architect.*

*Copyright by designer/architect.*

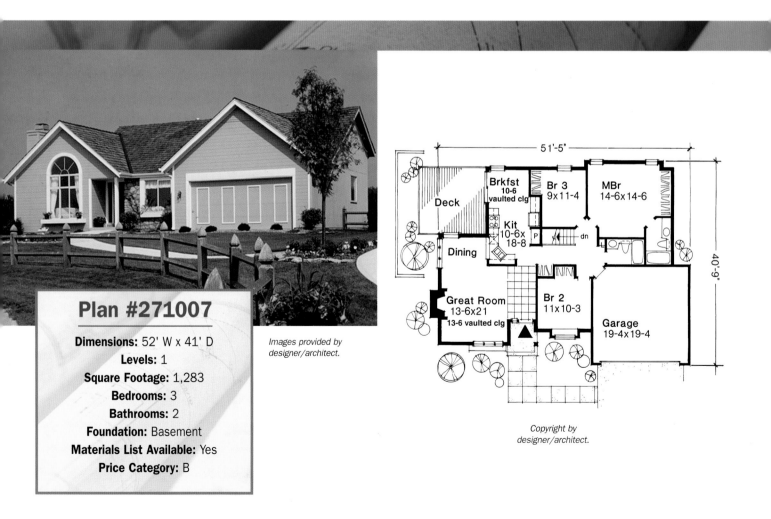

## Plan #271007

**Dimensions:** 52' W x 41' D
**Levels:** 1
**Square Footage:** 1,283
**Bedrooms:** 3
**Bathrooms:** 2
**Foundation:** Basement
**Materials List Available:** Yes
**Price Category:** B

*Images provided by designer/architect.*

*Copyright by designer/architect.*

# Plan #141004

**Dimensions:** 48' W x 29' D
**Levels:** 1
**Square Footage:** 1,514
**Bedrooms:** 3
**Bathrooms:** 2
**Foundation:** Slab, basement
**Materials List Available:** No
**Price Category:** C

*Images provided by designer/architect.*

Designed for the narrow lot, this cottage-style home features Craftsman-style exterior columns.

**Features:**

- Ceiling Height: 8 ft. unless otherwise noted.

- Entry: There's no defined foyer, so you enter immediately into the living area, with its vaulted ceiling that flattens over the dining area at a soaring 14 ft.

- Living/Dining Areas: The see-through fireplace flanked by bookcases is a main focal point of the home. It serves as the divider between the living room and dining room.

- Kitchen: This kitchen shares the vaulted ceiling with the dining room and living room. A plant shelf over the cabinets facing the dining room defines the space without obstructing the view of the fireplace.

- Master Suite: This private retreat has its own entrance away from the other bedrooms and boasts a cathedral ceiling over both bedroom and bath.

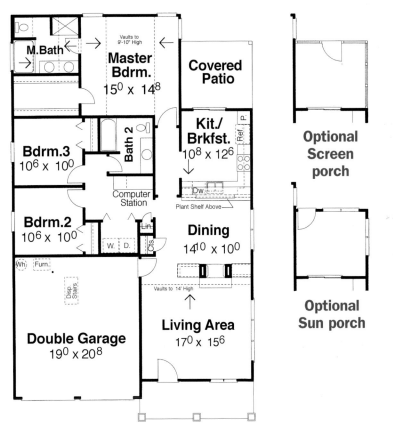

*Copyright by designer/architect.*

Images provided by designer/architect.

## Plan #141002

**Dimensions:** 48' W x 29' D
**Levels:** 1
**Square Footage:** 1,365
**Bedrooms:** 3
**Bathrooms:** 2
**Foundation:** Slab, basement
**Materials List Available:** No
**Price Category:** B

This warm country cottage-style house is perfect for the growing family.

**Features:**

- Ceiling Height: 8 ft. unless otherwise noted.

- Foyer: Guests will be greeted by a full vaulted ceiling that soars to a height of 11 ft. 8 in.

- Dining Area: This dining area flows from the foyer but is defined by a plant shelf over a column.

- Kitchen: This kitchen is open and spacious, with large windows facing the front of the house so that the cook can keep an eye on the kids playing in the front yard. It includes a pass-through over the sink.

- Master Bedroom: This bedroom is separated from the others to create more privacy. Its distinctive look comes from a ceiling that slopes to flat at 9 ft. 6 in.

- Laundry: For maximum efficiency, the washer and dryer are closeted in the hall of the secondary bedrooms.

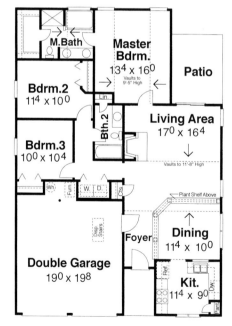

Copyright by designer/architect.

SMARTtip

## Contemporary Style in Your Bathroom

Incorporate elements of Arts and Crafts, Art Deco, or other designs associated with the modern movement of the twentieth century (International Style, Bauhaus, Memphis, and the influence of Scandinavian design). Their clean geometric lines are quite compatible with this environment. This eclectic approach can be very sophisticated. Look for framed art prints, a vintage-inspired wallpaper, or reproduction hardware, faucets, or light fixtures to underscore your theme. Fortunately, manufacturers are reproducing art tiles from original molds or designs that can be used as accents.

# Plan #161009

**Dimensions:** 60'9" W x 49' D

**Levels:** 1

**Square Footage:** 1,651

**Bedrooms:** 3

**Bathrooms:** 2

**Foundation:** Slab

**Materials List Available:** Yes

**Price Category:** C

The warm, textured exterior combines with the elegance of double-entry doors to preview both the casual lifestyle and formal entertaining capabilities of this versatile home.

**Features:**

- **Great Room:** Experience the openness provided by the sloped ceiling topping both this great room and the formal dining area. Enjoy the warmth and light supplied by the gas fireplace and dual sliding doors.

- **Kitchen:** This kitchen, convenient to the living space, is designed for easy work patterns and features an open bar that separates the work area from the more richly decorated gathering rooms.

- **Master Bedroom:** Separated for privacy, this master bedroom includes a tray ceiling and lavishly equipped bath.

- **Basement:** This full basement allows you to expand your living space to meet your needs.

*Images provided by designer/architect.*

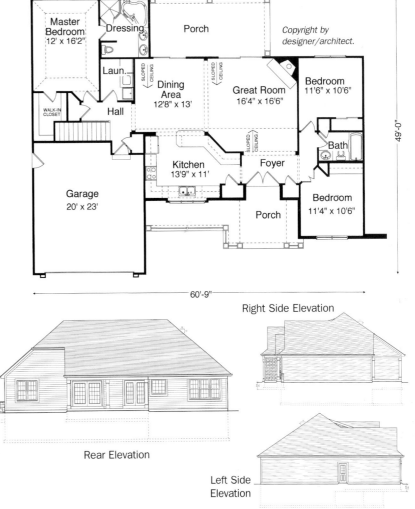

www.ultimateplans.com    199

# Easy-Care Surfaces

**B**uilding a new home means you will be making a number of decisions on the many materials that will be visible throughout your cottage-style house. Your builder won't ask you which brand of drywall to buy, but he or she will ask what color to paint the walls, what material to use on the kitchen counters, and what type of finish you want on the faucets in the master bathroom. It is a lot to think about, but the following will help you make decisions on some of the major materials.

## Countertop Materials

The market offers lots of countertop materials, all of which are worth consideration for your kitchen and bathroom surfaces. Pick the materials and designs that best suit your needs and the look of the room. You can also enhance a basic design by combining it with an eye-catching edge treatment. Another option is to combine different materials on the same surface.

**Plastic Laminate.** This thin, durable surface comes in hundreds of colors, textures, and patterns. The material is relatively easy to install; its smooth surface washes easily and can stand up well to everyday wear and tear. It is heat-resistant, although very hot pots can discolor or even burn it, and it will show scratches from knives and other sharp utensils; surface damage is difficult to repair.

Home centers and kitchen supply dealers sell post-formed counters. These are the types that come in 8- or 10-foot lengths that you or your builder will trim to fit. Both the laminate sheets and the post-form counters are available in a limited number of colors and patterns. Another option is to order a laminate counter from a counter fabricator—some home centers and kitchen dealers offer this service as well.

The counter will be built to your measurements, and you will get a wide variety of colors and patterns from which to choose. Most fabricators also offer a variety of edge treatments.

**Ceramic Tile.** Glazed tile can be magnificently decorative for counters, backsplashes, and walls, or as a display inset in another material. Tile is smooth and easy to wipe off, and it can't be burned by hot pots. In addition to the standard square tiles, ceramic tiles are available in a number of specialty shapes and sizes, allowing you to create a truly custom look. Ceramic tile costs more than laminate, but you can save money by doing the installation yourself.

When shopping, you should also consider the finish. There are two kinds: unglazed and glazed. Unglazed tiles are not sealed and always come in a matte look. They are not practical for use near water unless you apply a sealant. On the other hand, glazed

tiles are coated with a material that makes them impervious to water—or spills and stains from other liquids, too. This glaze on the tile can be matte or highly polished. The upkeep of tile is fairly easy, but you must regrout and reseal periodically. White grout shows dirt easily, but a dark-color mix can camouflage stains. Still, unless it is sealed, grout will harbor bacteria. So clean the countertop regularly with a nonabrasive antibacterial cleanser. Tile that is well-maintained will last a lifetime.

**Ceramic tile** provides a clean, nonporous surface for countertops, opposite.

**Colorful tiles** make a strong design statement in the bath shown bottom left.

**Solid surfacing,** right, resists burns and scratches.

**Plastic laminates,** below, are available in a variety of colors and patterns.

**Solid-Surfacing Material**. Made of acrylics and composite materials, solid surfacing comes in ½ inch and ¾ inch thicknesses. This is a premium material that resists moisture, heat, stains, and cracks.

There is almost no limit to the colors and patterns of solid surfacing. It can be fabricated to resemble marble and granite, or it can be a block of solid color. Either way, the material can be carved or beveled for decorative effects just like wood. Manufacturers recommend professional installation.

The surface becomes scratched fairly easily, but the scratches are not readily appar-

ent. Because the material is a solid color, serious blemishes can be removed by sanding or buffing.

**Natural Stone.** Marble, slate, and granite can be formed into beautiful but expensive counters. Of the three, granite is probably the most popular because it cannot be hurt by moisture or heat, nor does it stain if finished properly. Installers polish granite to produce a high-gloss finish.

Marble scratches, cracks, and stains easily, even if waxed. Slate can be easily scratched and cracked and cannot take a high polish.

These are heavy materials that should be installed by a professional. However, you can get the look of granite and marble by installing granite or marble tiles. Cut from the natural stones, these products are available in 12 x 12-inch tiles and are installed and cut in much the same way as ceramic tiles.

**Wood.** Butcher block consists of hardwood laminated under pressure and sealed with oil or a polymer finish. Because it's thicker than other materials, butcher block will raise the counter level about ¾ inch above standard height. Also, wood is sub-

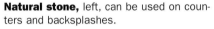

**Natural stone,** left, can be used on counters and backsplashes.

**Counter fabricators** can create decorative edge treatments such as the one above.

**A bathroom vanity,** above right, benefits from a polished quartz counter.

**Strong countertop color,** right, can set off neutral-color cabinets.

ject to damage by standing water or hot pans. Butcher-block tops are moderately expensive but can be installed by amateurs.

Other kinds of wood counters may be used, especially in serving areas. Any wood used near water must be resistant to moisture or well sealed to prevent water from penetrating below the surface.

**Concrete.** There aren't a great number of concrete counters, but the material is catching on with some in the kitchen design community. If your goal is to install a cutting-edge material that can still have a traditional look, concrete is it. Thanks to new

staining techniques, concrete can be saturated with color all the way through, and it can be preformed to any shape and finished to any texture. Set stone or ceramic tile chips into the surface for a decorative effect. Form it to drain off water at the sink. Be cautious, however, as a concrete countertop must be sealed, and it may crack. Installation is best left to a professional.

**Stainless Steel.** Stainless steel used for a countertop, whether it is for the entire counter or just a section of it, can look quite sophisticated, especially with a wood trim. What's practical about it is its capaci-

ty to take high heat without scorching, which makes it suitable as a landing strip for pots and pans straight from the cooktop. It is also impervious to water, so it's practical at the sink. On the negative side, stainless steel can be noisy to work on, and it will show smudges. Depending on the grade of the material, it may also be vulnerable to scrapes, stains, and corrosion. The higher the chromium and nickel content (and therefore the grade), the better. Also, look for a thick-gauge stainless steel that won't dent easily. If you prefer not to have a stainless-steel counter but like the look, consider a stainless-steel sink.

**Selecting colors** for walls can be intimidating. Fortunately, kitchens, above, usually have small unused wall areas so you can experiment more freely than you would in other rooms.

## Wall Treatments

It's hard to beat the ease of a coat of paint for decorating a room. But there are other ways to finish off the walls, too, such as vinyl wallcovering and paneling. You can go with one, two, or all three of these options in several combinations to achieve the cottage decor that will complement your new house.

**Paint.** Basically, there are two kinds of paint: latex, which is a water-based formulation, and oil-based products. You can buy latex and oil paint in at least four finishes: flat, eggshell, semigloss, and gloss. In general, stay away from flat paint in the kitchen because it is difficult to keep clean. The other finishes, or sheens, resist dirt better than flat paint and are easier to clean.

Latex is a term used to describe a variety of water-based paints. They are recommended for most interior surfaces, including walls, woodwork, and cabinets. Latex paints come in a huge assortment of colors,

clean up with soap and water, and dry quickly.

Oil-based paint refers to products that use alkyd resins as the solvent. Manufacturers once used linseed or some other type of oil as the solvent and the name stuck. They provide tough, long-lasting finishes. However, the convenience of latex products, along with government regulations limiting the amount of volatile organic compounds oil-based products produce, has forced their use to decline. This kind of paint is especially good for use over bare wood and surfaces that have been

previously painted. If you plan to use it (or latex, for that matter) on new wallboard, you'll have to apply a primer first.

### Wallcoverings.

Vinyl wallcoverings and coordinated borders offer an easy, low-cost way to put style into your new cottage kitchen. Practical because they are nonporous, stain resistant, and washable, vinyl coatings are available in a great variety of colors, textures, and patterns. Prepasted, pretrimmed rolls are the easiest for a novice to install. Just remember to remove any old wallpaper before applying new covering to walls.

### Paneling.

If you're looking for a simple way to create a "cottage" feel, paneling is it. Today's paneling options include prefinished softwood- or hardwood-veneered plywood, simulated wood grain on plywood or hardboard, prehung wallpaper on plywood, simulated wood grain or decorative finish panel board, tile board, or other decorative hardboard paneling, and solid pine or cedar plank paneling. For a versatile look, apply wainscoting, which is paneling that goes halfway or three-quarters of the way up the wall. Top it off with chair rail molding; paint or wallpaper the rest of the wall. Depending on how you install it, you can create horizontal, diagonal, or herringbone patterns.

**Wallpaper and borders** are an easy, inexpensive way to enliven a room's design, above. Pick colors and patterns to set off your cabinet finishes.

**Ceramic tile** is a popular choice for bathroom walls. Note how the tiles below contain decorative inlays to add sparkle to what would otherwise be a white wall.

# Flooring

Floor coverings fall into two broad categories: resilient flooring, which has some resiliency, or bounce, and hard flooring, with no flex whatsoever. Resilient floors are less tiring to stand on than hard-surface floors and less likely to produce instant disaster for dropped glasses or chinaware. But the flooring you select plays more than a practical role in your kitchen.

## Resilient Vinyl Tile and Sheet Flooring.

Vinyl flooring wears fairly well to very well, needs only occasional waxing or polishing (in some cases none at all), and is easy to clean. It comes in a wide variety of colors and patterns suitable to the cottage style, and is an economical alternative among flooring choices.

These products are available in individual tiles or in large sheets. (The sheets can look like individual tiles as well as a wide range of designs.) Installing vinyl tile is a popular do-it-yourself project. Installing sheet goods is a bit more complex but well within the skills of an experienced do-it-yourselfer.

**Laminate.** This type of flooring consists of laminate material, a tougher version of the material used on counters, bonded to fiberboard core. The decorative top layer of material can be made to look like just about anything. Currently, wood-grain patterns are the most popular, but laminates are available in many colors and patterns, including tile and natural stone designs.

**Vinyl flooring,** left, comes in a variety of patterns.

**Carpeting,** below, adds warmth to most rooms.

Available in both plank and tile form, they are easy to install, hold up well to normal traffic, and are easy to clean.

**Wood.** Thanks largely to polyurethane coatings that are impervious to water, wood flooring continues to be a popular choice for just about any room of the home, except bathrooms. Wood can be finished any way you like, though much of the wood flooring available today comes prefinished in an assortment of shades.

Hardwoods like oak and maple are popular and stand up to a lot of abuse. Softwoods like pine give a more distressed, countrified look. Flooring comes in 2¼-inch strips as well as variable-width planks. Parquet flooring, another good option, consists of wood pieces glued together into

**Stone flooring** imparts a feeling of solidity to an area, such as the foyer above. Inlay designs such as this one are the mark of a true stone craftsman.

a geometric pattern. These prefinished squares can be installed in a way similar to that used for vinyl tiles.

**Hard-Surface Flooring.** Ceramic tile, stone, and slate floors are hard, durable, and easy to clean, especially when you use grout sealers. Because these floors are so inflexible, anything fragile dropped on them is likely to break. Also, they are tiring to stand on and noisy, and they conduct extremes of temperature. For those who love the look of this kind of flooring, however, the drawbacks can be mitigated with accent and area rugs that add a cushion.

Ceramic tile makes an excellent kitchen or bathroom floor when installed with proper grout and sealants. The tiles range from the earth tones of unglazed, solid-color quarry tile to the great array of colors, patterns, and finishes in surface-glazed tiles. Grout comes color-keyed, so it can be

either inconspicuous or a design element. Ceramic and quarry tiles are best suited to a concrete subfloor, though you can lay them over any firm base. Cost ranges from moderate to expensive.

Stone and slate are cut into small slabs and can be laid in a regular or random pattern. Materials are inexpensive or costly, depending on quality and local availability. Even if you find these materials more expensive than other floor coverings, don't dismiss them because of price. They will never need to be replaced, making your initial investment your final one. Because stone and slate are laid in mortar and are themselves weighty materials, a concrete slab makes the ideal subfloor. In other situations, the subfloor must be able to carry a significantly heavy load. Installation is a complex job that should be left to contractors with experience in this type of stone work.

**Carpeting and Rugs.** The terms carpet and rug are often used interchangeably, but they're not the same. Carpeting is manufactured in rolls ranging from just over 2 feet wide to broadlooms that measure as much as 18 feet wide. Carpeting is usually laid wall-to-wall and can be installed over raw subflooring. Rugs are soft floor coverings that don't extend wall-to-wall and are used over another finished flooring surface. A mat is a small rug.

Differences in fiber composition, construction, color, texture, and cost make choosing a carpet or rug a complex job. Carpeting can be made of natural wool, synthetic fibers, or blends of wool and synthetics. Other natural fibers commonly used in area rugs, scatter rugs, and mats are cotton or plant materials known as cellulosics—hemp, jute, sisal, or grasses. Synthetic fibers are acrylics, nylon, olefin, and polyester.

# Plan #161002

**Dimensions:** 64'2" W x 44'2" D
**Levels:** 1
**Square Footage:** 1,860
**Bedrooms:** 3
**Bathrooms:** 2
**Foundation:** Basement
**Materials List Available:** Yes
**Price Category:** D

*Images provided by designer/architect.*

The brick, stone, and cedar shake facade provides color and texture to the exterior, while the unique nooks and angles inside this delightful one-level home give it character.

### Features:

- **Great Room/Dining Room:** This spacious great room is furnished with a wood-burning fireplace, a high ceiling, and French doors. Wide entrances to the breakfast room and dining room expand its space to comfortably hold large gatherings.

- **Kitchen:** The breakfast bar offers additional seating. The covered porch lets you enjoy a view of the landscape and is conveniently located for outdoor meals off this kitchen and breakfast area.

- **Master Bedroom:** The master bedroom is a private retreat. An alcove creates a comfortable sitting area, and an angled entry leads to the bath with whirlpool and a double-bowl vanity.

Left Side Elevation

Right Side Elevation

Rear Elevation

*Copyright by designer/architect.*

Dining Room

Great Room/Breakfast Area

Great Room

Living Room / Dining Room

## SMARTtip

## Installing Rods and Poles

The way to install a rod or pole depends on the type it is, the brackets that will hold it, the weight of the window treatment, and the surface to which it is being fastened. Given below are some general guidelines, but for specific installation procedures, refer to the instructions that accompany the rod or pole.

- Use a stepladder to reach high places.

- Use the proper tools.

- Take accurate measurements.

- Work with a helper.

- If attaching a bracket to wood, first drill small pilot holes to avoid splitting the wood.

- Consider using wall anchors, particularly for the heavier window treatments.

- Use a level as needed to help you position the brackets for the pole or rod.

- Take care not to drill or hammer into any pipes or electrical wiring.

Because they're designed to stand out, decorative poles and their finials require more room for installation than conventional drapery rods. Finials add inches to the ends of a window treatment, so make sure you have enough wall room to display your hardware to its full advantage. And because decorative rods are often heavy, be certain your window frames and walls can support the weight.

## Plan #171008

**Dimensions:** 72' W x 40' D
**Levels:** 1
**Square Footage:** 1,652
**Bedrooms:** 3
**Bathrooms:** 2
**Foundation:** Slab, crawl space
**Materials List Available:** Yes
**Price Category:** C

*Images provided by designer/architect.*

Copyright by designer/architect.

## SMARTtip

### Lighting for Decorative Shadows

Use lighting to create decorative shadows. For interesting, undefined shadows, set lights at ground level aiming upward in front of a shrub or tree that is close to a wall. For silhouetting, place lights directly behind a plant or garden statue that is near a wall. In both cases, using a wide beam will increase the effect.

## Plan #281009

**Dimensions:** 46' W x 52' D
**Levels:** 1
**Square Footage:** 1,423
**Bedrooms:** 3
**Bathrooms:** 2
**Foundation:** Walk-out basement
**Materials List Available:** Yes
**Price Category:** B

*Images provided by designer/architect.*

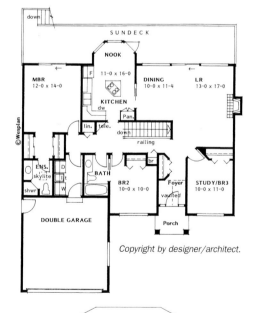

Copyright by designer/architect.

Rear Elevation

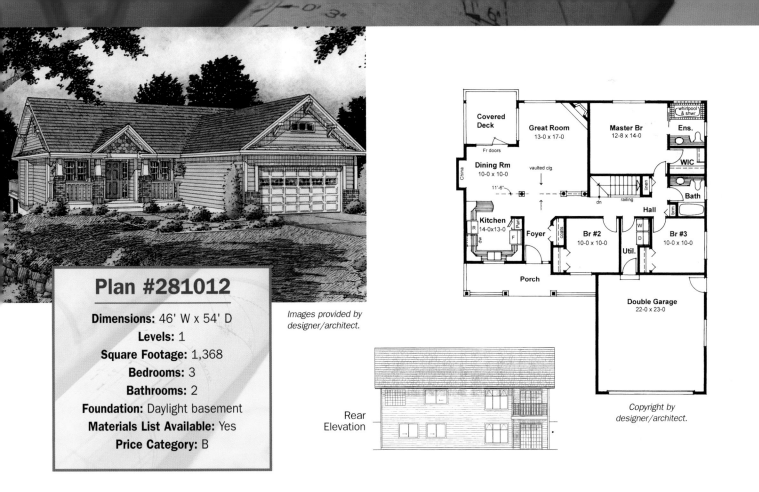

## Plan #281012

**Dimensions:** 46' W x 54' D

**Levels:** 1

**Square Footage:** 1,368

**Bedrooms:** 3

**Bathrooms:** 2

**Foundation:** Daylight basement

**Materials List Available:** Yes

**Price Category:** B

*Images provided by designer/architect.*

Rear Elevation

*Copyright by designer/architect.*

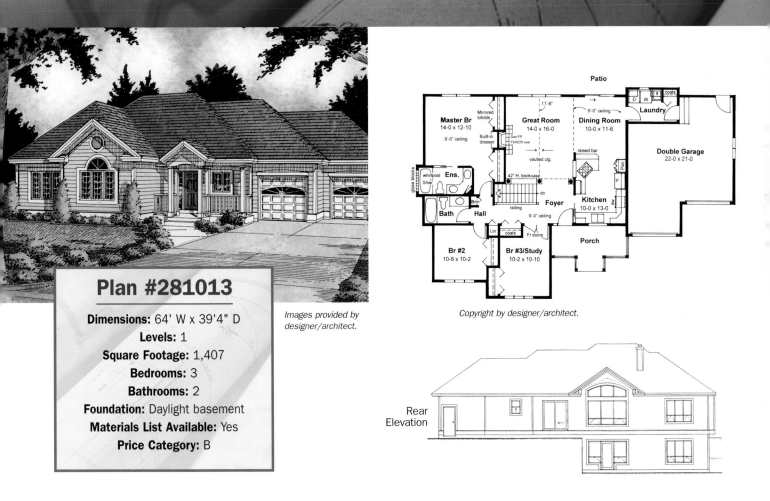

## Plan #281013

**Dimensions:** 64' W x 39'4" D

**Levels:** 1

**Square Footage:** 1,407

**Bedrooms:** 3

**Bathrooms:** 2

**Foundation:** Daylight basement

**Materials List Available:** Yes

**Price Category:** B

*Images provided by designer/architect.*

*Copyright by designer/architect.*

Rear Elevation

Images provided by designer/architect.

## Plan #251005

**Dimensions:** 50' W x 44'2" D
**Levels:** 1
**Square Footage:** 1,631
**Bedrooms:** 3
**Bathrooms:** 2
**Foundation:** Basement
**Materials List Available:** Yes
**Price Category:** C

This elegant home features hip roof lines that will add appeal in any neighborhood.

**Features:**

- Ceiling Height: 9 ft.

- Front Porch: The porch stretches across the entire front of the home, offering plenty of space to sit and enjoy evening breezes.

- Family Room: This family room features a handsome fireplace and has plenty of room for all kinds of family activities.

- Dining Room: This dining room has plenty of room for dinner parties. After dinner, guests can step through French doors onto the rear deck.

- Kitchen: This kitchen is a pleasure in which to work. It features an angled snack bar with plenty of room for informal family meals.

- Master Bedroom: You'll enjoy retiring at day's end to this master bedroom, with its large walk-in closet.

- Master Bath. This master bath features a double vanity, a deluxe tub, and a walk-in shower.

SMARTtip

### Victorian Style

Victorian, today, is a very romantic look. To underscore this, add the scent of lavender or some other dried flower to the room or use potpourri, which you can keep in a bowl on the vanity. Hang a fragrant pomander on a hook, display lavender soaps on a wall shelf, or tuck sachets between towels on a shelf. For an authentic touch, display a Victorian favorite, the spider plant.

*Copyright by designer/architect.*

# Plan #161004

**Dimensions:** 50' W x 54'8" D

**Levels:** 1

**Square Footage:** 1,315

**Bedrooms:** 3

**Bathrooms:** 2

**Foundation:** Slab

**Materials List Available:** Yes

**Price Category:** B

*Images provided by designer/architect.*

*Copyright by designer/architect.*

This multi-featured ranch has a covered porch, a ceiling that slopes to an 11-ft. height, an optional library, and a full basement to enhance your living enjoyment.

## Features:

- **Great Room:** Experience the expansive entertainment area created by this open great room and the dining area. Enjoy the lovely fireplace, with full glass on both sides.

- **Kitchen:** This kitchen is designed for total convenience and easy work patterns with immediate access to the first-floor laundry area.

- **Master Bedroom:** This master bedroom, split from the other bedrooms, offers privacy and features tray ceiling design.

- **Basement:** Designed with the future in mind, this full basement has open stairs leading to it and can be updated to expand your living space.

**Deck**

**Master Bedroom** 12'-4" x 13'-0"

**Great Room** 18'-8" x 17'-4"

**Bedroom** 11'-4" x 10'-8"

**Bath**

**Dining**

**Bath**

**Kitchen** 13'-4" x 9'-11"

**Foyer**

**Bedroom** 12'-4" x 10'-10"

**Laun.**

**Porch**

**Garage** 20'-0" x 26'-2"

54'-8"

50'-0"

**Bath**

**Optional Library**

**Rear Elevation**

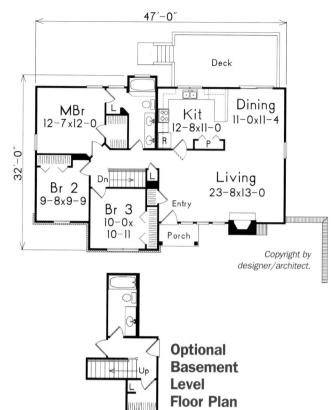

Deck

| MBr 12-7x12-0 | Kit 12-8x11-0 | Dining 11-0x11-4 |

Br 2 9-8x9-9

Dn

Br 3 10-0x 10-11

Living 23-8x13-0

Entry

Porch

47'-0"

32'-0"

*Copyright by designer/architect.*

## Plan #321024

**Dimensions:** 47' W x 32' D

**Levels:** 1

**Square Footage:** 1,403

**Bedrooms:** 3

**Bathrooms:** 1-2

**Foundation:** Daylight basement

**Materials List Available:** Yes

**Price Category:** B

*Images provided by designer/architect.*

**Optional Basement Level Floor Plan**

Up

---

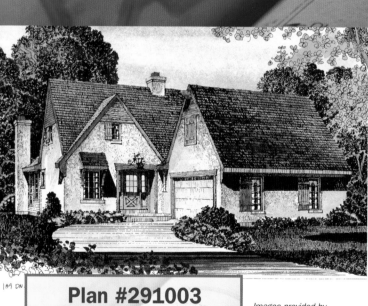

## Plan #291003

**Dimensions:** 42'4" W x 73'4" D

**Levels:** 1

**Square Footage:** 1,890

**Bedrooms:** 3

**Bathrooms:** 2

**Foundation:** Crawl space

**Materials List Available:** No

**Price Category:** D

*Images provided by designer/architect.*

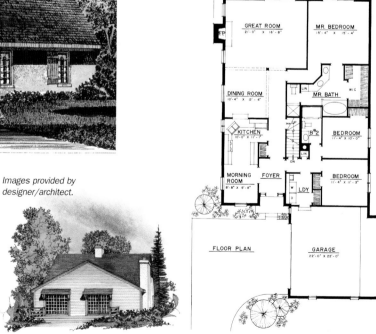

DECK

42'-4"

GREAT ROOM 21'-0" x 16'-8"

MR. BEDROOM 15'-4" x 15'-4"

DINING ROOM 10'-4" x 12'-4"

MR. BATH

WIC

KITCHEN 10'-0" x 11'-0"

BEDROOM 11'-4" x 10'-0"

MORNING ROOM 6'-8" x 9'-8"

FOYER

LDY

BEDROOM 11'-4" x 11'-3"

FLOOR PLAN

GARAGE 22'-0" x 22'-0"

*Copyright by designer/architect.*

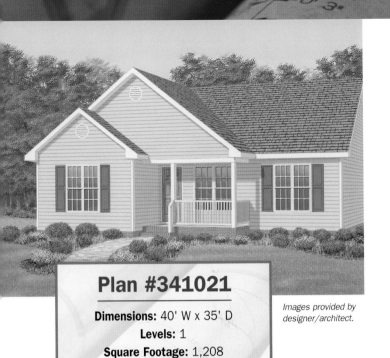

## Plan #341021

**Dimensions:** 40' W x 35' D

**Levels:** 1

**Square Footage:** 1,208

**Bedrooms:** 3

**Bathrooms:** 2

**Foundation:** Crawl space, slab, or basement

**Materials List Available:** Yes

**Price Category:** B

*Images provided by designer/architect.*

DECK

BEDROOM 3
11'-8"X10'-0"

KITCHEN
15'-6"X11'-4"

DINING

BA. 2

LIN

COAT

VAULTED
CEILING

D

W

GREAT ROOM
14'-8"X12'-4"

BEDROOM 1
12'-7"X15'-0"

BEDROOM 2
11'-8"X11'-0"

PORCH

35'-0"

40'-0"

*Copyright by designer/architect.*

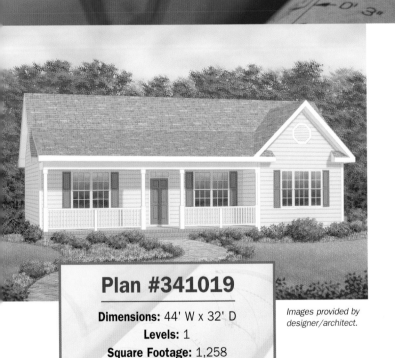

## Plan #341019

**Dimensions:** 44' W x 32' D

**Levels:** 1

**Square Footage:** 1,258

**Bedrooms:** 3

**Bathrooms:** 2

**Foundation:** Crawl space, slab, or basement

**Materials List Available:** Yes

**Price Category:** B

*Images provided by designer/architect.*

DECK
10'-0" X 10'-0"

BEDROOM 3
10'-0" X 10'-2"

CLOSET

COATS

SINK

DW

KITCHEN/DINING
15'-9" X 10'-2"

RANGE

REF

WASH

DRY

SHWR

WH

BATH 1

GARDEN TUB

CLOSET

LINENS

BATH 2

BEDROOM 2
11'-0" X 10'-2"

CLOSET

FAMILY ROOM
15'-9" X 15'-7"

VAULTED CEILING

MASTER SUITE
13'-3" X 16'-5"

PORCH

32'-0"

44'-0"

*Copyright by designer/architect.*

## Plan #221013

**Dimensions:** 48' W x 58'8" D

**Levels:** 1

**Square Footage:** 1,495

**Bedrooms:** 3

**Bathrooms:** 2

**Foundation:** Basement

**Materials List Available:** No

**Price Category:** B

If you love rooms with unusual shapes, angled features, and interesting ceilings, this could be the home of your dreams.

**Features:**

- Ceiling Height: 8 ft.

- Great Room: A cathedral ceiling complements this huge room, and the fireplace and flanking windows make a lovely focal point.

- Dining Room: You'll love the cathedral ceiling that gives elegance to this open dining room, as well as its doors, which lead to both the backyard and the screened-in porch.

- Kitchen: Arched openings let you look into the dining room and the great room, and the angled counter area gives distinction to this room, with its step-saving floor plan.

- Master Suite: Enjoy the tray ceiling, walk-in closet, plant ledge, and luxurious bath.

- Additional Bedrooms: Bedroom #2 has a cathedral ceiling, and shares a bath with bedroom #3.

Rear Elevation

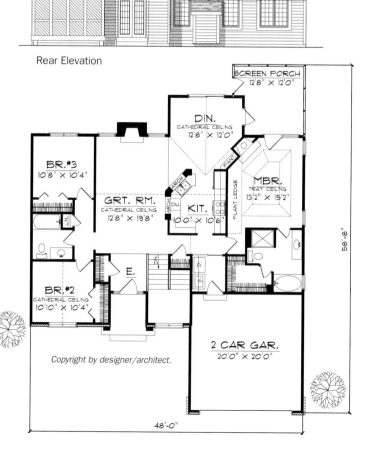

Copyright by designer/architect.

## Plan #301002

**Dimensions:** 57'2" W x 54'10" D

**Levels:** 1

**Square Footage:** 1,845

**Bedrooms:** 3

**Bathrooms:** 2½

**Foundation:** Crawl space, slab

**Materials List Available:** Yes

**Price Category:** D

*Images provided by designer/architect.*

Although compact, this home is filled with surprisingly luxurious features.

**Features:**

• Ceiling Height: 8 ft. unless otherwise noted.

• Front Porch: Guests will be sheltered from the rain by this lovely little porch.

• Foyer: This elegant foyer features a 10-ft. ceiling and is open to the dining room and the rear great room.

• Dining Room: The 10-ft. ceiling from the foyer continues into this spacious dining room.

• Family Room: This family room features a vaulted ceiling and a fireplace with built-in bookcases.

• Kitchen: This kitchen boasts a pantry and plenty of storage and counter space.

• Master Bedroom: This master bedroom includes a cathedral ceiling and two walk-in closets. The master bath has two vanities, a corner spa, and a walk-in closet.

*Copyright by designer/architect.*

## Plan #341033

**Dimensions:** 57' W x 32'3" D

**Levels:** 1

**Square Footage:** 1,297

**Bedrooms:** 3

**Bathrooms:** 2

**Foundation:** Crawl space, slab, or basement

**Materials List Available:** Yes

**Price Category:** B

*Images provided by designer/architect.*

*Copyright by designer/architect.*

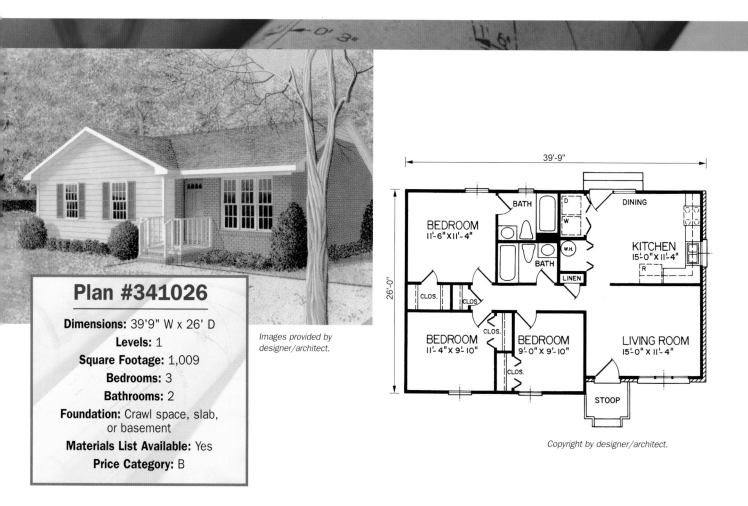

## Plan #341026

**Dimensions:** 39'9" W x 26' D

**Levels:** 1

**Square Footage:** 1,009

**Bedrooms:** 3

**Bathrooms:** 2

**Foundation:** Crawl space, slab, or basement

**Materials List Available:** Yes

**Price Category:** B

*Images provided by designer/architect.*

*Copyright by designer/architect.*

## Plan #341029

**Dimensions:** 49' W x 57' D

**Levels:** 1

**Square Footage:** 1,737

**Bedrooms:** 3

**Bathrooms:** 2

**Foundation:** Crawl space, slab, or basement

**Materials List Available:** Yes

**Price Category:** C

*Images provided by designer/architect.*

*Copyright by designer/architect.*

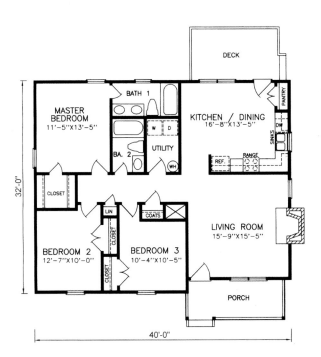

## Plan #341028

**Dimensions:** 40' W x 32' D

**Levels:** 1

**Square Footage:** 1,248

**Bedrooms:** 3

**Bathrooms:** 2

**Foundation:** Crawl space, slab, or basement

**Materials List Available:** Yes

**Price Category:** B

*Images provided by designer/architect.*

*Copyright by designer/architect.*

## Plan #321001

**Dimensions:** 83' W x 42' D

**Levels:** 1

**Square Footage:** 1,721

**Bedrooms:** 3

**Bathrooms:** 2

**Foundation:** Basement, crawl space, or slab

**Materials List Available:** Yes

**Price Category:** C

*Images provided by designer/architect.*

You'll love the atrium that creates a warm, naturally lit space inside this gracious home, as well as the roof dormers that give it wonderful curb appeal from the outside.

**Features:**

- **Great Room:** Bathed in light from the atrium window wall, this room, with its vaulted ceiling, will be the hub of your family life.

- **Dining Room:** This room also has a vaulted ceiling and is lit by the atrium, but you can draw drapes at night to create a cozy, warm feeling.

- **Kitchen:** Designed for functionality, this step-saving kitchen is easy to organize and makes cooking a pleasure.

- **Breakfast Room:** For convenience, this room is located between the kitchen and the rear covered porch.

- **Master Suite:** Retire with pleasure to this lovely retreat, with its luxurious bath.

Rear View

*Copyright by designer/architect.*

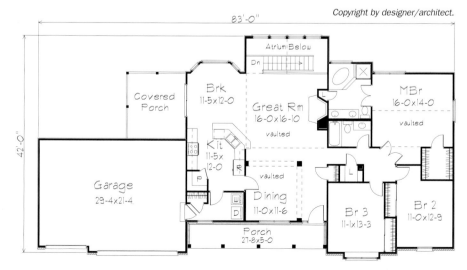

## Plan #181159

**Dimensions:** 37' W x 31' D
**Levels:** 2
**Square Footage:** 1,992
**Main Level Sq. Ft.:** 996
**Finished Basement Sq. Ft.:** 996
**Bedrooms:** 3
**Bathrooms:** 2
**Foundation:** Walk-out basement
**Materials List Available:** Yes
**Price Category:** D

*Images provided by designer/architect.*

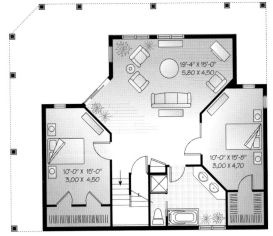

**Basement Level
Floor Plan**

*Copyright by
designer/architect.*

Ideal for the family who loves the outdoors, this charmer features a wraparound porch that creates a covered pavilion and roofed terrace.

**Features:**

- Ceiling Height: 9-ft. ceilings enhance the airy feeling given by the many windows here.

- Family Rooms: These family rooms (one on each floor) allow a busy family adequate space for entertaining a crowd.

- Kitchen: Designed for efficient work patterns, this kitchen features ample work and storage space, as well as an island that can double as a

- Bedrooms: Each bedroom features a large, walk-in closet and easy access to a large, amenity-filled bathroom with a double vanity, tub, enclosed shower, and a private toilet.

- Porch: Enjoy the panoramic view from this spacious covered porch at any time of day.

**Main Level
Floor Plan**

31'-0"
9,3 m

37'-0"
11,1 m

Images provided by designer/architect.

Copyright by designer/architect.

## Plan #151043

**Dimensions:** 53' W x 64' D

**Levels:** 1

**Square Footage:** 1,636

**Bedrooms:** 3

**Bathrooms:** 2

**Foundation:** Crawl space, slab (basement option for fee)

**Materials List Available:** Yes

**Price Category:** C

Copyright by designer/architect.

Images provided by designer/architect.

## Plan #161014

**Dimensions:** 51'8" W x 49'8" D

**Levels:** 1

**Square Footage:** 1,698

**Bedrooms:** 3

**Bathrooms:** 2

**Foundation:** Slab

**Materials List Available:** Yes

**Price Category:** C

Rear Elevation

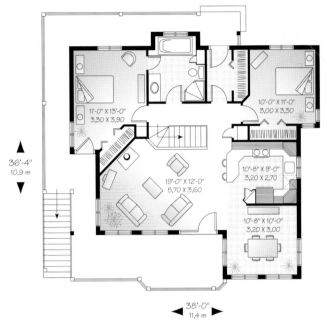

# Plan #181143

**Dimensions:** 38' W x 36'4" D

**Levels:** 1

**Square Footage:** 1,056

**Bedrooms:** 2

**Bathrooms:** 1

**Foundation:** Full basement with walkout

**Materials List Available:** Yes

**Price Category:** B

*Images provided by designer/architect.*

36'-4"
10,9 m

38'-0"
11,4 m

*Copyright by designer/architect.*

# Plan #181147

**Dimensions:** 52' W x 40' D

**Levels:** 1

**Square Footage:** 1,360

**Bedrooms:** 2

**Bathrooms:** 2

**Foundation:** Full basement with walkout

**Materials List Available:** Yes

**Price Category:** B

*Images provided by designer/architect.*

40'-0"
12,0 m

52'-0"
15,6 m

*Copyright by designer/architect.*

## Plan #291002

**Dimensions:** 62'8" W x 38'4" D

**Levels:** 1

**Square Footage:** 1,550

**Bedrooms:** 3

**Bathrooms:** 2

**Foundation:** Basement

**Materials List Available:** No

**Price Category:** C

This comfortable Southwestern-style ranch house will fit perfectly into any setting.

**Features:**

- Ceiling Height: 8 ft. unless otherwise noted.

- Front Porch: This scalloped front porch offers plenty of room for enjoying a cool summer breeze.

- Foyer: Upon entering this impressive foyer you'll be greeted by a soaring space encompassing the living room and dining room.

- Living/Dining Area: This combined living room and dining room has a handsome fireplace as its focal point. When dinner is served, guests will flow casually into the dining area.

- Kitchen: Take your cooking up a notch in this terrific kitchen. It features a 42-in.-high counter that will do double-duty as a snack bar for family meals and a wet bar for entertaining.

- Master Suite: This master retreat is separated from the other bedrooms and features an elegant vaulted ceiling. The dressing area has a compartmentalized bath and a walk-in closet.

Rear View

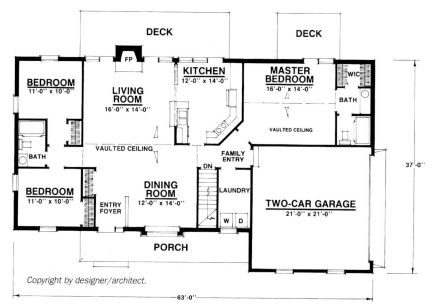

Copyright by designer/architect.

## Plan #161008

**Dimensions:** 64'2" W x 46'6" D
**Levels:** 1
**Square Footage:** 1,860
**Bedrooms:** 3
**Bathrooms:** 2
**Foundation:** Slab
**Materials List Available:** No
**Price Category:** D

*Images provided by designer/architect.*

If you enjoy casual living and formal entertaining, this delightful floor plan will attract your eye.

### Features:

- **Great Room:** A sloped ceiling and corner fireplace combine to provide this great room with an open and cozy atmosphere, perfect for relaxing evenings.

- **Kitchen:** This kitchen offers ample counter and cabinet space. A convenient snack bar provides a view to the breakfast area and great room

- **Master Suite:** Enjoy the elegance and style of this master suite, with its deluxe bath, large walk-in closet, and secluded alcove.

- **Laundry Room:** You will appreciate the ample counter space in this large laundry room with utility closet.

- **Porch:** From the breakfast area, enjoy a relaxed meal on this rear covered porch in warm weather.

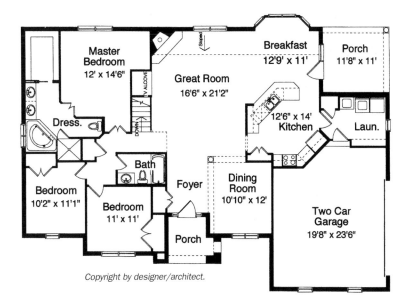

*Copyright by designer/architect.*

## SMARTtip

### Espaliered Fruit Trees

Try a technique used by the royal gardeners at Versailles—espalier. They trained the fruit trees to grow flat against the walls, creating patterns. It's not difficult, especially if you go to a reputable nursery and purchase an apple or pear tree that has already been espaliered. Plant it against a flat surface that's in a sunny spot.

Rear Elevation

## Plan #221012

**Dimensions:** 71' W x 51' D

**Levels:** 1

**Square Footage:** 1,802

**Bedrooms:** 3

**Bathrooms:** 2½

**Foundation:** Basement

**Materials List Available:** No

**Price Category:** D

*Images provided by designer/architect.*

## Plan #231004

**Dimensions:** 44' W x 37'6" D

**Levels:** 1

**Square Footage:** 1,463

**Bedrooms:** 2

**Bathrooms:** 2

**Foundation:** Crawl space

**Materials List Available:** No

**Price Category:** A

*Images provided by designer/architect.*

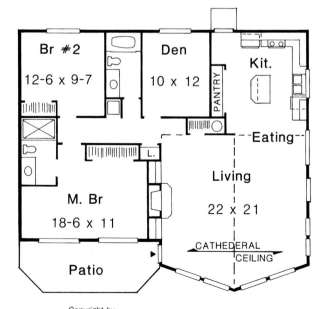

## Plan #251006

**Dimensions:** 65'5" W x 59'11" D

**Levels:** 1

**Square Footage:** 1,849

**Bedrooms:** 3

**Bathrooms:** 2

**Foundation:** Crawl space

**Materials List Available:** Yes

**Price Category:** D

*Images provided by designer/architect.*

*Copyright by designer/architect.*

## Plan #321035

**Dimensions:** 55'8" W x 46' D

**Levels:** 1

**Square Footage:** 1,384

**Bedrooms:** 2

**Bathrooms:** 2

**Foundation:** Basement

**Materials List Available:** Yes

**Price Category:** B

*Images provided by designer/architect.*

Rear View

*Copyright by designer/architect.*

**Optional Basement Level Floor Plan**

# Plan #341013

**Dimensions:** 44' W x 34' D

**Levels:** 1

**Square Footage:** 1,363

**Bedrooms:** 3

**Bathrooms:** 2

**Foundation:** Crawl space, slab, or basement

**Materials List Available:** Yes

**Price Category:** B

*Images provided by designer/architect.*

The luxurious amenities in this compact, well designed home are sure to delight everyone in the family.

**Features:**

- Ceiling Height: 9-ft. ceilings add to the spacious feeling created by the open design.

- Family Room: A vaulted ceiling and large window area add elegance to this comfortable room, which will be the heart of this home.

- Dining Area: Adjoining the kitchen, this room features a large bayed area as well as French doors that open onto the back deck.

- Kitchen: This step-saving design will make cooking a joy for everyone in the family.

- Utility Room: Near the kitchen, this room includes cabinets and shelves for extra storage space.

- Master Suite: A triple window, tray ceiling, walk-in closet, and luxurious bath make this area a treat.

*Copyright by designer/architect.*

## Plan #131008

**Dimensions:** 45'4" W x 36'4" D
**Levels:** 1
**Square Footage:** 1,299
**Bedrooms:** 3
**Bathrooms:** 2
**Foundation:** Crawl space, basement
**Materials List Available:** Yes
**Price Category:** C

*Images provided by designer/architect.*

Build this home in a vacation spot or any other location where you'll treasure the convenience of having three different outdoor entrances.

**Features:**

- Ceiling Height: 8 ft.

- Living Room: Sliding glass doors open onto the large deck area and serve to let bright, natural light stream into the home during the day. Add drapes to keep the house cozy at night and on cloudy winter days.

- Kitchen: Shaped like a galley, this kitchen is so well designed that you'll love working in it. Counter space and cabinets add to its practicality, and a windowed nook makes it charming.

- Master Suite: Enjoy the private bath attached to the bedroom in this quiet area.

- Additional Bedrooms: These nicely sized rooms share another full bathroom.

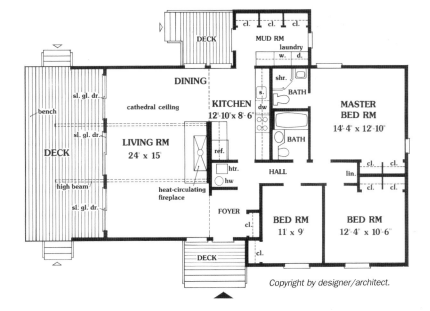

*Copyright by designer/architect.*

Rear View

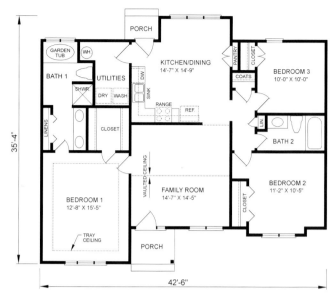

## Plan #341010

**Dimensions:** 42'6" W x 35'4" D

**Levels:** 1

**Square Footage:** 1,261

**Bedrooms:** 3

**Bathrooms:** 2

**Foundation:** Crawl space, slab, or basement

**Materials List Available:** Yes

**Price Category:** B

## Plan #341012

**Dimensions:** 43'2" W x 33'6" D

**Levels:** 1

**Square Footage:** 1,316

**Bedrooms:** 3

**Bathrooms:** 2

**Foundation:** Crawl space, slab, or basement

**Materials List Available:** Yes

**Price Category:** B

Images provided by
designer/architect.

## Plan #341027

**Dimensions:** 54' W x 55'10" D

**Levels:** 1

**Square Footage:** 1,657

**Bedrooms:** 3

**Bathrooms:** 2

**Foundation:** Crawl space, slab,
or basement

**Materials List Available:** Yes

**Price Category:** C

Copyright by designer/architect.

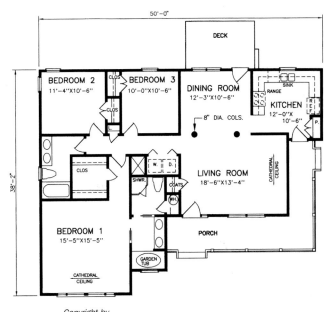

Images provided by
designer/architect.

## Plan #341034

**Dimensions:** 50' W x 38'2" D

**Levels:** 1

**Square Footage:** 1,445

**Bedrooms:** 3

**Bathrooms:** 2

**Foundation:** Crawl space, slab,
or basement

**Materials List Available:** Yes

**Price Category:** B

Copyright by
designer/architect.

## Plan #131015

**Dimensions:** 57'4" W x 56'10" D
**Levels:** 1
**Square Footage:** 1,860
**Bedrooms:** 3
**Bathrooms:** 2
**Foundation:** Basement, crawl space, or slab
**Materials List Available:** Yes
**Price Category:** E

*Images provided by designer/architect.*

The mixture of country charm and formal elegance is sure to thrill any family looking for a distinctive and comfortable home.

**Features:**

• Great Room: Separated from the dining room by a columned arch, this spacious room has a stepped ceiling, a built-in media center, and a fireplace. French doors within a rear bay lead to the large backyard patio at the rear of the house.

• Dining Room: Graced by a bay window, this formal room has an impressive 11-ft. 6-in.-high stepped ceiling.

• Breakfast Room: With a 12-ft. sloped ceiling, this room shares an eating bar with the kitchen.

• Master Bedroom: The 10-ft. tray ceiling and bay window contribute elegance, and the walk-in closet and bath with a bayed nook, whirlpool tub, and separate shower make it practical.

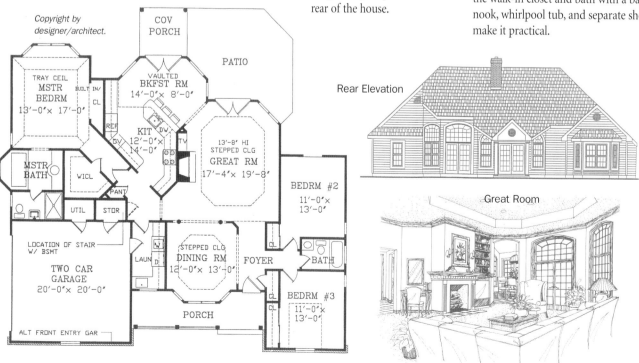

*Copyright by designer/architect.*

Rear Elevation

Great Room

## Plan #121059

**Dimensions:** 52' W x 59'4" D
**Levels:** 1
**Square Footage:** 1,782
**Bedrooms:** 3
**Bathrooms:** 2
**Foundation:** Basement
**Materials List Available:** Yes
**Price Category:** C

*Images provided by designer/architect.*

This home is ideal for families looking for luxury and style mixed with convenience.

**Features:**

- Great Room: This large room is enhanced by the three-sided fireplace it shares with adjacent living areas.

- Hearth Room: Enjoy the fireplace here, too, and decorate to emphasize the bayed windows.

- Kitchen: This kitchen was designed for efficiency and is flooded with natural light.

- Breakfast Area: Picture-awing windows are the highlight in this area.

- Master Suite: A boxed ceiling and walk-in closet as well as a bath with a double-vanity, whirlpool tub, shower, and window with a plant ledge make this suite a true retreat.

- Bedrooms: These lovely bedrooms are served by a luxurious full bath.

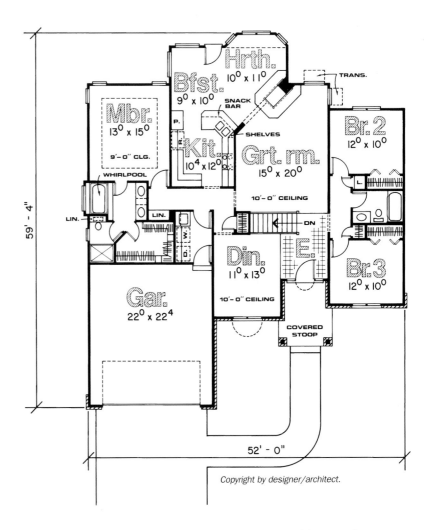

*Copyright by designer/architect.*

## Plan #131002

**Dimensions:** 70'1" W x 60'7" D
**Levels:** 1
**Square Footage:** 1,709
**Bedrooms:** 3
**Bathrooms:** 2½
**Foundation:** Basement, crawl space, or slab
**Materials List Available:** Yes
**Price Category:** D

*Images provided by designer/architect.*

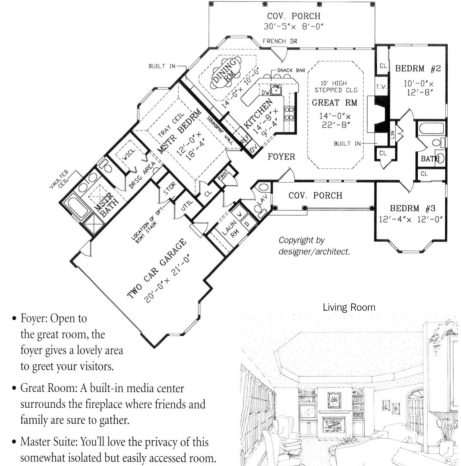

**Living Room**

Rear View

You'll love the way this angled ranch brings out the best in a corner lot or on a slope.

**Features:**

Ceiling Height: 8 ft.

- Front Porch: Hang baskets of plants from the roof of this porch, which is just the right size for a couple of rockers and a side table.

- Dining Room: Well-placed windows flood this room with sunlight during the day and a built-in cabinet gives ample storage space for all your china, linens, and collectables.

- Foyer: Open to the great room, the foyer gives a lovely area to greet your visitors.

- Great Room: A built-in media center surrounds the fireplace where friends and family are sure to gather.

- Master Suite: You'll love the privacy of this somewhat isolated but easily accessed room. Decorate to show off the large bay window and tray ceiling, and enjoy the luxury of a compartmented bathroom.

## Plan #271001

**Dimensions:** 55' W x 36' D
**Levels:** 1
**Square Footage:** 1,400
**Bedrooms:** 3
**Bathrooms:** 2
**Foundation:** Basement
**Materials List Available:** Yes
**Price Category:** B

This contemporary design builds on the basics, creating a comfortable home that offers possibilities for entertaining or quiet downtime.

**Features:**

- Great room: The heart of the home, this massive gathering room features a handsome fireplace and a handy wet bar, and flows into the dining space. Sliding glass doors between the two spaces lead to a deck.

- Kitchen/Breakfast: This combination space uses available space efficiently and comfortably.

- Master Suite: The inviting master bedroom includes a private bath.

*Images provided by designer/architect.*

Deck

Master Br
15-4x11

Great Room
16-8x19

Dining

Kitchen/ Brkfst
13-8x12-8

Bar

dn

Den/Br 3
11-4x12-4

Br 2
11x10

Garage
19-4x19-4

35'-4"

52'-8"

*Copyright by designer/architect.*

## SMARTtip

### Candid Camera for Your Landscaping

To see your home and yard as others see them, take some camera shots. Seeing your house and landscaping on film will create an opportunity for objectivity. Problems will become more obvious, and you will then be better able to prioritize your home improvements, as well as your landscaping plan.

## Plan #151070

**Dimensions:** 54'2" W x 57'4" D

**Levels:** 1

**Square Footage:** 1,786

**Bedrooms:** 3

**Bathrooms:** 2

**Foundation:** Crawl space, slab (basement option for fee)

**Materials List Available:** Yes

**Price Category:** C

*Images provided by designer/architect.*

*Copyright by designer/architect.*

## SMARTtip

### Using Wall Anchors

Where a pilaster doesn't fall over a stud, use a combination of construction adhesive and an anchor-type fastener.

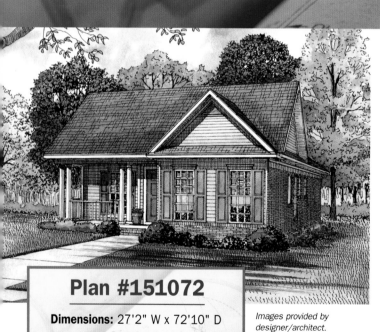

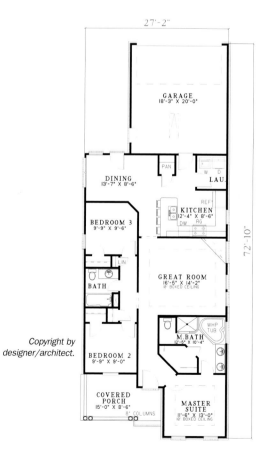

## Plan #151072

**Dimensions:** 27'2" W x 72'10" D

**Levels:** 1

**Square Footage:** 1,263

**Bedrooms:** 3

**Bathrooms:** 2

**Foundation:** Crawl space, slab

**Materials List Available:** Yes

**Price Category:** B

*Images provided by designer/architect.*

*Copyright by designer/architect.*

## Plan #131040

**Dimensions:** 50' W x 37' D
**Levels:** 1
**Square Footage:** 1,630
**Bedrooms:** 3
**Bathrooms:** 2
**Foundation:** Basement, crawl space, or slab
**Materials List Available:** Yes
**Price Category:** D

The raised main level of this home makes this plan ideal for any site that has an expansive view, and you can finish the lower level as an office, library, or space for the kids to play.

**Features:**

- **Living Room:** This sunken living room with a prow-shaped front is sure to be a focal point where both guests and family gather in this lovely ranch home. A see-through fireplace separates this room from the dining room.

- **Dining Room:** A dramatic vaulted ceiling covers both this room and the adjacent living room, creating a spacious feeling.

- **Kitchen:** Designed for efficiency, you'll love the features and location of this convenient kitchen.

- **Master Suite:** Luxuriate in the privacy this suite affords and enjoy the two large closets, sumptuous private bath, and sliding glass doors that can open to the optional rear deck.

**Rear Elevation**

## Main Level Floor Plan

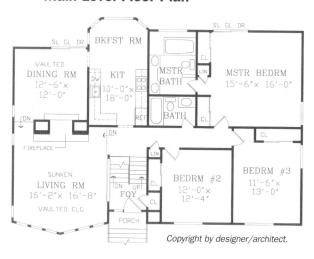

*Copyright by designer/architect.*

## Lower Level Floor Plan

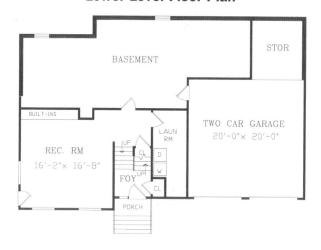

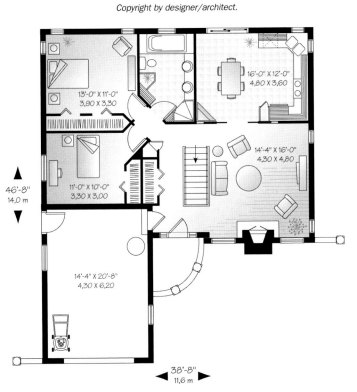

## Plan #181019

**Dimensions:** 59'8" W x 44'4" D

**Levels:** 1

**Square Footage:** 1,494

**Bedrooms:** 3

**Bathrooms:** 1

**Foundation:** Full basement

**Materials List Available:** Yes

**Price Category:** B

*Images provided by designer/architect.*

*Copyright by designer/architect.*

*Copyright by designer/architect.*

## Plan #181016

**Dimensions:** 38'8" W x 46'8" D

**Levels:** 1

**Square Footage:** 1,080

**Bedrooms:** 2

**Bathrooms:** 1

**Foundation:** Full basement

**Materials List Available:** Yes

**Price Category:** B

*Images provided by designer/architect.*

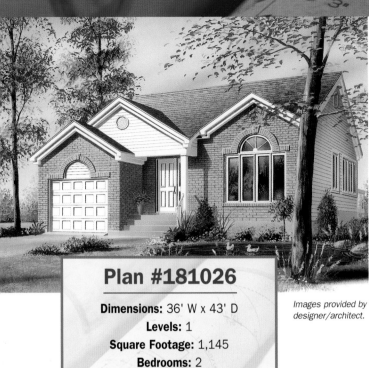

## Plan #181026

**Dimensions:** 36' W x 43' D

**Levels:** 1

**Square Footage:** 1,145

**Bedrooms:** 2

**Bathrooms:** 1

**Foundation:** Full basement

**Materials List Available:** Yes

**Price Category:** B

*Images provided by designer/architect.*

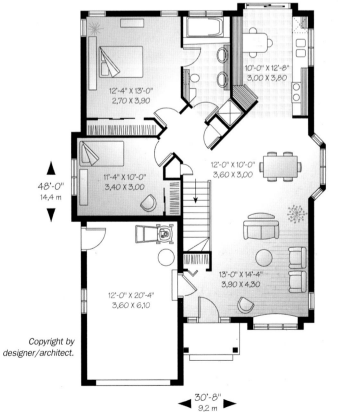

43'-0"
12,9 m

36'-0"
10,8 m

11'-4" X 13'-0"
3,40 X 3,90

12'-4" X 9'-8"
3,70 X 2,90

8'-4" X 12'-8"
2,50 X 3,80

10'-8" X 8'-8"
3,20 X 2,60

12'-0" X 11'-0"
3,60 X 3,30

12'-0" X 20'-4"
3,60 X 6,10

14'-8" X 11'-8"
4,40 X 3,50

*Copyright by designer/architect.*

## Plan #181027

**Dimensions:** 30'8" W x 48' D

**Levels:** 1

**Square Footage:** 1,103

**Bedrooms:** 2

**Bathrooms:** 1

**Foundation:** Full basement

**Materials List Available:** Yes

**Price Category:** B

*Images provided by designer/architect.*

48'-0"
14,4 m

30'-8"
9,2 m

12'-4" X 13'-0"
2,70 X 3,90

10'-0" X 12'-8"
3,00 X 3,80

11'-4" X 10'-0"
3,40 X 3,00

12'-0" X 10'-0"
3,60 X 3,00

12'-0" X 20'-4"
3,60 X 6,10

13'-0" X 14'-4"
3,90 X 4,30

*Copyright by designer/architect.*

## Plan #151036

**Dimensions:** 46'10" W x 56'4" D
**Levels:** 1
**Square Footage:** 1,474
**Bedrooms:** 3
**Bathrooms:** 2
**Foundation:** Crawl space or slab; basement with fee
**Materials List Available:** Yes
**Price Category:** B

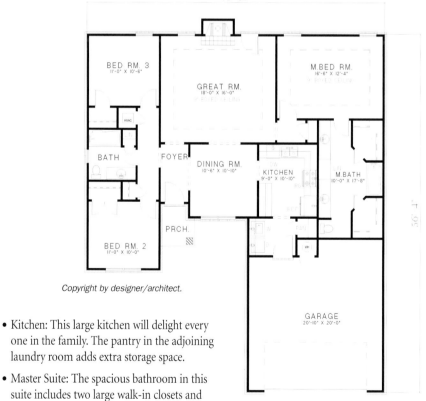

Copyright by designer/architect.

You'll love the elegant exterior design of this home and be delighted with the many features that make it ideal for a rich family life.

**Features:**

- Great Room: A stunning boxed ceiling and handsome gas fireplace make this room a beauty, and a door to the back adds practicality.

- Dining Room: Open to the foyer and great room, this room lets you dine formally as well as casually.

- Kitchen: This large kitchen will delight every one in the family. The pantry in the adjoining laundry room adds extra storage space.

- Master Suite: The spacious bathroom in this suite includes two large walk-in closets and two vanities. In the spacious bedroom, a boxed ceiling adds an elegant note.

- Additional Bedrooms: Both rooms feature walk-in closets and easy access to a shared bath.

## Plan #151049

**Dimensions:** 41'6" W x 57'8" D
**Levels:** 1
**Square Footage:** 1,355
**Bedrooms:** 3
**Bathrooms:** 2
**Foundation:** Crawl space or slab; basement with fee
**Materials List Available:** Yes
**Price Category:** B

Your whole family will love this home, with its elegant public areas and large, comfortable bedrooms for the family.

### Features:

- **Great Room:** Just off the foyer, this great room features a boxed ceiling and a gas fireplace. A doorway leads to the rear covered porch.

- **Dining Room:** A vaulted ceiling sets the tone for this lovely room, which is open to the kitchen for ease of serving.

- **Kitchen:** This spacious room includes a pantry for extra storage area and a snack bar where friends and family can sit and visit with the cook.

- **Master Suite:** A boxed ceiling gives grandeur to the bedroom in this spacious suite, and a walk-in closet gives practicality. The double vanity in the bath is separated from the tub and toilet.

- **Laundry Area:** This spacious area opens to the garage beyond for cover on those rainy days.

*Images provided by designer/architect.*

*Copyright by designer/architect.*

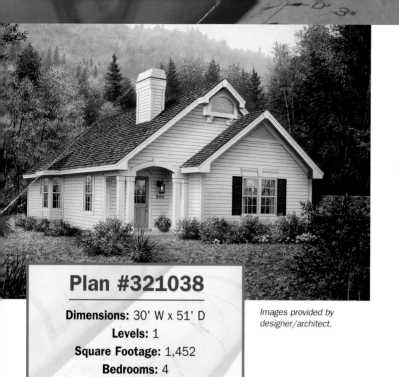

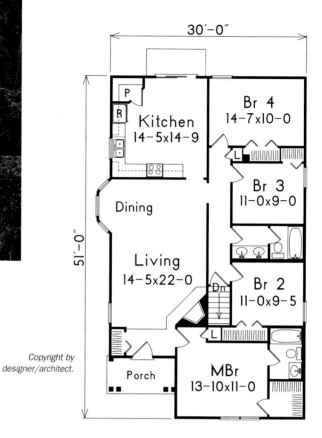

## Plan #321038

**Dimensions:** 30' W x 51' D

**Levels:** 1

**Square Footage:** 1,452

**Bedrooms:** 4

**Bathrooms:** 2

**Foundation:** Basement

**Materials List Available:** Yes

**Price Category:** B

*Images provided by designer/architect.*

*Copyright by designer/architect.*

30'-0"

51'-0"

P
R
Kitchen
14-5x14-9

Br 4
14-7x10-0

Dining

Br 3
11-0x9-0

Living
14-5x22-0

Dn

Br 2
11-0x9-5

Porch

MBr
13-10x11-0

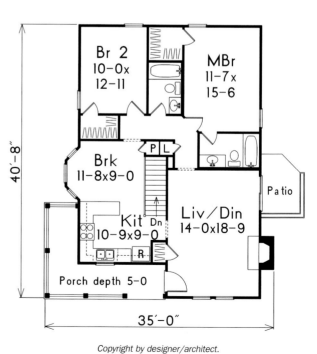

## Plan #321040

**Dimensions:** 35' W x 40'8" D

**Levels:** 1

**Square Footage:** 1,084

**Bedrooms:** 2

**Bathrooms:** 2

**Foundation:** Basement

**Materials List Available:** Yes

**Price Category:** B

*Images provided by designer/architect.*

40'-8"

Br 2
10-0x
12-11

MBr
11-7x
15-6

Brk
11-8x9-0

Patio

P L

Kit
10-9x9-0

Dn

Liv/Din
14-0x18-9

R

Porch depth 5-0

35'-0"

*Copyright by designer/architect.*

## Plan #151052

**Dimensions:** 33'10" W x 69'6" D
**Levels:** 1
**Square Footage:** 1,660
**Bedrooms:** 3
**Bathrooms:** 2
**Foundation:** Crawl space, slab
**Materials List Available:** Yes
**Price Category:** C

*Images provided by designer/architect.*

*Copyright by designer/architect.*

## Plan #151078

**Dimensions:** 73'4" W x 51'8" D
**Levels:** 1
**Square Footage:** 1,871
**Bedrooms:** 3
**Bathrooms:** 3½
**Foundation:** Crawl space, slab, or basement
**Materials List Available:** Yes
**Price Category:** D

*Images provided by designer/architect.*

*Copyright by designer/architect.*

**Bonus Area**

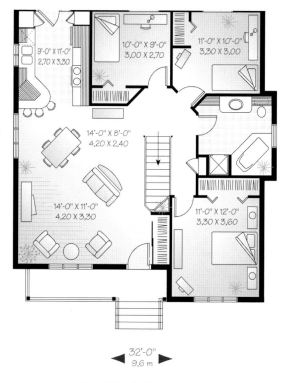

## Plan #181007

**Dimensions:** : 32' W x 36' D

**Levels:** 1

**Square Footage:** 1,090

**Bedrooms:** 3

**Bathrooms:** 1

**Foundation:** Full basement

**Materials List Available:** Yes

**Price Category:** B

*Images provided by designer/architect.*

36'-0"
10,8 m

32'-0"
9,6 m

*Copyright by designer/architect.*

---

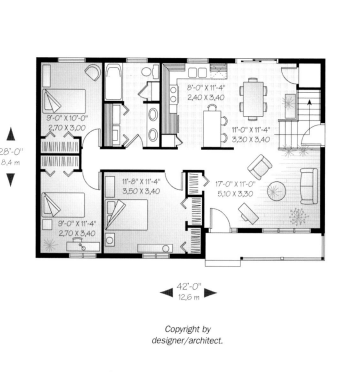

## Plan #181008

**Dimensions:** : 42' W x 28' D

**Levels:** 1

**Square Footage:** 1,106

**Bedrooms:** 3

**Bathrooms:** 1

**Foundation:** Full basement

**Materials List Available:** Yes

**Price Category:** B

*Images provided by designer/architect.*

28'-0"
8,4 m

42'-0"
12,6 m

*Copyright by designer/architect.*

Copyright by designer/architect.

## Plan #181017

**Dimensions:** 62' W x 43' D
**Levels:** 1
**Square Footage:** 1,736
**Bedrooms:** 3
**Bathrooms:** 2
**Foundation:** Full basement
**Materials List Available:** Yes
**Price Category:** C

*Images provided by designer/architect.*

## SMARTtip
## Simplify Your Deck Design

If your railing is an elaborate Chinese-Chippendale style, you may want to keep the design of benches, planters, and decking basic to prevent visual competition between the elements.

## Plan #181022

**Dimensions:** 46' W x 40'4" D
**Levels:** 1
**Square Footage:** 1,098
**Bedrooms:** 2
**Bathrooms:** 1
**Foundation:** Full basement
**Materials List Available:** Yes
**Price Category:** B

*Images provided by designer/architect.*

Copyright by designer/architect.

## Plan #291009

**Dimensions:** 74'8" W x 41'4" D

**Levels:** 2

**Square Footage:** 1,655

**Main Level Sq. Ft.:** 1,277

**Upper Level Sq. Ft.:** 378

**Bedrooms:** 3

**Bathrooms:** 2

**Foundation:** Basement

**Materials List Available:** No

**Price Category:** C

If your family loves a northern European look, they'll appreciate the curved eaves and arched window that give this lovely home its character.

**Features:**

- **Entryway:** The front door welcomes both friends and family into a lovely open design on the first floor of this home.

- **Living Room:** The enormous arched window floods this room with natural light in the daytime. At night, draw drapes across it to create a warm, intimate feeling.

- **Dining Room:** Windows are the highlight of this room, too, but here, the angled bay window area opens to the rear deck.

- **Kitchen:** The family cook will be delighted with this well-planned kitchen, which is a snap to organize.

- **Master Suite:** Located on the first floor, this suite includes a private bath for total convenience.

*Images provided by designer/architect.*

### Main Level Floor Plan

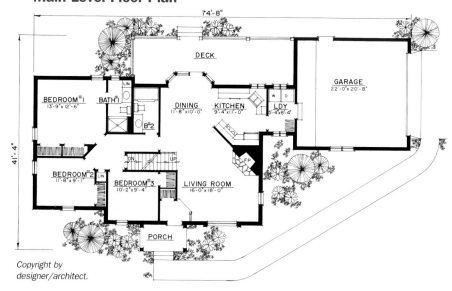

*Copyright by designer/architect.*

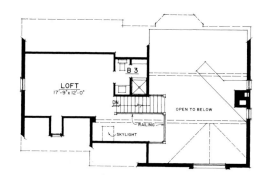

### Upper Level Floor Plan

## Plan #221019

**Dimensions:** 64'8" W x 57' D

**Levels:** 1

**Square Footage:** 1,591

**Bedrooms:** 3

**Bathrooms:** 2

**Foundation:** Basement

**Materials List Available:** No

**Price Category:** C

*Images provided by designer/architect.*

You'll be delighted with the many luxurious elements included in this compact home.

**Features:**

• Ceiling Height: 9 ft.

• Great Room: A vaulted ceiling sets the elegant tone you'll find reflected in the rest of this gracious home. The fireplace, flanked by windows, and the open entry to the dining room make everyone feel comfortable.

• Dining Room: A tray ceiling distinguishes this formal room. You'll find a door to the large screened porch from this room, so it's easy to serve meals here when the weather's fine or relax with a beverage at the end of the day.

• Kitchen: The ample counter and cabinet space make this kitchen a delight, and the eating bar encourages lots of little visitors.

• Master Suite: With a tray ceiling and huge walk-in closet, this suite's bedroom makes you feel elegant. The large bathroom, with its whirlpool tub, standing shower, and dual-sink vanity, confirms the feeling.

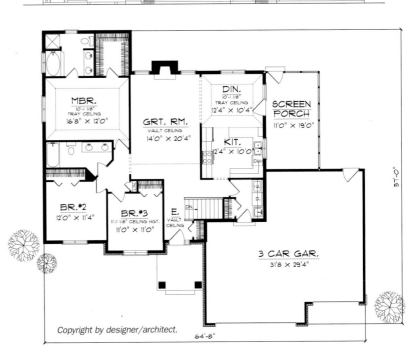

Rear Elevation

*Copyright by designer/architect.*

*Copyright by designer/architect.*

## Plan #321012

**Dimensions:** 58'8" W x 51'2" D

**Levels:** 1

**Square Footage:** 1,882

**Bedrooms:** 3

**Bathrooms:** 2

**Foundation:** Basement

**Materials List Available:** Yes

**Price Category:** D

*Images provided by designer/architect.*

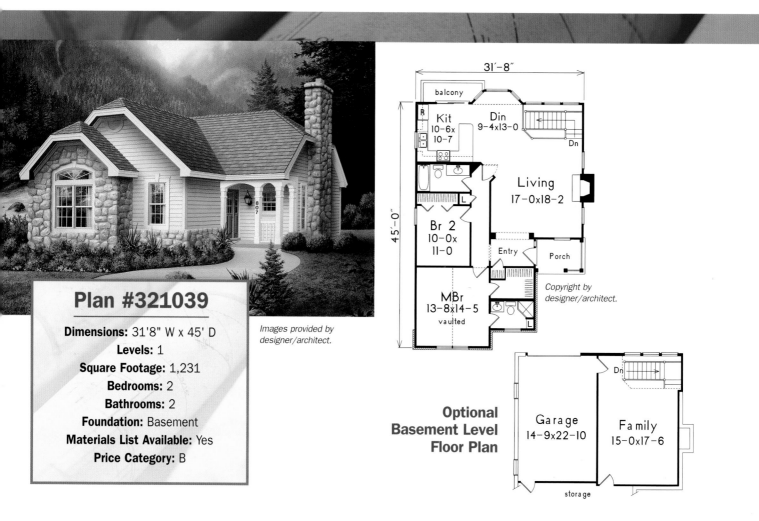

*Copyright by designer/architect.*

**Optional Basement Level Floor Plan**

## Plan #321039

**Dimensions:** 31'8" W x 45' D

**Levels:** 1

**Square Footage:** 1,231

**Bedrooms:** 2

**Bathrooms:** 2

**Foundation:** Basement

**Materials List Available:** Yes

**Price Category:** B

*Images provided by designer/architect.*

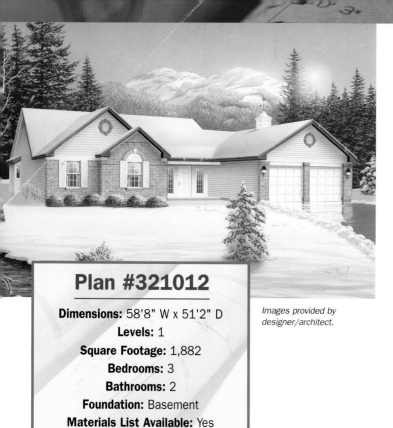

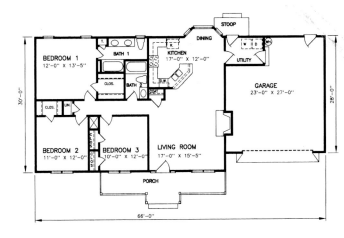

*Images provided by designer/architect.*

## Plan #341005

**Dimensions:** 66' W x 30' D

**Levels:** 1

**Square Footage:** 1,334

**Bedrooms:** 3

**Bathrooms:** 2

**Foundation:** Crawl space, slab, or basement

**Materials List Available:** Yes

**Price Category:** B

*Copyright by designer/architect.*

## Plan #341022

**Dimensions:** 58'4" W x 31'10" D

**Levels:** 1

**Square Footage:** 1,281

**Bedrooms:** 3

**Bathrooms:** 2

**Foundation:** Crawl space, slab, or basement

**Materials List Available:** Yes

**Price Category:** B

*Images provided by designer/architect.*

*Copyright by designer/architect.*

## Plan #181018

**Dimensions:** 39' W x 45' D
**Levels:** 1
**Square Footage:** 1,231
**Bedrooms:** 2
**Bathrooms:** 1
**Foundation:** Basement
**Materials List Available:** Yes
**Price Category:** B

*Images provided by designer/architect.*

The dramatic double-glass-door arched entry sets the tone for this elegant European beauty.

**Features:**

• Ceiling Height: 8 ft.

• Family Room: Family and friends will be drawn to the warmth and grace of this room, which is filled with natural light streaming

from the spectacular full wall of windows. Warm yourself by the fireplace.

• Kitchen: This kitchen shares the fireplace with the adjoining family room. Cooking will be a pleasure, thanks to plenty of counter space and a double pantry.

• Breakfast Area: This eat-in area off the kitchen offers plenty of room for the whole family to enjoy informal meals.

• Bedrooms: The flexible floor plan offers either one large master suite with a walk-in closet or two nicely sized bedrooms, each with its own closets. Both options include a luxurious full bathroom with a relaxing whirlpool tub.

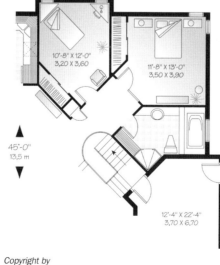

**Alternate Floor Plan**

45'-0"
13,5 m

*Copyright by designer/architect.*

39'-0"
11,7 m

## Plan #241006

**Dimensions:** 51' W x 53' D
**Levels:** 1
**Square Footage:** 1,744
**Bedrooms:** 3
**Bathrooms:** 2
**Foundation:** Slab
**Materials List Available:** No
**Price Category:** C

The striking rooflines and arched window of this split-bedroom home will captivate onlookers and guests.

**Features:**

- Great Room: A spacious foyer introduces this great room, which features a cozy corner fireplace. Guests will enjoy a natural flow through a columned entry to the formal dining room or through a French door to the rear yard.

- Kitchen: Designed for total convenience, this kitchen features ample counter space, an eating bar, a pantry, and a roomy breakfast area. A 42-in.-high wall separating it from the dining room maximizes the openness of the kitchen.

- Master Suite: You will enjoy the comfort and privacy of this master suite, which features a whirlpool tub, dual vanities, a corner glass shower, and a large walk-in closet.

- Additional Bedrooms: Two secondary bedrooms share a common bath.

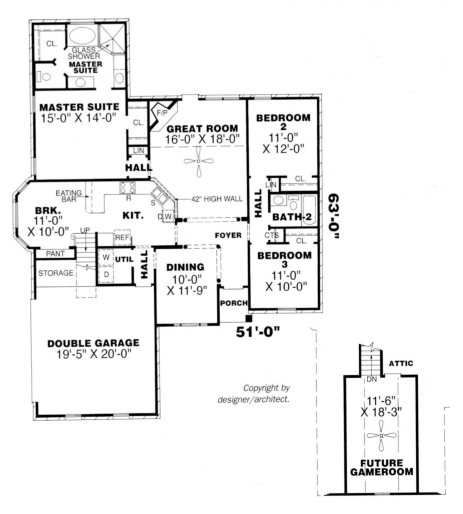

# Plan #131007

**Dimensions:** 59'10" W x 47'8" D
**Levels:** 1
**Square Footage:** 1,595
**Bedrooms:** 3
**Bathrooms:** 2
**Foundation:** Crawl space, slab, basement, or walkout
**Materials List Available:** Yes
**Price Category:** D

*Images provided by designer/architect.*

Imagine living in this home, with its traditional country comfort and individual brand of charm.

**Features:**

- Exterior elements: The mixture of a front porch with a cameo front door, decorative posts, bay windows, and dormers will delight you.

- Great Room: A tray ceiling gives distinction to this large room, and a wet bar eases entertaining.

- Screened Porch: At dusk and dawn, this porch is sure to be your favorite outdoor spot.

- Kitchen: Eat any meal in this large kitchen for a touch of homey charm.

- Dining Room: Perfect for hosting a formal dinner, this bayed dining room can increase your enjoyment of simple family meals.

- Master Bedroom: For the sake of privacy, this room is somewhat secluded. Decorate to emphasize the elegant tray ceiling.

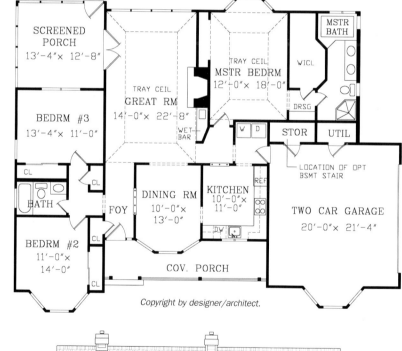

*Copyright by designer/architect.*

Rear Elevation

## Plan #211002

**Dimensions:** 68' W x 62' D
**Levels:** 1
**Square Footage:** 1,792
**Bedrooms:** 3
**Bathrooms:** 2
**Foundation:** Crawl space
**Materials List Available:** Yes
**Price Category:** C

Arched windows on the front of this home give it a European style that you're sure to love.

## SMARTtip

### Water Features

Water features create the ambiance of a soothing oasis on a deck. A water-filled urn becomes a mirror that reflects the sky—making a small deck look larger. Fish flashing in an ornamental pool add color and act as a focal point for a deck with no view.

A water fountain introduces a pleasant rhythmical sound that helps drown out the background noises of traffic and nearby neighbors.

**Features:**

• Living Room: The 12-ft. ceiling in this large, open room enhances its spacious feeling. A fireplace adds warmth on chilly days and cool evenings.

• Dining Room: Decorate to accentuate the 12-ft. ceiling and formal feeling of this room.

• Kitchen: Designed for comfort and efficiency, this room also has a 12-ft. ceiling. The cozy breakfast bar is a natural gathering spot for friends and family.

• Master Suite: A split design guarantees privacy here. A sloped cathedral ceiling adds elegance, and a walk-in closet makes it practical. The bath has two vanities, a tub, and a walk-in shower.

• Garage: Park two cars here, and use the balance of this 520 sq. ft. area as a handy storage area.

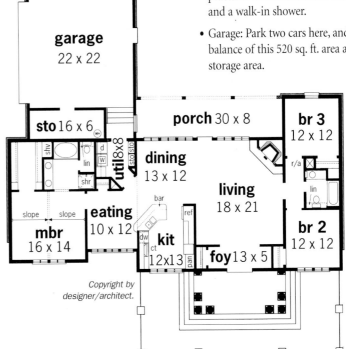

*Copyright by designer/architect.*

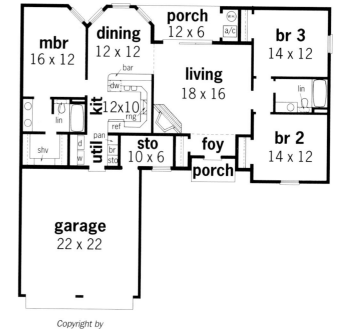

*Images provided by designer/architect.*

*Copyright by designer/architect.*

## Plan #211026

**Dimensions:** 56' W x 50' D
**Levels:** 1
**Square Footage:** 1,415
**Bedrooms:** 3
**Bathrooms:** 2
**Foundation:** Slab
**Materials List Available:** Yes
**Price Category:** B

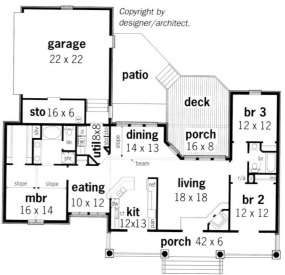

*Copyright by designer/architect.*

*Images provided by designer/architect.*

## Plan #211029

**Dimensions:** 68' W x 60' D
**Levels:** 1
**Square Footage:** 1,672
**Bedrooms:** 3
**Bathrooms:** 2
**Foundation:** Crawl space
**Materials List Available:** Yes
**Price Category:** C

## SMARTtip

### Ponds

If a pond or small body of water already exists on your property, arrange your garden elements to take advantage of it. Build a bridge over it to connect it to other areas of the garden. If there's a dock already in place, make use of it for an instant midday picnic for one.

*Copyright by designer/architect.*

## Plan #151054

**Dimensions:** 71'2" W x 54'10" D

**Levels:** 1

**Square Footage:** 1,746

**Bedrooms:** 3

**Bathrooms:** 2

**Foundation:** Crawl space, slab, with basement option for fee

**Materials List Available:** Yes

**Price Category:** C

*Images provided by designer/architect.*

*Copyright by designer/architect.*

## Plan #211037

**Dimensions:** 66' W x 60' D

**Levels:** 1

**Square Footage:** 1,800

**Bedrooms:** 3

**Bathrooms:** 2

**Foundation:** Crawl space

**Materials List Available:** Yes

**Price Category:** D

*Images provided by designer/architect.*

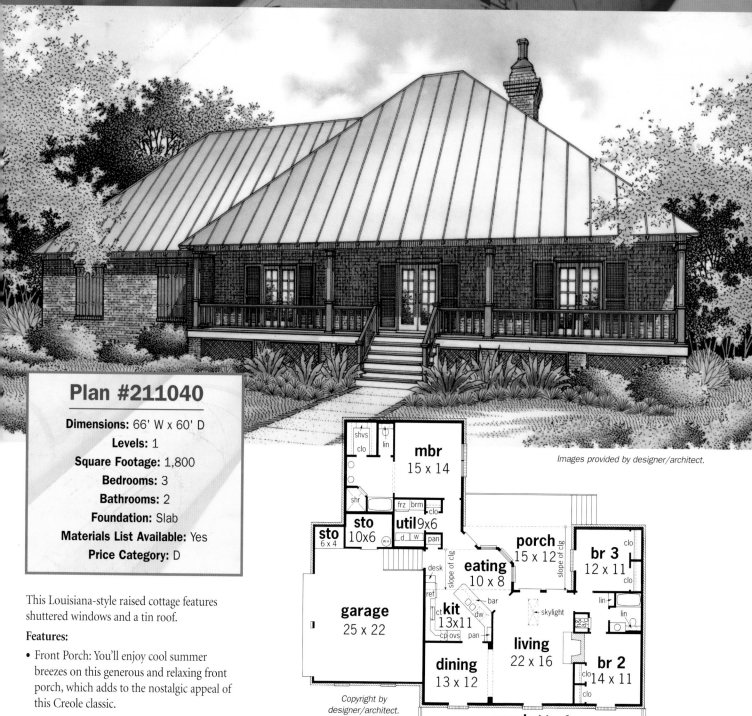

## Plan #211040

**Dimensions:** 66' W x 60' D
**Levels:** 1
**Square Footage:** 1,800
**Bedrooms:** 3
**Bathrooms:** 2
**Foundation:** Slab
**Materials List Available:** Yes
**Price Category:** D

*Images provided by designer/architect.*

*Copyright by designer/architect.*

This Louisiana-style raised cottage features shuttered windows and a tin roof.

**Features:**

- **Front Porch:** You'll enjoy cool summer breezes on this generous and relaxing front porch, which adds to the nostalgic appeal of this Creole classic.

- **French Doors:** These elegant doors lead from the front porch to the formal living areas and the front bedroom.

- **Master Bedroom Suite:** You'll enjoy the open space, walk-in closet, and master bath amenities.

### Floor plan labels

mbr 15 x 14 · sto 10x6 · sto 6 x 4 · util 9x6 · garage 25 x 22 · eating 10 x 8 · porch 15 x 12 · br 3 12 x 11 · kit 13x11 · living 22 x 16 · dining 13 x 12 · br 2 14 x 11 · porch 44 x 6 · skylight · desk · ref · bar

## SMARTtip

### Folding and Draping Swags

Plaids and stripes are a traditional choice for swags and jabots. But how they are folded and draped has a significant effect on the resulting overall pattern. For example, the lines can be positioned to be vertical and horizontal, or they can be draped as a diagonal. In addition, installing the darker-value stripes as the outer part of the pleat will create a totally different look from the one produced by setting the lighter value there. Try folding the fabric in different ways and pleat depths before you finally decide on the look that you prefer.

## Plan #131042

**Dimensions:** 75' W x 43'4" D
**Levels:** 2
**Square Footage:** 1,815
**Main Level Sq. Ft.:** 1,815
**Upper Level:** Unfinished bonus room
**Bedrooms:** 3
**Bathrooms:** 2
**Foundation:** Crawl space, slab, or basement
**Materials List Available:** Yes
**Price Category:** E

*Images provided by designer/architect.*

If family life is important to you, you'll love the design of this gracious home.

**Features:**

• Great Room: The location of this pavilion-styled room—from front to back and between the kitchen and the bedroom wing—make it the natural hub of the house. The 10-ft. ceiling and built-in fireplace add to the comfort.

• Kitchen: Beyond the great room, you'll find this warm kitchen, which is visually connected to the breakfast area and just around the corner from the formal dining room. Good counter space and a thoughtful design make it a pleasure to cook in this room.

• Master Suite: Tucked away for privacy, this master suite is sure to be your favorite place to relax and unwind at the end of a busy day.

• Rear Porch: Entertain here, or save the space for family activities.

• Bonus Room: The kids will love this extra space.

### Upper Level Floor Plan

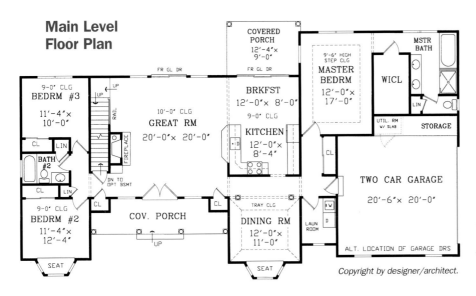

**Main Level Floor Plan**

*Copyright by designer/architect.*

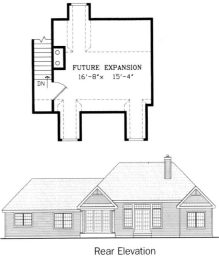

*Rear Elevation*

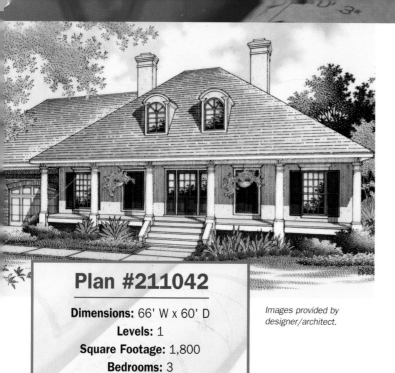

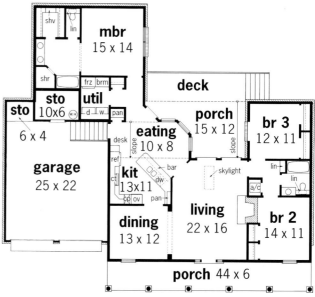

## Plan #211042

**Dimensions:** 66' W x 60' D

**Levels:** 1

**Square Footage:** 1,800

**Bedrooms:** 3

**Bathrooms:** 2

**Foundation:** Crawl space

**Materials List Available:** Yes

**Price Category:** D

*Images provided by designer/architect.*

mbr 15 x 14

deck

sto 10x6

util

sto 6 x 4

porch 15 x 12

br 3 12 x 11

eating 10 x 8

garage 25 x 22

kit 13x11

bar

skylight

living 22 x 16

br 2 14 x 11

dining 13 x 12

porch 44 x 6

*Copyright by designer/architect.*

---

## Plan #291010

**Dimensions:** 68' W x 33' D

**Levels:** 2

**Square Footage:** 1,776

**Main Level Sq. Ft.:** 1,182

**Upper Level Sq. Ft.:** 594

**Bedrooms:** 3

**Bathrooms:** 2½

**Foundation:** Basement

**Materials List Available:** No

**Price Category:** C

*Images provided by designer/architect.*

### Main Level Floor Plan

MASTER BEDROOM 15'-8"x 12'-9"

MR. BATH

GREAT ROOM 21'-3" x 12'-9"

GARAGE 20'-6"x22'-0"

DINING ROOM 12'-10"x 11'-2"

KIT. 8'-6" 10'-6"

LDY

ENTRY

MORNING RM 8'-6" x 7'-9"

MORNING PATIO

FIRST FLOOR PLAN

*Copyright by designer/architect.*

### Upper Level Floor Plan

BATH #2

OPEN TO VAULTED CEILING

BEDROOM #2 13'-4"x14'-4"

RAILING

BEDROOM #3 11'-0"x14'-11"

## Main Level Floor Plan

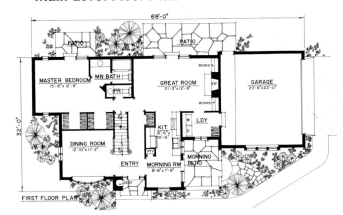

Copyright by designer/architect.

*Images provided by designer/architect.*

## Upper Level Floor Plan

## Plan #291011

**Dimensions:** 68'6" W x 33' D

**Levels:** 2

**Square Footage:** 1,898

**Main Level Sq. Ft.:** 1,182

**Upper Level Sq. Ft.:** 716

**Bedrooms:** 4

**Bathrooms:** 2½

**Foundation:** Basement

**Materials List Available:** No

**Price Category:** D

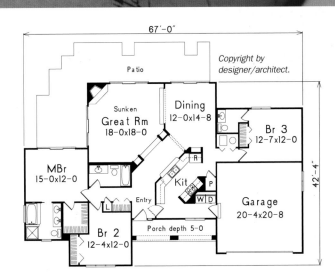

Copyright by designer/architect.

## Plan #321026

**Dimensions:** 67' W x 42'4" D

**Levels:** 1

**Square Footage:** 1,712

**Bedrooms:** 3

**Bathrooms:** 2½

**Foundation:** Crawl space

**Materials List Available:** Yes

**Price Category:** C

*Images provided by designer/architect.*

## SMARTtip

## Deck Design with Computers

Consider using a computer-aided design (CAD) program to plan your deck. Some programs let you see three-dimensional views of your design complete with railings, stairs, planters, hot tubs, and the surrounding landscaping.

## Plan #291001

**Dimensions:** 62'8" W x 38'4" D

**Levels:** 1

**Square Footage:** 1,550

**Bedrooms:** 3

**Bathrooms:** 2

**Foundation:** Basement

**Materials List Available:** No

**Price Category:** C

*Images provided by designer/architect.*

A handsome porch with Greek Revival details greets visitors to this Early-American style home.

### Features:

- Ceiling Height: 8 ft. unless otherwise noted.

- Foyer: Upon entering this foyer you'll be struck by the space provided by the vaulted ceiling in the dining room, living room, and kitchen.

- Dining Room: This dining room is perfectly suited for formal dinner parties as well as less formal family meals.

- Decks: Two rear decks are conveniently accessible from the master bedroom, kitchen, and living room.

- Kitchen: You'll enjoy cooking in this well-designed kitchen, which features an eating area that is perfect for informal family meals.

- Master Bedroom: This master retreat is separated from the other bedrooms for additional privacy. It features an elegant vaulted ceiling and is graced with a dressing area, private bath, and walk-in closet.

Rear View

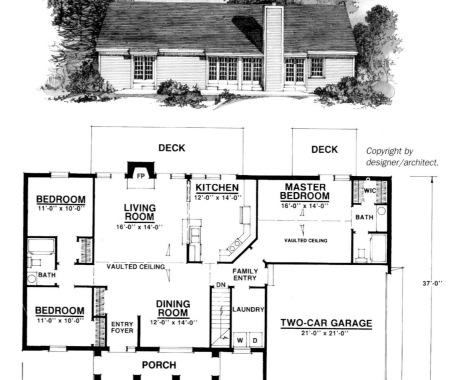

*Copyright by designer/architect.*

## Plan #181021

**Dimensions:** 37' W x 44' D

**Levels:** 1

**Square Footage:** 1,124

**Bedrooms:** 2

**Bathrooms:** 1

**Foundation:** Basement

**Materials List Available:** Yes

**Price Category:** B

*Images provided by designer/architect.*

This cozy country cottage is enhanced by lattice trim details over the porch and garage.

**Features:**

- Ceiling Height: 8 ft.

- Living Room: This living room gets extra architectural interest from a sunken floor. The room, located directly to the left of the entry hall, has plenty of space for entertaining.

- Dining Room: This dining room is located in center of the home. It's adjacent to the kitchen to make it easy to serve meals.

- Kitchen: This bright and efficient kitchen is a real pleasure in which to work. It includes a pantry and double sinks. There's a breakfast bar that will see plenty of informal meals for families on the go.

- Covered Porch: This is the perfect place to which to retire after dinner on a warm summer evening.

- Bedrooms: Each of the two bedrooms has its own closet. They share a full bathroom.

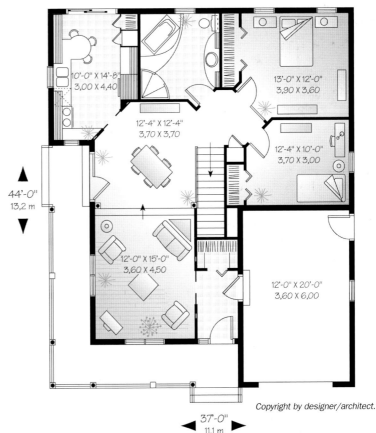

*Copyright by designer/architect.*

## Plan #211033

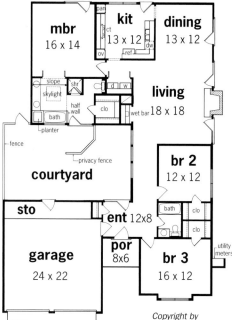

**Dimensions:** 46' W x 66' D
**Levels:** 1
**Square Footage:** 1,732
**Bedrooms:** 3
**Bathrooms:** 2
**Foundation:** Slab
**Materials List Available:** Yes
**Price Category:** C

You'll love the good taste with which this home was designed, as well as the versatility its mixture of formal and informal areas affords.

**Features:**

- Ceiling Height: 9-ft. ceilings.
- Living Room: The dimensions of this room make it easy to decorate for either formal or informal occasions and entertaining.
- Dining Room: Close to the kitchen for convenience, this dining room is also versatile enough to be appropriate for any sort of entertaining.
- Kitchen: The practical design here allows you to work without needlessly wasting precious time or energy, and the location of this kitchen means that serving and clearing-up chores are eased.
- Master Suite: Retreat to this area after a long, stressful day so that you can recharge your batteries—either by resting or showering.

*Copyright by designer/architect.*

## SMARTtip

### Types of Paintbrush Bristles

**Nylon Bristles.** Bristles made of nylon are most suitable for latex paint, although they can also be used with solvent-based paint.

**Natural Bristles.** Also called "China bristle," natural bristle brushes are preferred for use with solvent-based paints and varnishes because they tend to hold more paint and generally brush out to a smoother looking finish. Natural bristle brushes should not be used with latex paint. The water in the paint will cause the bristles to expand and ruin the brush.

**Choosing Brushes.** When buying a brush, check for thick, resilient bristles that are firmly held in place. Be sure, also, to get the proper type brush for the job.

# Let Us Help You
## Plan Your
# Dream Home

**W**hether you've always dreamed of building your own home or you can't find the right house from among the dozens you've toured, our collection of cottage-style plans can help you achieve the home of your dreams. You could have an architect create a one-of-a-kind home for you, but the design services alone could end up costing up to 15 percent of the cost of construction—a hefty premium for any building project. Isn't it a better idea to select from among the hundreds of unique designs shown in our collection for a fraction of the cost?

### What does Creative Homeowner Offer?

In this book, Creative Homeowner provides hundreds of home plans from the country's best architects and designers. Our designs are among the most popular available. Whether your taste runs from traditional to contemporary, Victorian to early American, you are sure to find the best house design for you and your family. Our plans packages include detailed drawings to help you or your builder construct your dream house. **(See page 280.)**

### Can I Make Changes to the Plans?

Creative Homeowner offers three ways to help you achieve a truly unique home design. Our customizing service allows for extensive changes to our designs. **(See page 281.)** We also provide reverse images of our plans, or we can give you and your builder the tools for making minor changes on your own. **(See page 282.)**

### Can You Help Me Stay on Budget?

Building a house is a large financial investment. To help you stay within your budget, Creative Homeowner can provide you with general construction costs based on your zip code. **(See page 282.)** Also, many of our plans come with the option of buying detailed materials lists to help you price out construction costs.

### Is There Anything I Missed?

A typical construction crew consists of a number of skilled professionals. If you plan on doing all or part of the work yourself, or you want to keep tabs on your builder, we offer best-selling building and design books at attractive prices. Our book packages cover all phases of home construction, including framing and drywalling, interior decorating, kitchen and bath design, landscaping, and outdoor living. **(See pages 287–288.)**

# Our Plans Packages Offer:

All of our home plans are the result of many hours of work by leading architects and professional designers. When you place an order for one of our home plans, you will receive the following.

## Frontal Sheet

This artist's rendering of the front of the house gives you an idea of how the house will look once it is completed and the property landscaped.

## Detailed Floor Plans

These plans show the size and layout of the rooms. They also provide the locations of doors, windows, fireplaces, closets, stairs, and electrical outlets and switches.

## Foundation Plan

A foundation plan gives the dimensions of basements, walk-out basements, crawl spaces, pier foundations, and slab construction. Each house design lists the type of foundation included. If the plan you choose does not have the foundation type you require, our customer service department can help you customize the plan to meet your needs.

## Roof Plan

In addition to providing the pitch of the roof, these plans also show the locations of dormers, skylights, and other elements.

## Exterior Elevations

These drawings show the front, rear, and sides of the house as if you were looking at it head on. Elevations also provide information about architectural features and finish materials.

## Interior Elevations and Details

Interior elevations show specific details of such elements as fireplaces, kitchen and bathroom cabinets, built-ins, and other unique features of the design.

## Cross Sections

These show the structure as if it were sliced to reveal construction requirements, such as insulation, flooring, and roofing details.

**Frontal Sheet**

**Floor Plan**

**Foundation Plan**

**Roof Plan**

**Cross Sections**

**Stair Details**

**Elevation**

Illustrations provided by designer/architect

# Customize Your Plans in 4 Easy Steps

**1** **Select the home plan** that most closely meets your needs. Purchase of a reproducible master is necessary in order to make changes to a plan.

**2** **Call 1-800-523-6789 to place your order.** Tell our sales representative you are interested in customizing your plan. To receive your customization cost estimate, we will send you a checklist (via fax or email) for you to complete indicating the changes you would like to make to your plan. There is a $50 nonrefundable consultation fee for this service. If you decide to continue with the custom changes, the $50 fee is credited to the total amount charged.

**3** **Fax the completed checklist** to 1-201-760-2431 or email it to us at customize@creativehomeowner.com. Within three business days of receipt of your checklist, a detailed cost estimate will be provided to you.

**4** **Once you approve the estimate,** a 75% retainer fee is collected and customization work begins. Preliminary drawings typically take 10 to 15 business days. After approval, we will collect the balance of your customization order cost before shipping the completed plans. You will receive five sets of blueprints or a reproducible master, plus a customized materials list if desired.

## Modification Pricing Guide

| Categories | Average Cost From... | To |
|---|---|---|
| Add or remove living space | Quote required | |
| Bathroom layout redesign | $120 | $280 |
| Kitchen layout redesign | $120 | $280 |
| Garage: add or remove | $400 | $680 |
| Garage: front entry to side load or vice versa | Starting at $300 | |
| Foundation changes | Starting at $220 | |
| Exterior building materials change | Starting at $200 | |
| Exterior openings: add, move, or remove | $55 per opening | |
| Roof line changes | $360 | $630 |
| Ceiling height adjustments | $280 | $500 |
| Fireplace: add or remove | $90 | $200 |
| Screened porch: add | $280 | $600 |
| Wall framing change from 2x4 to 2x6 | Starting at $200 | |
| Bearing and/or exterior walls changes | Quote required | |
| Non-bearing wall or room changes | $55 per room | |
| Metric conversion of home plan | $400 | |
| Adjust plan for handicapped accessibility | Quote required | |
| Adapt plans for local building code requirements | Quote required | |
| Engineering stamping only | Quote required | |
| Any other engineering services | Quote required | |
| Interactive illustrations (choices of exterior materials) | Quote required | |

**Note:** *Any home plan can be customized to accommodate your desired changes. The average prices above are provided only as examples of the most commonly requested changes, and are subject to change without notice. Prices for changes will vary according to the number of modifications requested, plan size, style, and method of design used by the original designer. To obtain a detailed cost estimate, please contact us.*

## Architectural Seals

Because of differences in building codes, some cities and states now require an architect or engineer licensed in that state to review and "seal" a blueprint, or officially approve it, prior to construction. Delaware, Nevada, New Jersey, and New York require that all plans for houses built in those states be redrawn by an architect licensed in the state in which the home will be built.

**Before Customization**

**After**

# Decide What Type of Plan Package You Need

## How many Plans Should You Order?

**Standard 8-Set Package.** We've found that our 8-set package is the best value for someone who is ready to start building. Once the process begins, a number of people will require their own set of blueprints. The 8-set package provides plans for you, your builder, the subcontractors, mortgage lender, and the building department.

**Minimum 4-Set Package.** If you are in the bidding process, you may want to order only four sets for the bidding round and reorder additional sets as needed.

**1-Set Study Package.** The 1-set package allows you to review your home plan in detail. The plan will be marked as a study print, and it is illegal to build a house from a study print alone. It is a violation of copyright law to reproduce a blueprint without permission.

## Buying Additional Sets

If you require additional copies of blueprints for your home construction, you can order additional sets within 60 days of the original order date at a reduced price. The cost is $45.00 for each additional set. For more information, contact customer service.

## Reproducible Masters

If you plan to make minor changes to one of our home plans, you can purchase reproducible masters. Drawn on vellum paper, an erasable paper that you can reproduce in a copying machine, reproducible masters allow an architect, designer, or builder to alter our plans to give you a customized home design. This package also allows you to print as many copies of the modified plans as you need for construction.

## Mirror-Reverse Sets

Plans can be printed in mirror-reverse—we can "flip" plans to create a mirror image of the design. This is useful when the house would fit your site or personal preferences if all the rooms were on the opposite side than shown. As the image is reversed, the lettering and dimensions will also be reversed, meaning they will read backwards. Therefore, when ordering mirror-reverse drawings, you must order at least one set of right-reading plans. A $50.00 fee per order will be charged for mirror-reverse (regardless of the number of mirror-reverse sets ordered).

# Determine Your Construction Costs

## EZ Quote: Home Cost Estimator

EZ Quote is our response to one of the most frequently asked questions we hear from customers: "How much will the house cost me to build?" EZ Quote: Home Cost Estimator will enable you to obtain a calculated building cost to construct your new home, based on labor rates and building material costs within your zip code area. This summary building cost report is particularly useful for first-time buyers who might be concerned with the total construction costs before purchasing sets of home plans. It will also provide a certain level of comfort when you begin soliciting bids from builders. The cost is $29.95 for the first EZ Quote and $14.95 for each additional EZ Quote.

## Materials List

Available for most of our plans, the Materials List provides you an invaluable resource in planning and estimating the cost of your home. Each Materials List outlines the quantity, dimensions, and type of materials needed to build your home (with the exception of mechanical systems). You will get faster, more-accurate bids from your contractors and building suppliers—and avoid paying for unused materials. A Materials List may only be ordered with the purchase of a set of home plans.

**Order Toll Free by Phone**
**1-800-523-6789**
**By Fax: 201-760-2431**

Regular office hours are
8:30AM–9:00PM ET, Mon–Fri

Orders received 3PM ET, will be processed
and shipped within two business days.

**Order Online**
**www.ultimateplans.com**

**Mail Your Order**
Creative Homeowner
Attn: Home Plans
24 Park Way
Upper Saddle River, NJ 07458

**Canadian Customers**
**Order Toll Free 1-800-393-1883**

# Index

# Index

# Books To Help You Build

Creative Homeowner offers an extensive selection of leading how-to books.
Choose any of the book packages below to get started.

## Home Building Package

*Build and repair your home—inside and out—with these essential titles.*

Retail Price: $74.80
**Your Price: $65.95**
Order #: 267095

### Wiring: Complete Projects for the Home
Provides comprehensive information about the home electrical system. Over 750 color photos and 75 illustrations. 288 pages.

### Plumbing: Basic, Intermediate & Advanced Projects
An overview of the plumbing system with code-compliant, step-by-step projects. Over 750 full-color photos, illustrations. 272 pages.

### House Framing
Walks you through the framing basics, from assembling simple partitions to cutting compound angles for dormers. 500 full-color illustrations and photos. 208 pages.

### Drywall: Pro Tips for Hanging and Finishing
Covers tools and materials, estimating, cutting, hanging, and finishing gypsum wallboard. 250 color photos and illustrations. 144 pages.

## Kitchen & Bath Package

*Learn to design and build kitchens and bathrooms like a pro.*

Retail Price: $79.80
**Your Price: $69.95**
Order #267080

### The *New* Smart Approach to Kitchen Design
Includes all the answers to help plan a project, hire a contractor, shop for appliances, and decorate like a design pro. More than 260 color photos. 208 pages.

### Kitchens: Plan, Remodel, Build
A complete design and installation package, including design trends and step-by-step projects. More than 550 full-color photos and illustrations. 256 pages.

### The *New* Smart Approach to Bath Design
The latest and best materials and products on the market for master baths, family baths, and powder rooms. More than 260 color photos. 208 pages.

### Bathrooms: Plan, Remodel, Build
Includes step-by-step projects, storage options, products, materials, and lighting possibilities. Over 100 illustrations and 550 color photographs. 256 pages.

## Landscaping Package

*Create a yard you'll love with these comprehensive landscape guides.*

Retail Price: $73.80
**Your Price: $64.95**
Order # 267075

### Complete Home Landscaping
Covers everything from design principles to construction projects, from plant selection to plant care. More than 800 full-color photos and illustrations. 320 pages.

### Trees, Shrubs & Hedges
Create a landscape, match plants to growing conditions, and learn to plant, transplant, and prune. Over 500 color photos and paintings. 208 pages.

### Smart Guide: Ponds & Fountains
Plan, build, and maintain with projects and easy-to-understand text. Covers plant and fish selection. 175 -color illustrations, 40 color photos. 80 pages.

### Annuals, Perennials & Bulbs
Lavishly illustrated with portraits of over 100 flowering plants; filled with instructional techniques and tips. More than 500 color photos and illustrations. 208 pages.

## Decks & Patios Package

*Design and build decks and patios for your new home.*

Retail Price$66.80
**Your Price $55.95**
Order # 267090

### Decks: Planning, Designing, Building
Takes you through every step involved in designing and building a beautiful deck. 600 color photos and illustrations. 192 pages.

### Deck Designs Plus Railings, Planters, Benches
The best plans from top deck designers. Includes planters, railings, benches, and trellises. 300 color photos and drawings. 192 pages.

### Walks, Walls & Patios: Design, Plan & Build
Includes the ideas and how-to you'll need to integrate popular hardscape designs into a home landscape. Over 500 color photos and illustrations. 240 pages.

### Design Ideas for Decks
Everything you'll need to create a beautiful deck for your home. Learn about the newest deck styles, designs, and patterns. More than 250 photos. 128 pages.

## Decorating Package

*Save money and design like a professional with these must-have decorating books.*

Retail Price $66.85
**Your Price: $59.95**
Order # 267085

### The New Smart Approach to Home Decorating
Introduces the classic design theories, showcases interior design trends, and teaches how to make the most of any space. Over 440 color photos. 288 pages.

### Lyn Peterson's Real Life Decorating
Noted interior designer gives easy-to-live-with solutions to the most daunting decorating dilemmas. More than 300 color photos and illustrations. 304 pages.

### Color in the American Home
Shows how the power of color can transform even the plainest room into a beauty. Over 200 color photos. 176 pages.

## Outdoor Projects Package

*Use these project guides to accessorize the largest room in your home—your yard.*

Retail Price $51.85
**Your Price: $45.95**
Order # 267060

### Trellises & Arbors
Features inspiring photos, planning advice, design ideas, plant information, and 10 step-by-step trellis projects. Over 450 photos and illustrations. 160 pages.

### Yard & Garden Furniture
Contains 20 step-by-step projects, from the comfortable lines of an Adirondack chair to the sturdy serviceability- of a family picnic table. Over 600 color photos and illustrations. 208 pages.

### Gazebos & Other Outdoor Structures
Design fundamentals, step-by-step building techniques, and custom options for the perfect gazebo, arbor, or pavilion. 480 color illustrations and photos. 160 pages.

## Home Reference Package

*Find it, fix it, design it, create it—*
*if it's in your home, it's in here.*

Retail Price: $59.90
**Your Cost: $49.95**
Order # 267070

### The Home Book
The largest, most complete home improvement book on the market—608 pages packed with over 2,300 photos, 800 drawings, and an understandable, practical text that covers your home top to bottom, inside and out. 608 pages.

### The *New* Smart Approach to Home Decorating
Decorate every room in your home with the same confidence and flair as a professional designer. More than 440 color photos. 288 pages.

## Family-Living Package

*Start your home off right with these family-oriented ideas*
*for the home and garden.*

Retail Price: $69.80
**Your Cost: $59.95**
Order # 267065

### Lyn Peterson's Real Life Decorating
Noted interior designer gives easy-to-live-with solutions to the most daunting decorating dilemmas. More than 300 color photos and illustrations. 304 pages.

### Smart Approach to Kids' Rooms
Ideas for decorating, furnishing, designing, and organizing space for children with practical design advice and safety tips. Over 200 color photos. 176 pages.

### Build a Kids' Play Yard
How to build a swing set, monkey bars, balance beam, playhouse, and more. Over 200 color photos and drawings. 144 pages.

### National Wildlife Federation®
### Attracting Birds, Butterflies and Other Backyard Wildlife
Wildlife-friendly gardening, landscape designs, and family projects from the National Wildlife Federation. Over 200 color photos and illustrations. 128 pages.

- - - - - - - - - - - - - - - - - - - - - - - - - - - - - - - - - - - -

# Order Form for Books to Help Complete Your Home

| Qty. | Description | Order # | Price | Cost |
|---|---|---|---|---|
| **Book Packages:** | | | | |
| ___ | Home Building Package . . . . . . . . . . . . . . . .267095 | | $65.95 | ___ |
| ___ | Kitchen & Bath Package . . . . . . . . . . . . . . . .267080 | | 69.95 | ___ |
| ___ | Landscaping Package . . . . . . . . . . . . . . . .267075 | | 64.95 | ___ |
| ___ | Decks & Patios Package . . . . . . . . . . . . . .267090 | | 55.95 | ___ |
| ___ | Decorating Package . . . . . . . . . . . . . . . . .267085 | | 59.95 | ___ |
| ___ | Outdoor Projects Package . . . . . . . . . . . . .267060 | | 45.95 | ___ |
| ___ | Home Reference Package . . . . . . . . . . . . .267070 | | 49.95 | ___ |
| ___ | Family-Living Package . . . . . . . . . . . . . . . .267065 | | 59.95 | ___ |
| **Individual Titles from Creative Homeowner:** | | | | |
| ___ | Wiring: Basic and Advanced Projects . . . . . . .278237 | | $19.95 | ___ |
| ___ | Plumbing: Basic, Intermediate & Advanced Projects . . . . . . . . . . . . . . . . . .278210 | | 19.95 | ___ |
| ___ | House Framing . . . . . . . . . . . . . . . . . . . . . .277655 | | 19.95 | ___ |
| ___ | Drywall: Pro Tips for Hanging and Finishing . . .278315 | | 14.95 | ___ |
| ___ | The New Smart Approach to Kitchen Design . .279946 | | 19.95 | ___ |
| ___ | Kitchens: Plan, Remodel, Build . . . . . . . . . . .277061 | | 19.95 | ___ |
| ___ | The New Smart Approach to Bath Design . . . .279234 | | 19.95 | ___ |
| ___ | Bathrooms: Plan, Remodel, Build . . . . . . . . .278627 | | 19.95 | ___ |
| ___ | Complete Home Landscaping . . . . . . . . . . . .274615 | | 24.95 | ___ |
| ___ | Trees, Shrubs & Hedges . . . . . . . . . . . . . . .274238 | | 19.95 | ___ |
| ___ | Smart Guide: Ponds & Fountains . . . . . . . . .274643 | | 8.95 | ___ |
| ___ | Annuals, Perennials & Bulbs . . . . . . . . . . .274032 | | 19.95 | ___ |
| ___ | The New Smart Approach to Home Decorating . . . . . . . . . . . . . . . . . . . .279672 | | 24.95 | ___ |
| ___ | Lyn Peterson's Real Life Decorating . . . . . . .279382 | | 21.95 | ___ |
| ___ | Color in the American Home . . . . . . . . . . . . .287264 | | 19.95 | ___ |
| ___ | Decks: Planning, Designing, Building . . . . . . .277162 | | 16.95 | ___ |
| ___ | Deck Designs . . . . . . . . . . . . . . . . . . . . . . .277369 | | 16.95 | ___ |
| ___ | Walks, Walls & Patios . . . . . . . . . . . . . . . . .277997 | | 19.95 | ___ |
| ___ | Design Ideas for Decks . . . . . . . . . . . . . . . .277155 | | 12.95 | ___ |
| ___ | Trellises & Arbors . . . . . . . . . . . . . . . . . . . .274804 | | 16.95 | ___ |

| Qty. | Description | Order # | Price | Cost |
|---|---|---|---|---|
| **Individual Titles from Creative Homeowner:** | | | | |
| ___ | Yard & Garden Furniture . . . . . . . . . . . . . . . .277462 | | $19.95 | ___ |
| ___ | Gazebos & Other Outdoor Structures . . . . . . .277138 | | 14.95 | ___ |
| ___ | The Home Book . . . . . . . . . . . . . . . . . . . . . .267855 | | 34.95 | ___ |
| ___ | The Smart Approach to Kids' Rooms . . . . . . .279473 | | 19.95 | ___ |
| ___ | Build a Kids' Play Yard . . . . . . . . . . . . . . . . .277662 | | 14.95 | ___ |
| ___ | Attracting Birds, Butterflies & and Other Backyard Wildlife . . . . . . . . . . .274955 | | 12.95 | ___ |

Shipping* _____

SUBTOTAL _____

Sales Tax (NJ residents add 6%) _____

TOTAL _____

*Shipping Costs:
For book packages: $5.95 per package
For individual titles: $4.75 for first book
$1.75 for each additional book

Make check payable to Creative Homeowner
To order, send form to:
Creative Homeowner
P.O. Box 38
24 Park Way
Upper Saddle River, NJ 07458

Or call
1-800-523-6789

# CRE▲TIVE
# HOMEOWNER®

SHIP TO:

Name _____
*(Please print)*

Address _____

City _____ State:____ Zip:_____ Phone #_____